WHEN
TIME
ENDS

WHEN
TIME
ENDS

The Victory of Forgiveness
at Armageddon

BRUCE W. SCOTT

ROCKWOOD PRESS

When Time Ends © 2010 Bruce W. Scott

www.WhenTimeEnds.net

Book design by Cat Scott, www.catscott.com

Cover: *The Raising of Lazarus,* Rembrandt [Public domain], via Wikimedia Commons

ISBN #: 978-0-615-43425-4

TABLE OF CONTENTS

And the angel which I saw stand upon the sea and upon the earth lifted up his hand to heaven, and sware by him that liveth for ever and ever, who created heaven, and the things that therein are, and the earth, and the things that therein are, and the sea, and the things which are therein, that there should be time no longer.

—Revelation 10:5-6 KJV

PREFACE

When I graduated from the Louisville Presbyterian Theological Seminary, my late grandfather, Penn R. Watson II, gave me several hundred dollars to establish a theological library. With it I bought some books that I hoped, someday, would be the basis of a study of the apocalyptic literature of the Bible.

What motivated me then was my interest in how the Bible's prophets and apocalyptic visionaries addressed war, injustice, and empire in their times. How might they address these issues in times dominated by controversy over poverty, civil rights, and the war in Vietnam? Compounding my interest over the years has been the rising political fortunes of the religious right, which interprets biblical prophecy quite differently from me. I watched astonished as religious conservatives used their fundamentalist beliefs about prophecy and apocalypse to justify their indifference to the consequences of our wars in the Middle East and to the increasing numbers of imprisoned, impoverished, and despised people at home. I believe those attitudes are the opposite of the prophetic voices of the Old Testament and the good news of the New. Using the term of John in his first letter in the New Testament, the warmongering, exceptionalism, bigotry, and intolerance of the religious right are "the antichrist."

I finally found time to begin my study. The books I bought thirty years earlier with my grandfather's money, most importantly D. S. Russell's volume for the Westminster Old Testament Library, *The Methods and Message of Jewish Apocalyptic*, were useful but dated. An enormous amount of research into biblical history and literature had become available in the intervening years. My theological reeducation began.

This book aims to correct the biblical interpretations of end-times writers and television evangelists who warn of a coming tribulation caused by an antichrist and urge us to escape it through the rapture by embracing Jesus as a personal savior.

The first part of my book lays out recent end-times scenarios, one published by megachurch pastor John Hagee and the other from the popular *Left Behind* series of novels written by Tim LaHaye and Jerry Jenkins. Hagee, LaHaye, and Jenkins are contemporary manifestations of a fundamentalist theology from the late nineteenth century called premillennial dispensationalism, and the first part will spend some time on its strange history. The part concludes by identifying the biblical sources of their scenarios for discussion in the parts that follow.

The next three parts consider the biblical sources of the dispensationalist end-time scenario in the historical order modern scholars believe they were created. The second part focuses on Old Testament prophets like Isaiah, Ezekiel, and Zechariah who wrote centuries before Jesus walked the earth, but who influenced Jesus and, after his death, his apostles. The third and fourth parts review biblical books created closer to Jesus' times. These books (like Daniel and Revelation) are more revelatory than prophetic: they unveil God's hidden purposes for the creation using the literature of visions. Indeed, "unveiling" is a translation of the Greek word *apokolypsis*, the source of the word "apocalyptic." Fundamentalists misinterpret apocalyptic visions and their prophetic precursors as predictive evidence for their ghastly end-times scenarios.

Prophetic and apocalyptic voices in the Bible should not be dismissed out of hand because of their misuse by fundamentalists. The final, fifth part of my book discusses ways that apocalyptic thinking underlies common Christian practices and beliefs, particularly table fellowship and the recital of the Lord's Prayer. These practices, among the many other hopeful and loving things that Christians do, bring the kingdom of heaven to earth in our time, and without human or divine violence. This is the good news that the biblical record reveals.

I am grateful to Patrick Clark, Dr. Arthur Mielke, and the Reverend Dr. G. David Hawley for their reviews of a first draft of this book. Their questions and suggestions prompted a thorough revision that sharpened my thoughts and hopefully made the book more interesting and readable. I also need to thank my mother, Barbara Scott, for checking Bible references. Any remaining errors are mine.

—Bruce W. Scott
Silver Bay, New York
August 2010

Part One
RAPTURE
AND
TRIBULATION

The king sent an Athenian senator to compel the Jews to forsake the laws of their ancestors and no longer to live by the laws of God; also to pollute the temple in Jerusalem and to call it the temple of Olympian Zeus. . . .

Harsh and utterly grievous was the onslaught of evil. For the temple was filled with debauchery and reveling by the Gentiles. . . . The altar was covered with abominable offerings that were forbidden by the laws. People could neither keep the sabbath, nor observe the festivals of their ancestors, nor so much as confess themselves to be Jews.

On the monthly celebration of the king's birthday, the Jews were taken, under bitter constraint, to partake of the sacrifices . . . Two women were brought in for having circumcised their children. They publicly paraded them around the city, with their babies hanging at their breasts, and then hurled them down headlong from the wall. Others who had assembled in the caves nearby, in order to observe the seventh day secretly, were betrayed to [the Governor] and were all burned together, because their piety kept them from defending themselves, in view of their regard for that most holy day.

—2 Maccabees 6:1-11, describing the repression of Judaism by King Antiochus IV Epiphanes in 171 BCE

Chapter 1
THE EVANGELICAL PURPOSE OF END-TIMES BOOKS

A reader of one of the sixty-five million volumes in print[1] of *Left Behind*, the first in a series of novels by Tim LaHaye and Jerry B. Jenkins, learns that the end of the world begins something like this:

Over the Atlantic Ocean, Rayford Steele puts his Boeing 747 on autopilot and enters the passenger cabin to flirt with a pretty stewardess. But she's upset—many of her passengers have simply vanished, leaving their clothing behind in their seats. When he lands the plane amid chaos on the ground, he learns that millions of people everywhere are gone, among them his wife, who had joined an evangelical church not long ago, and their young son. Good people everywhere, children less than twelve, and unborn fetuses are all missing. There's speculation that they have risen into the upper atmosphere in what Christians call *the rapture*, but that notion is ridiculed by almost everybody, who are also being uncommonly rude.

Meanwhile, arriving back in the United States on Steele's plane is Cameron "Buck" Williams, a cable news reporter who has just witnessed the miraculous destruction in Israel of swarms of attacking Russian bombers. The airplanes had unexplainably exploded in midair, harming nothing in Israel but littering the landscape with their mangled superstructures and their crews' bodies.

In the wider world, a charismatic leader backed by shadowy financiers emerges from Romania. He's named Nicolae Carpathia, invoking two specters: soviet communism (the West's nickname for the leader of the Bolshevik revolution, Vladimir Ilyich Lenin, was "Nikolae") and vampires (Dracula's castle is in the Carpathian Mountains of Eastern Europe).[2] He seduces the

---

[1] From the cover of my paperback copy of Left Behind, purchased in 2008.
[2] LaHaye may also be alluding to the "Nicolaitans," a group of "false teachers" in an early church identified in Rev 2:6 and 15.

people of the world with his promises to end famine and bring peace.

Traumatized by the disappearance of so many people, the representatives of the world assemble at the United Nations to welcome Carpathia as a leader who can bring order out of chaos. Carpathia is thirty-three and "handsome as a young Robert Redford";[3] he's tall, blond, blue-eyed, and impeccably dressed; he fluently speaks nine languages. The first novel in the series tells us three separate times that he's been chosen as the "Sexiest Man Alive" by People Magazine.[4]

Carpathia streamlines the United Nations, reducing the size of the Security Council to representatives of ten nations who are loyal to him and proposing to locate a more efficient complex for UN bureaucrats in Babylon, the ancient capital of civilizations in Iraq. He invites the world to disarm after the nations cede to the UN (under his power) ten percent of their weaponry. He encourages the establishment of a single religion, "probably headquartered in Italy,"[5] that unites all faiths under the rubric "the lovers of humankind."[6] He requires the consolidation of national currencies into a single global one.

But some Christians who were left behind because of their shallow faith realize, tardily, that these otherwise popular initiatives are signs of the end times, about which they had been warned. Nicolae Carpathia is evil, and they recognize him as the antichrist prophesied in the Bible. His initiatives to end hunger and bring peace are not what they seem; his real interest is in control, and he will use manipulation and violence to achieve world domination.

Chastened by the disappearance of his wife and son, Rayford Steele joins a cell of repentant Christians meeting with a minister at his missing wife's church. Assistant Pastor Bruce Barnes, himself left behind but now committed to resistance, warns the group about the events predicted in the Bible that follow the rapture of the church and the rise of the antichrist. They should expect seven years of civil unrest and war, divided into two three-and-a-half year periods. During the first period, Pastor Barnes warns the group, a few months of peace and diplomacy will be followed by thermonuclear war. After the war, famine and a plague will kill a fourth of the world's population. An earthquake will follow, then calamities that are "progressively worse."[7] Their mission is "to stand up to oppression, to big government, to bigotry."[8]

In the novels that follow in the series, LaHaye and Jenkins describe how

---

[3] LaHaye and Jenkins, *Left Behind*, 232.

[4] Ibid., 270-1, 303, 362. As a point of reference, the "Sexiest Men Alive" in 1995, the year *Left Behind* was first published, was Brad Pitt. "People Magazine," Wikipedia. Online at: http://en.wikipedia.org/wiki/People_Magazine.

[5] Ibid., 353. LaHaye isn't always so subtle about equating Roman Catholicism with the forces who oppose Christ, as we will see.

[6] Ibid., 414

[7] Ibid., 312.

[8] Ibid., 429.

Carpathia consolidates his power and repentant Christians resist it. Armies rise to oppose Carpathia and they converge on the Holy Land; a great battle among them ensues. Closing the battle, Jesus Christ descends from heaven with an army of people lifted up in the rapture along with everyone in history who died believing in him, and he destroys the worldly forces in a bloodbath. Carpathia survives but is rendered harmless.

After the battle, Jesus Christ judges people who survive to determine whether their faith has earned them membership in the kingdom on earth that he will establish. He also holds nations accountable for their persecution of Israel, the Jews, and his early church. Those found wanting are condemned to Hell.

Jesus Christ then reigns in Israel for a thousand years, a period of peace and prosperity for the Christians who have been faithful to him and the Jews who have accepted him as the Messiah. When his reign (and the series of novels) concludes, Jesus Christ has a final battle with the antichrist, who is defeated forever. The world ends and eternity begins.

†

The repentant Christians in *Left Behind* learn that the catastrophes unfolding around them were foretold in the Bible. For example, passages in the Apostle Paul's first letter to the church in Thessalonica speak of a time coming soon when the faithful will suddenly join Jesus in heaven. The Old Testament prophet Ezekiel describes a battle between God and the villainous Gog of Magog who invades Israel with his armies but is utterly destroyed. Other Old Testament prophets, Zephaniah and Zechariah, describe a battle for Jerusalem on the "day of the Lord." The book of Daniel warns of a beast that will desecrate the Jerusalem temple to begin a three-and-a-half-year-long pogrom against the Jews. In the gospels, Jesus reminds his followers about Daniel's warning and adds his own about deceivers and false prophets. A New Testament letter from John speaks of the antichrist; another letter, from Peter, warns of a fiery trial. The book of Revelation describes a satanic beast that marks his followers with a sign and is defeated by the armies of Jesus Christ at a place called Armageddon.

The novel's readers may conclude that the fictional people who weren't lifted up in the rapture should have listened to ministers when they preached about the scriptural signs of the end times. They should have heeded their friends and relatives who urged them to be born again. Had they repented their sins and accepted Jesus as their savior, they could have risen in the rapture, too, and avoided the tribulation. But there's still time to avoid the judgment of eternal damnation that will come at the close of the tribulation. They can accept Jesus, follow the Ten Commandments, resist the forces of the antichrist, and pray for forgiveness.

As should we, LaHaye and Jenkins would say. Their novels have a purpose that's rooted in the authors' evangelical beliefs. After his early retirement from a successful career as pastor of a large church in the San Diego area, Tim LaHaye became a prolific end-times author and a political activist in the religious right; he's been characterized by *Time* magazine as one of twenty-five of the most influential evangelicals of contemporary times.[9] For his part, Jerry Jenkins, the author of the books based on LaHaye's detailed scenarios, worked for years as a publicist and writer for the Moody Bible Institute, one of the pillars of the modern conservative evangelical movement, before moving into freelance writing.

LaHaye's ambitions aren't only pastoral and literary. Among his considerable activities, LaHaye has been cofounder of the Institute for Creation Research, which supports a literal reading of the Bible for describing the origins of life, and a board member of the late Jerry Falwell's once-influential political action organization of conservative evangelicals, Moral Majority.[10] He was honorary cochairman of Jack Kemp's unsuccessful 1987 Republican primary campaign for President, but resigned after the Baltimore *Sun*, newspaper to a historically Catholic state, printed excerpts from a commentary he had written on the book of Revelation where he "referred to Roman Catholicism as a 'false religion.'"[11] With Paul Weyrich, who founded the conservative think tank The Heritage Foundation, LaHaye cofounded the shadowy Council for National Policy to influence conservative political leaders.[12] As an indication of its influence, five Republican contenders came hat in hand to the Council during the 2008 presidential election season: Mike Huckabee, Duncan Hunter, Rick Santorum, Fred Thompson, and the eventual Republican candidate, John McCain.[13]

Despite his conservative political goals, LaHaye is also interested in his scholastic legacy. He founded the "Pre-Trib Research Center" to advance the discussion of end-times beliefs in an academic setting, and he and his wife, Beverly, herself an influential evangelical light, have donated money for two buildings at Liberty University, the university founded by Jerry Falwell: a School of Prophecy that houses the Pre-Trib Research Center, and an ice-hockey rink. The university, in turn, has awarded LaHaye an honorary doctorate in literature. Of *Left Behind*, Falwell has said, "In terms of its impact

---

[9] "The 25 Most Influential Evangelicals in America," *Time* Magazine, February 7, 2005. Online at http://www.time.com/time/covers/1101050207/photoessay/15.html

[10] "How Popular Are the Left Behind Books . . . and Why?" in Forbes and Kilde, eds., *Rapture, Revelation, and the End Times*, 12-13.

[11] Boyd, Gerald M. "Official in Kemp's Campaign Quits After Report on Books," *New York Times*, December 8, 1987. Online at http://www.nytimes.com/1987/12/08/us/official-in-kemp-s-campaign-quits-after-report-on-books.html

[12] Kirkpatrick, David D., "Club of the Most Powerful Gathers in Strictest Privacy." *New York Times*, August 28, 2004. Online at http://query.nytimes.com/gst/fullpage.html?res=9C0CE3DA1E3EF93BA1575BC0A9629C8B63.

[13] Council for National Policy, "2007 Spring Policy Counsel [sic] Speeches," Online at http://www.policycounsel.org

on Christianity, it's probably greater than that of any other book in modern times, outside the Bible."[14]

The *Left Behind* novels fall on fertile ground. Polling in the 1980s confirmed that belief in end-times scenarios like the one offered in the *Left Behind* series is widespread in the United States. A Gallup poll in 1983 found that 62 percent of Americans had "'no doubts' that Jesus will come to earth again"; in a 1988 poll, 80 percent "expressed the conviction that they will appear before God on Judgment Day."[15]

LaHaye isn't alone in promoting the evangelical scenario of imminent rapture, tribulation, and judgment. His peers include Paul Crouch, the founder of the Trinity Broadcasting Network, which with Falwell's Christian Broadcasting Network is a staple of community cable television lineups; John Hagee, pastor of a megachurch in San Antonio and president of Global Evangelism Television, another cable syndicate; and Hal Lindsey, probably the best-known end-times writer of the late twentieth century until LaHaye's and Jenkins' books hit the market. Lindsey wrote *The Late, Great Planet Earth*, which outsold all other American nonfiction books during the 1970s[16] (but was a poor predictor of the Jesus' second coming, which Lindsey said would occur in the 1980s and of course didn't). Lindsey has written several books since then, including two recent ones warning about militant Islam, the demon of conservatism since the collapse of soviet communism. He is a regular contributor to Crouch's cable network and a columnist for World Net Daily, a website of news and comment (and marketing) for the religious right.[17]

Tim LaHaye, John Hagee, and their peers in the modern end-times publishing business shape the beliefs and political activities of many conservative evangelical Christians today by asserting that current events reveal that prophecies about the end-times are being fulfilled in our times. These are signs they commonly identify in world events: after two thousand years of exile and oppression, the Jews have resettled the Holy Land and formed a nation. Transnational organizations like the European Union are adopting common laws, institutions, and currencies. The cyber-revolution includes research into microchips that could embed health or financial histories in people's skins. The United Nations intervenes in conflicts and promotes peace, justice, and health. Based on fundamentalist interpretations of certain passages in the Bible, these trends are signs that the rise of the antichrist will begin soon.

End-times writers also view changes in social order as signs of the imminence of apocalyptic catastrophe. John Hagee warns of these signs in a book from 1999:

---

[14] Quoted in "The 25 Most Influential Evangelicals in America," *Time* Magazine, February 7, 2005. Online at http://www.time.com/time/covers/1101050207/photoessay/15.html

[15] Boyer, *When Time Shall Be No More*, 2.

[16] Wojcik, *The End of the World As We Know It*, 8.

[17] Online at http://www.worldnetdaily.com./WND%20Columnists

My friend, every time I pick up a newspaper, I grow more and more convinced that God's doomsday clock is ticking out the final seconds on the last hour. On one page I read of children killing other children on school playgrounds; on another page I read about parents stuffing their young children into hot ovens. The headlines are filled with stories about our president committing vulgar acts and flagrant infidelity in the Oval Office itself, while our country applauds and his approval ratings rise to new heights! America has become a nation where a Vietnam veteran can walk the streets homeless while a draft dodger sleeps in the White House.[18]

To the extent our government supports immorality, the United States risks damnation at the close of the tribulation because Jesus Christ will judge not just persons, but *nations*. National responsibility for sin and faithlessness is an important theme in end-times writing; the concern may result from the disproportionate occurrence of the word *nations* in Daniel, Ezekiel, and Revelation,[19] the books of the Bible most used by end-time writers to predict a catastrophic future, such as these passages:

> To [God] was given dominion
>   and glory and kingship,
> that all peoples, *nations*, and languages
>   should serve him. (Dan 7:14, emphasis added)

> "Lord, who will not fear and glorify your name? For you alone are holy. All *nations* will come and worship before you, for your judgments have been revealed." (Rev 15:4, emphasis added)

To a more critical student, the frequency of the word *nations* in the Bible's prophetic books reflects the focus of their authors on the role of Israel in history as a redeemer of the entire world, not just its own people. Still, conflict among nations, especially involving the modern state of Israel, is an essential feature of end-times scenarios. Cooperative international initiatives to reduce conflicts and their causes are futile; instead, conflicts in the Middle East are inevitable harbingers of the end-times.

†

International conflicts in our present age always risk nuclear confrontation, and the devastation and plague-like consequences of nuclear warfare create the biblical proportions of chaos and suffering that the antichrist can exploit. We shouldn't be surprised, then, when nuclear war figures in most end-times books written after nuclear bombs devastated Hiroshima and Nagasaki and ended

---

[18] Hagee, *From Daniel to Doomsday*, 85-6. The book was written when Bill Clinton, who received a student draft deferment during the Vietnam War and was impeached for lying about extra-marital sexual liaisons, was President. Hagee fails to cite the newspaper he was reading.

[19] Boyer, *When Time Shall Be No More*, 148.

the American war with Japan.[20] Looking forward to global thermonuclear annihilation in fulfillment of biblical prophecy might seem uncharacteristic of Christian charity, but modern end-times writers often seize on the following passage from the second letter of Peter (in its King James Version translation) to predict it: ·

> But the day of the Lord will come as a thief in the night; in the which the heavens shall pass away with a great noise, and the elements shall melt with fervent heat, the earth also and the works therein shall be burned up.
> Seeing then that all these things shall be dissolved, what manner of persons ought ye to be in all holy conversations and godliness,
> Looking for and hasting unto the coming of the day of God, wherein the heavens being on fire shall be dissolved, and the elements shall melt with fervent heat? (2 Peter 3:10-12 KJV, emphasis added)

A verse with similar sentiments in the *first* letter of Peter is also commonly identified to make the nuclear end-times case, but its metaphorical flourish is more subdued:

> Beloved, think it not strange concerning the *fiery trial* which is to try you, as though some strange thing happened unto you. (1 Peter 4:12 KJV, emphasis added)

Using these passages as a factual basis for predicting global thermonuclear war requires ripping them from their contexts and ignoring biblical scholarship since the King James Version was first published in 1611. The New Revised Standard Version (NRSV), published in 1989 and benefiting from research and scholarship over four intervening centuries, translates the last verse in the appropriate *present* tense: "Beloved, do not be surprised at the fiery ordeal *that is taking place* among you to test you, as though something strange were happening to you" (emphasis added). The letter writer completes his thought in the verse that follows: "But rejoice insofar as you are sharing Christ's sufferings, so that you may also be glad and shout for joy when his glory is revealed" (1 Peter 4:12-13). The "fiery" passage of the second letter concludes similarly with this epitome of apocalyptic hope in its more modern translation: "In accordance with his promise, we wait for new heavens and a new earth, where righteousness is at home" (2 Peter 3:13).

Both letters identify their author as Peter, the disciple in the Garden of Gethsemane when Jesus was arrested before his crucifixion who told the temple police that he didn't know him. Like many stories about Jesus' teaching, the last becomes first, and the disciple who abandoned his loyalty became by tradition the founder of the church in Rome, where Peter likely died during Nero's persecution of Christians about thirty years later. The first letter exhorts Christians to hew to Christian moral and religious codes even though it results

---

[20] Boyer, *When Time Shall Be No More*, 118-20.

in their ostracism from mainstream Greco-Roman society. Peter encourages his flock to live "as aliens and exiles," conducting themselves "honorably" (1 Pet 2:11). The second letter is similarly encouraging, but it primarily addresses doctrinal squabbles typical of a maturing institution that is dealing with pressures to assimilate to Roman values and practices.

From a historical perspective, scholars agree that the second letter of Peter was written long after the first, perhaps sixty years later in about 130 CE by someone using Peter's traditional authority to address a later crisis in the church.[21] (Using the name of a respected predecessor as the author of a book is a common device in biblical literature, as we will see.) That the second letter's apocalyptic imagery is so much more detailed reflects Christians' disappointment that the fulfillment of time, promised by Jesus within the lifetimes of members of his generation, has been postponed, perhaps indefinitely. As we review other apocalyptic literature in the Bible, we'll see the effect of the postponement on Christian thinking about the fulfillment of time: as the years pass, Jesus' original revelation of the kingdom of God as an unexpected event revealed to the faithful in everyday ways (through forgiveness, peacemaking, or sharing) is replaced by notions of a violent global upheaval in the future that restores an idealized, messianic kingdom.

From a literary perspective, *Fiery ordeal* was a well-established metaphor in popular apocalyptic writings of the time. In the Bible, its most memorable use is in the book of Daniel, which was popular at the time the first letter from Peter was written; in it, three of Daniel's colleagues are thrown into a *fiery* furnace in Babylon but emerge unscathed (Dan 3:19-30). Both letters use the metaphor; the second, typical of the apocalyptic thought of its time, projects a current crisis onto a vivid futuristic screen displaying a titanic struggle with spectacular heavenly effects where God triumphs, later, over evil.

Using a modern translation and considering the literary and historical contexts of the two letters, it's easy to conclude that passages in the letters from Peter about a *fiery ordeal* were written to encourage Christians' perseverance in their faithful conduct, not to predict nuclear war two thousand years later. In the first letter, the writer is not looking forward; he is looking back, encouraging those who suffer by recalling a story in the Old Testament (and perhaps alluding to the persecution under the Roman emperor Nero, who blamed Christians for the fire that almost destroyed Rome). *Fiery ordeal* is not an end-times catastrophe; it is a metaphor appropriated from the book of Daniel and perhaps recent events to describe the sacred significance of the alienation and persecution readers of his letter presently endure in their own times.

Misinterpretation of a metaphor like Peter's *fiery ordeal* is not an unusual failure by end-times writers. Many of the isolated biblical passages they use to build their end-times scenarios were assembled from the King James Version

---

[21] Brown, Raymond F., *An Introduction to the New Testament*, 767.

of the Bible in the nineteenth century by the founders of fundamentalism as proofs for their ideas. The meanings of these passages have become clearer more recently with better translations and historical, literary, and archaeological research. End-times writers constantly update their interpretations to be topical (like the new focus on militant Islam); however, the orthodox suite of apocalyptic scriptures they use in a beloved but dated translation doesn't change over time..

✝

For end-times writers in our nuclear age who require a worldwide conflict among nations to fulfill their frightening interpretations of prophetic and apocalyptic scripture, *fiery ordeal* precisely describes a thermonuclear catastrophe, and it isn't hard to find other apocalyptic metaphors in the Bible to tease out the details. Considering Hal Lindsey's 1970 best seller, *The Late Great Planet Earth*, for example, social historian Paul Boyer observes:

> Assuming that all scriptural allusions to fiery destruction and mass suffering foreshadowed nuclear war, Lindsey (usually with a qualifying phrase such as "quite possible" or "may very well be") relentlessly turned the Bible into a manual of atomic-age combat: Zechariah's image of human flesh consuming away portrays "exactly what happens to those who are in a thermonuclear blast"; "fire and brimstone" means tactical nuclear weapons; the falling stars and stinging locusts of Revelation are warheads fired from space platforms and Cobra helicopters spraying nerve gas; the scorching heat and awful sores mentioned in Revelation describe the effects of radiation as observed a Hiroshima and Nagasaki. For page after mind-numbing page, Lindsey systematically went through the apocalyptic scriptures, mechanically transcribing every phrase and image into the vocabulary of Pentagon strategists.[22]

Boyer also observes end-times thermonuclear fascination in late-twentieth century television evangelists who sought to influence national affairs, such as Pat Robertson (who ran for President in 1988) and Billy Graham, spiritual advisor to many presidents. In a troubling excursion into the recent past, Boyer wonders about the influence of ideas about a nuclear apocalypse on the late President Ronald Reagan, who publicly acknowledged his end-times beliefs; commenting in 1971 (before his presidency) on a political coup in Libya, which we will later learn is part of the "Gog of Magog" alliance that end-times writers claim will invade Israel to begin the tribulation, Reagan said:

> That's a sign that the Day of Armageddon isn't far off. . . . Everything is falling into place. It can't be long now. Ezekiel says that fire and brimstone will be rained upon the enemies of God's people. That must mean that they'll be destroyed by nuclear weapons.[23]

---

[22] Boyer, *When Time Shall Be No More*, 127.
[23] Quoted in ibid., 142.

Because many Americans are swimming in a fearful soup of millennial pessimism, terrorist catastrophe, and reactionary politics, it's not surprising that a significant number of them discount the effectiveness of international cooperation and nuclear disarmament treaties. Indeed, a Yankelovich poll taken in 1984 found that thirty-nine percent of respondents agreed with this statement: "When the Bible predicts that the earth will be destroyed by fire, it's telling us that a nuclear war is inevitable." A 1985 Nielsen survey found that approximately "61 million television viewers . . . regularly listen to preachers who tell them nothing can be done to prevent a nuclear war in our lifetime." [24]

Modern end-time writers interpret nuclear proliferation and, in their view, the decay of social morals as proving two things: the truth of biblical prophecy, which they believe predicted these things, and the literal nearness of the end times, of which these things are signs. If the biblical predictions are true, then saving the willing and reforming the nation are urgent tasks requiring aggressive action.

And evangelicals feel an obligation to act. The evangelical tradition derives from the charge given by Jesus to his disciples in "The Great Commission" after his resurrection: "'Go into all the world and proclaim the good news [in Greek, *euangelion*] to the whole creation. The one who believes and is baptized will be saved; but the one who does not believe will be condemned'" (Mark 16:15-16). Although the scenarios of the *Left Behind* novels and other end-times writings are difficult to characterize as *good* news, evangelicals believe they must carry their understanding of it to others who will remain at risk of judgment if they do not accept their offer of salvation from the tribulation.

Evangelicals also feel obliged to reform the United States, which as a nation risks judgment, too. Tim LaHaye and John Hagee aren't simply the authors of popular books; they are significant players on the political right. They urge Congressional support of the expansion of the modern nation of Israel, regardless of international rules of warfare and the claims of Palestinians, because the restoration of that nation to its "promised Land" is God's will. [25] They urge states to erect icons of the Ten Commandments on the grounds of their capitols as the basis of laws that will regulate people's sinful behavior. [26] They vilify international initiatives for peacemaking as antireligious

---

[24] Quoted in Wojcik, *The End of the World As We Know It*, 1, 7.

[25] For example, Hagee, "Five Bible Reasons Christians Should Support Israel," *Jerusalem Countdown*, 229 ff. Hagee solicits donations on his website for his "Exodus II" project whose mission is "Helping with the end-gathering of exiles, orphans, education and other humanitarian causes" in Israel and claims to have raised over $48 million. Online at: www.jhm.org/ME2. See also David D. Kirkpatrick, "For Evangelicals, Supporting Israel is 'God's Foreign Policy.'" New York Times, November 14, 2006. Online at: www.nytimes.com/2006/11/14/washington/14israel. html.

[26] For example, Hagee, *The Revelation of Truth*, 161.

conspiracies,[27] and they support preemptive wars that target nations of a rival Abrahamic faith, Islam.[28] For individual Americans and the nation alike, the literal consequences coming soon for our failure to embrace the social and foreign policy prescriptions of their militant theologies are the horrors of the tribulation and confinement in a lake of fire.

[27] For example, Lindsey, *The Apocalypse Code*, 102 ff.

[28] For example, "President George Bush has given moral clarity to this clash of civilizations, saying, 'This nation is at war with Islamic fascists.'" Hagee, *Jerusalem Countdown*, 3.

Chapter 2
DISPENSATIONAL PREMILLENIALISM

Tim LaHaye, John Hagee, and their peers in the end-times publishing business are heirs to a nineteenth-century theology called *dispensational premillennialism*, which interprets the Bible to divide human history into seven ages that they call *dispensations*.[29] At the opening of each dispensation, God enters into a covenant with God's people. As each dispensation proceeds, people rebel; eventually, God judges them, punishing the unfaithful but preserving a remnant, and the dispensation ends. The current age will end similarly with a horrific judgment—*tribulation*. Before this tribulation, the faithful in the church and innocent children, the remnant, will be lifted into the air to be with Jesus Christ—*rapture*. The tribulation at the end of the present age will usher in the final age of history, the one-thousand-year reign of Jesus Christ in the now-Christian nation of Israel—*millennium*. The rapture and tribulation precede the millennium—*premillenialism*.

The beginning of dispensational premillenialism is attributed to John Nelson Darby (1800-1882), a renegade Church of Ireland minister who lectured widely in the British Isles and the United States in the nineteenth century. Darby drew on beliefs about the end of history that had been around for at least two thousand years, and his particular end-times scenario can be traced to Joachim of Fiore (ca. 1135-1202), a medieval scholar who identified three ages of history, each associated with a member of the Holy Trinity: the Age of Law, associated with God the Father; the Age of Grace, beginning with the birth of Jesus Christ and including the present time; and the Age of the Spirit,

---

[29] Based on the KJV translations of Eph 1:9-10 and 3:1-9, which seem to identify different ages termed *dispensations*. More modern translations of these passages use *plan* instead of *dispensation* and are clearer as to Paul's purpose in writing, which was to explain how Jesus' sacrifice made possible the inclusion of non-Jews in God's plans a proposition rejected by some at the church in Jerusalem (see Acts 15).

associated with the Holy Spirit and following the future defeat of the antichrist, when people will live in spiritual contemplation. Joachim used charts filled with symbols to describe the flow of salvation history through the three ages, and many end-times writers such as Tim LaHaye continue to use complicated charts in their books.[30]

Darby modernized these medieval beliefs and organized them, Boyer writes, into "a tight and cohesive system that he buttressed at every point by copious biblical proof texts."[31] On speaking tours, Darby argued that all prophecy, including Jesus' own prophetic sayings, predicted the restoration of the Jews to the lands in Palestine that God had promised them in the Old Testament and the reconstruction of the great temple in Jerusalem that was destroyed in the first century, forty years after Jesus' death. Once Israel was restored and the temple rebuilt, the antichrist would instigate a "Great Tribulation," a remnant of 144,000 Jews would accept Jesus Christ as the Messiah, and the mother of all battles would occur in Israel. Jesus Christ would then descend from heaven, end the battle in a bloodbath, judge the survivors, and begin the millennium.

Darby made six speaking tours of the United States beginning in 1859. His organized and well-documented scheme of history and its purposes resonated with the millennial hopes of Americans nurtured by preachers in the revivals that had swept North America since European settlement.

Prerevolutionary America was characterized by end-times beliefs that were notably positive, in contrast to the fatalistic and scary beliefs of end-time writers today. While he was best known for his fiery sermons, among them the high school literature staple, "Sinners in the Hands of an Angry God," Jonathan Edwards (1703-1758) wondered whether America might be the seat of the utopian New Jerusalem promised for the end-times. Edwards believed that the end of the earth would occur only at the close of the millennium. After the faithful were safely removed to heaven, God would destroy the world, "there being no further use for it."[32] This type of belief is called *post*millennialism, because the tribulation and rapture come after the millennium, not before it.

But there was also a darker side to prerevolutionary American millennialism, represented by Increase Mather (1639-1723) and his son Cotton (1663-1728), both notorious in history for their sponsorship of the Salem witch trials. The father, Increase, viewed the emerging American democracy as a version of the New Jerusalem described in the book of Revelation, but he still warned of an imminent tribulation. He also taught that the saints would be lifted into the air beforehand to avoid it, an early formulation of the rapture.

---

[30] Boyer, *When Time Shall Be No More,* 52. For examples of modern end-times charts, see LaHaye, *Revelation Unveiled,* 12-13, 18, 24, etc.

[31] Boyer, *When Time Shall Be No More,* 88.

[32] Quoted in Boyer, *When Time Shall Be No More,* 71.

His son, Cotton, had a similarly positive view of America but a predilection for computing the date when the millennium would begin, first 1697, then 1736, then 1716. Although he gave current history a positive thrust, he warned, "God in 'an all-devouring rage' [would] unleash 'a terrible *Conflagration*' annihilating all evidence of human endeavor."[33]

After the American Revolution, millennial hope was nurtured not just by preachers but also by utopian communities that aspired to create perfect kingdoms on earth. The communities had mixed results. The Shaker movement, an exuberant and communalist outgrowth of Quakerism, built communities in New England and extended them southeast to Kentucky and Indiana. The Amana communities succeeded first in western New York and then Iowa, selling their refrigerator business during the Great Depression to assure their continuing survival; they continue as a community of faith but are no longer economically communal (their businesses, however, still share profits). The Oneida community, of silverware fame, reorganized along more secular lines after its founder, John Humphrey Noyes (1811-86), fled to Canada in 1879 to avoid warrants for his arrest for statutory rape. One of Noyes' beliefs was that "male continence" during sexual intercourse was sinless, in his case even with the adolescent daughters of the society's members, making the Oneida experiment one of the first evangelical shipwrecks on the shoals of human sexuality. Despite their high rate of failure, these utopian efforts shared a hopeful view of the millennium, encouraging their members to work cooperatively during their earthly lives toward its coming.

Also emerging with the Amana and Oneida communities (and with Joseph Smith, the founding visionary of the Latter Day Saints) from upstate New York's "burned-over district" was a movement around William Miller (1782-1849), who generated popular millennial excitement throughout the northeast by predicting that Jesus would appear on a certain date in 1843. When he didn't, Miller recalculated to a certain date in 1844, when Jesus again failed to appear. Miller's followers were scandalized, but their underlying beliefs persisted; the Seventh Day Adventist Church reinterpreted Miller's beliefs to emphasize, among other things, a healthful diet for the faithful who wished to hasten the millennium, and has had an enduring impact on American health as well as its religions, resulting for example in the invention of corn flakes by Adventist John Harvey Kellogg in Battle Creek, Michigan.[34]

Boyer observes that the Millerite movement influenced biblical prophecy and popular religion in three ways. One was obvious: Miller's date-setting fiasco persuaded future millennnialists to avoid calculation of the precise date of Jesus' second coming. Hal Lindsey is typical: in his 1970s best seller, *The Late Great Planet Earth*, he writes that "within forty years *or so* of 1948 [when Israel

---

[33] Ibid., 75, emphasis original.
[34] Wojcik, *The End of the World As We Know It*, 26.

declared its independence], all these things *could* take place."[35] Lindsey based his loose prediction on a saying by Jesus in the gospel of Matthew, identifying the spring leafing of the fig tree as a symbol for the establishment of Israel and a "generation" as forty years:

> "From the fig tree learn its lesson: as soon as its branch becomes tender and puts forth its leaves, you know that summer is near. So also, when you see *these things*, you know that he is near, at the very gates. Truly I tell you, this generation will not pass away until all *these things* have taken place." (Matt 24:32-34, emphasis added).

Lindsey is stretching the envelope of his avowed literalism. In this passage, Jesus is using the fig tree's early leaves as a metaphor, not a symbol. Jesus has been speaking in the preceding paragraphs of similar signs (*these things*) that indicate that the kingdom of God is near, not in some indefinite time but in the present. Jesus uses the fig tree, a commonplace in the life of first-century Palestinian peasants like Jesus and his disciples, to aid his disciples' understanding that the kingdom was imminent, like the arrival of summer after the fig tree blooms, and would be fulfilled in ordinary and not thermonuclear ways. We'll look more at Jesus' teaching about the imminence of the kingdom of God and its mundane manifestations in the third part.

A second way that Miller influenced the use of prophecy to predict the future was to encourage everyday people to use proof-texting methods to draw their own conclusions about how the end times would unfold. The presidency of Andrew Jackson a few decades earlier had opened American government to the participation of common people; Miller felt that study of the Bible should be similarly democratic. Boyle writes, "Just as the Jacksonians claimed that any (white male) citizen could perform the duties of government, so the Millerites insisted that untutored believers could unravel the apocalyptic mysteries."[36] Studying groups of Bible passages that might predict an end-times catastrophe became a grassroots enterprise with the enthusiasm (and distrust of disciplined scholarship) characteristic of those movements.

A third way Miller influenced the popular study of biblical prophecy was by using methods he believed were rational and scientific. Drawing on the contemporary interest in almanacs to predict the weather, he argued that his study methods were just as data-driven and rigorous; modern dispensationalist writing still uses pseudoscientific arguments adorned with tables and pictograms that array the biblical data on which they are based.

✝

---

[35] Lindsey, *The Late Great Planet Earth*, 43, emphasis added.
[36] Boyer, *When Time Shall Be No More*, 83.

Pastors influenced by John Darby's American speaking tours popularized dispensationalism in their churches, especially among Presbyterians and Baptists. A Presbyterian minister in St. Louis, James H. Brookes (1830-97), published an influential book about the end times, *The Lord Cometh*, and organized the Niagara Bible Conference, a series of summer conferences that eventually landed at Niagara-on-the-Lake, a resort on Lake Ontario. Prophecy conferences like Brookes' were attended by thousands, abetted by the development in the late nineteenth century of a rail network that made a family vacation at a conference center affordable on a preacher's salary.

Not all evangelicals at these conferences were dispensationalists, nor were they premillennarians. Some evangelicals, postmillennarians like the younger Mather, believed that the tribulation would occur at the close of the millennium; they were a remnant of the positivist strain of evangelicalism in the earlier nineteenth century that saw slavery, child labor, the denial of the vote to women, and alcoholism as impediments to the millennium's arrival that should be extirpated. This strand of optimistic and socially active millennialism would persist into the early twentieth century as the "Social Gospel," but its adherents were on the decline in the late nineteenth century, and the conferences increasingly embraced premillennialist views.[37]

Responding to demand for formal training in Bible prophecy prompted by conferences and revivals, fifty Bible institutes were established, foremost among them the Moody Bible Institute in Chicago, founded in 1886 by Dwight L. Moody (1837-99), an important figure in American evangelical history. After gaining fame in a revivalist tour of Great Britain, he returned to America and led a series of huge revivals here. Moody saw his mission as saving souls from the tribulation and from damnation: "I look upon this world as a wrecked vessel. God has given me a lifeboat and said to me, 'Moody, save as many as you can.'"[38]

Moody's message differed from the more positive views that had predominated in American evangelicalism until then. The late nineteenth century was a time of radical changes in people's economic and social lives: an influx of poor immigrants challenged the presumed homogeneity of American communities; the rise of large cities brought crime, poverty, and pollution; the role of the yeoman farmer as the building block of American democracy had diminished; large bureaucracies in finance and government had developed; and manufactured killing machines had emerged as the bloody instruments of war. In the United States, interest in the end-times was compounded by the horrors, moral acrimony, and divisiveness of the Civil War, which northern evangelicals (of the optimistic strain) had supported to end black slavery and hasten God's kingdom but which resulted, in the south, in violent, reactionary

---

[37] Wojcik, *The End of the World As We Know It*, 34-35.
[38] Quoted in Marsden, *Understanding Fundamentalism and Evangelicalism*, 21.

movements to undo new black freedoms by extralegal means.

To disseminate more widely the ideas emerging from Bible conferences and popularized by Moody and other evangelists, in 1910 two oil tycoons financed the printing of hundreds of thousands of copies of a four-volume set of lectures titled *The Fundamentals* and sent them free to hundreds of thousands of pastors, seminarians, and YMCAs.[39] The World's Christian Fundamentals Association was founded in 1919, and the term *fundamentalist* was first used during a conference held in 1920.[40] Within this movement emerged *five fundamentals* variously phrased in evangelical literature that can be summarized as follows:

1. The scriptures accurately depict historical events, including especially:
2. The virgin birth and deity of Jesus Christ, and
3. His bodily resurrection.
4. Scriptures also accurately depict future events at the close of history,
5. In particular Jesus Christ's return to hold sinners accountable.

To assess the dimensions of the key term in the fourth fundamental, "accurately depict future events," consider the following comment witnessed by journalist Craig Unger, who tagged along with Tim LaHaye and a tour group on a visit to the Megiddo valley in Israel, where the book of Revelation seems to locate the battle of Armageddon:

> "Can you imagine this entire valley filled with blood?' [the tourist] asks. "That would be a 200-mile-long river of blood, four and a half feet deep. We've done the math. That's the blood of as many as two and a half billion people."[41]

The tourist is interpreting this figurative passage, a vision in the book of Revelation, as literal:

> So the Angel swung his sickle over the earth and gathered the vintage of the earth, and he threw it into the great wine press of the wrath of God. And the wine press was trodden outside the city, and blood flowed from the wine press as high as a horse's bridle, for a distance of two hundred miles. (Rev 14:19-20)

In the passage to which the tourist refers, the author of the book of Revelation is alluding to prophecies in the Old Testament that talk about God's salvation using the metaphor of a *wine press*, a harvest tool; in biblical prophecy, *wine press* usually speaks to God's in-gathering and redemption of a faithful remnant during a time of judgment. *Blood* in this passage is better interpreted within the tradition of Jesus' sacrifice on the cross, where *blood* describes the wine used in the fellowship ritual of the Lord's Supper and symbolizes reconciliation ("for this is my blood of the covenant, which is poured out *for many* for the forgiveness of sins" [Matt 26:28, emphasis added]). The volume of

---

[39] *The Fundamentals* is still available from Baker Publishers and online at Christianbook. com.

[40] Marsden, *Understanding Fundamentalism and Evangelicalism*, 57.

[41] Quoted by Craig Unger, "American Rapture," *Vanity Fair*, December 2005.

the blood at Armageddon speaks to the incalculable number of people whom God will gather in a transformed world when time is fulfilled.

✝

The developmental stage of dispensational premillenialism in the United States reached its zenith in the *Scofield Reference Bible*, published in 1909. An annotation of the seventeenth-century King James Version of the Bible, it continues to be an essential reference today among fundamentalists and evangelicals. The book's editor, Cyrus I. Scofield (1843-1921), had early character problems but rediscovered his faith in prison (on charges of forgery) and began an association with James Brookes, the founder of the Niagara Bible Conference. Through Brookes, he met other emerging evangelical leaders including especially Dwight Moody, who thought so highly of him that he asked Scofield to be the pastor of his congregation; at Moody's death, Scofield presided at his funeral.[42]

The *Scofield Reference Bible* guides the reader through the Bible by framing the biblical text with headings and annotating it with comments in parallel columns that reflect Scofield's dispensationalist interpretation. The tone in his commentaries is authoritative and he hammers at dispensationalist and premillennialist themes: the corruption of the mainstream churches, the necessity of the return of the Jews to the Holy Land to reestablish Israel, pessimism that mankind will conform its behavior to God's commandments in this current age, and the inevitability of a tribulation at its close.

The *Scofield Reference Bible* was an extraordinary religious publishing success: sales reached one million copies by 1930.[43] The original entered the public domain long ago,[44] but new editions (using updated versions of the King James translation) are widely available at Christian bookstores. Its publisher, Oxford University Press, now offers a "2009 Centennial Edition." Indicating its continuing relevance to conservative interpreters of the Bible, Tim LaHaye's 1999 commentary on the book of Revelation opens with a quote from it:

> Almost one hundred years ago the author of the *Scofield Reference Bible* said in his notes on Revelation, "Doubtless, much which is designedly obscure to us will be clear to those for whom it was written as *the time approaches.*" Most prophecy scholars believe that time is at hand, and many things are clearer today than they were in Dr. Scofield's day.[45]

---

[42] Boyer, *When Time Shall Be No More*, 97.

[43] Karleen, Paul S., "The Centennial of the Scofield Study Bible." Online at http://g. christianbook.com/netstorage/pdf/more/7964X.pdf

[44] Searchable databases of the version of the Scofield Reference Bible in the public domain are online at http://www.studylight.org/com/srn/ and http://www.searchgodsword.org/com/srn/

[45] LaHaye, *Revelation Unveiled*, 13, emphasis original.

The *Scofield Reference Bible* continued the tradition of democratic Bible study begun by William Miller in the mid-nineteenth century. Scofield demystified the Bible for people who were deeply interested in it but didn't have the time to learn biblical languages or to debate alternative interpretations and theologies. Scofield's demystification was a radical interpretation of the Bible, but it conformed nicely to the pessimism of its times and the conservatism of fundamentalists, and it has been widely accepted in conservative evangelical circles as authoritative.

Dispensationalism, premillennialism, and fundamentalism were reactions to rationalism, the idea that science could be used to perfect society. Rationalism was a real threat to the popular religion that had marked American Protestantism during the colonial period. Scripture literally understood described the natural world in ways that simply weren't accurate, and science stood to make the religion of Edwards and the Mathers irrelevant. Liberal approaches that used the emerging disciplines of literature, history, and anthropology to aid the interpretation of the Bible were opportunities to make sense of religion in a secular age and they were embraced by many seminaries. However, religious conservatives observed brutal wars, civil discord, and the chaos of cities as manifestations of the errors of modernist theology and stolidly advanced their fundamentalism, firmly planting it on supernatural information in fantastic passages of scripture.[46] A huge divide had opened between conservative and progressive American Protestants, and the moat that separated them seems to widen even today.

---

[46] Marsden, "The Protestant Crisis and the Rise of Fundamentalism, 1870-1930," in *Understanding Fundamentalism and Evangelicalism*.

Chapter 3
THE DISPENSATIONALIST
FOCUS ON JUDGMENT

During his challenge in 2004 to the reelection of President George W. Bush, Senator John Kerry was the target of a withering attack on his faith by religious conservatives because of his accommodation, as a Roman Catholic, with the permissive Supreme Court decision on abortion in Roe *v.* Wade. Attempting (with many Democrats) to assert the strength of his religious faith, Senator Kerry addressed an audience at Pepperdine University on September 18, 2006, and said:

> I consider public leadership to be a form of Christian service and an expression of my faith. I believe the most important teaching of the Gospels is that it is not enough just to say one believes in Jesus. Believing in Jesus requires action—-it requires a bona fide effort—-commitment to live in the example of Jesus and nowhere in my judgment is the expectation of service more clearly stated than in Matthew 25:34:
> "For I was hungry and you gave me food, I was thirsty and you gave me something to drink, I was a stranger and you welcomed me,
> "I was naked and you gave me clothing, I was sick and you took care of me, I was in prison and you visited me."[47]

Senator Kerry was referring to a prophecy of Jesus, presented here in its entirety because it will come up again and again in this book:

> [Jesus said,] "When the Son of Man comes in his glory, and all the angels with him, then he will sit on the throne of his glory. All the nations will be gathered before him, and he will separate people one from another as a shepherd separates the sheep from the goats, and he will put the sheep at his right hand and the goats at the left. Then the king will say to those at his right

---

[47] "Text of John Kerry's Speech on Faith," Washington Post, September 18, 2006. Online at: http://www.washingtonpost.com/wp-dyn/content/article/2006/09/18/AR2006091801016.html?nav=hcmodule

hand, 'Come, you that are blessed by my Father, inherit the kingdom prepared for you from the foundation of the world; for I was hungry and you gave me food, I was thirsty and you gave me something to drink, I was a stranger and you welcomed me, I was naked and you gave me clothing, I was sick and you took care of me, I was in prison and you visited me.' Then the righteous will answer him, 'Lord, when was it that we saw you hungry and gave you food, or thirsty and gave you something to drink? And when was it that we saw you a stranger and welcomed you, or naked and gave you clothing? And when was it that we saw you sick or in prison and visited you?' And the king will answer them, 'Truly I tell you, just as you did it to one of the least of these who are members of my family, you did it to me.'" (Matthew 25:31-40)

Senator Kerry had chosen a passage that means one thing to progressive Christians and quite another to conservative evangelicals such as John Hagee, author of end-times books, founder and pastor of the 17,000-member Cornerstone Church in San Antonio, president of Global Evangelism Television, and outspoken advocate for the geographical expansion of the modern nation of Israel. Hagee caused a minor stir during the 2008 presidential election campaign reminiscent of the one caused by Tim LaHaye's involvement in Jack Kemp's presidential campaign twenty years earlier. Republican Party candidate John McCain received Hagee's endorsement, then rejected it after Hagee was denounced by the president of the otherwise conservative Catholic League, Bill Donohue, who said, "For the past few decades, [Hagee] has waged an unrelenting war against the Catholic Church. For example, he likes calling it 'The Great Whore,' an 'apostate church,' the 'anti-Christ,' and a 'false cult system.'" [48]

An assurance of harsh judgment, not a scolding from Jesus for a lack of compassion for the poor and oppressed, is what Hagee gleans from the passage Kerry used in his speech about public service. Hagee comments on Jesus' sermon about "the least of these" in one of his books about the end times, *The Revelation of Truth*, where we may observe the literal interpreter at work. First, Hagee limits the applicability of the passage. Considering the line, "Truly I tell you, just as you did it to one of the least of these who are members of my family, you did it to me," Hagee interprets "members of my family" as pertaining to the treatment of Jews by Gentiles.

Hagee then rejects a literal reading of the text:

> Upon a casual reading of Matthew's passage, you might think these Gentiles are being judged by their works—if they gave food and water to the ministering Jews, they would be allowed to obtain eternal life. The idea, however, contradicts the entire body of Scripture, for nowhere does God allow man to be saved through his own efforts. [49]

---

[48] Catholic League for Civil and Religious Rights, "McCain Embraces Bigot," online at http://www.catholicleague.org/release.php?id=1393.

[49] Hagee, The Revelation of Truth, 236.

His argument is the evangelical doctrine of "salvation by faith alone." That salvation comes by accepting it from a televangelist to the exclusion of acting on moral obligations to the poor is another arguable proposition, but it's one we won't pursue here. Hagee is more interested in a detail in the dispensationalist end-times scenario: the 144,000 Jewish converts to Christianity in Israel who, dispensationalists believe based on a passage in the book of Revelation (7:9-17), are the "least of these" and will be worldwide witnesses for Jesus during the tribulation.

The significance to Hagee of "the least of these" saying in Matthew is *not* Jesus' encouragement to heal the sick or feed the hungry, which Senator Kerry said drove his interest in public service. Rather, end-times writers like Hagee value the passage because it provides documentary evidence that Jesus Christ, amid the wreckage of the tribulation, will divide those of us who have been saved by their born-again faith from those who haven't, and judge us accordingly.

✝

God's repeated judgment of the faithless throughout history is a crucial theme in dispensationalist theology. Judgment, in fact, is the organizing principal of dispensationalism; fundamentalists like Hagee divide history into distinct ages that each end in judgment, portending that the current age will end similarly.

Hagee's book *The Revelation of Truth*, where he commented on the passage that drives Senator Kerry's public service, is a good example of popular end-times books that order biblical history using the dispensationalist scheme. Each division of the biblical history is a melodrama of promise, betrayal, punishment, and salvation. As each dispensation opens, God gives people rules and they enter into an agreement to heed them, a covenant to be God's people. But people inevitably rebel, and God intervenes to punish the rebellious and to defeat Satan, who is behind the rebellion. God preserves a righteous remnant with whom a new covenant is made to begin the following age. Here is how Hagee applies the dispensationalist regime of revelation, covenant, judgment, defeat of evil, and preservation of a remnant in each of the ages in the dispensationalist scheme of history:

Age of Innocence: God offers eternal life to Adam and Eve as long as they don't eat of the "tree of the knowledge of good and evil" (Gen 2:15-17). In the form of a snake, Satan successfully tempts Eve; the couple is expelled from the Garden of Eden to endure the hardships of life in the world outside God's garden and the snake is condemned to slither on the earth. Hagee writes: "Their failure was not only personal, but it also affected the entire world, plunging us all into the depravity of sin."[50]

---

[50] Ibid., 41

Age of Conscience: God expels Adam and Eve with a curse which Hagee identifies as a covenant that permits people to rule themselves and to dominate the rest of creation using their knowledge of good and evil. However, corruption and immorality become universal. God asks Noah and his family, who alone are righteous, to build and crew a boat to save two each of the creatures of the earth from the worldwide flood that God sends in judgment; humanity, except Noah's family, is destroyed. Hagee identifies the Flood story as an archetype of the end times: "God's purpose for the Tribulation is to punish the ungodly who have rejected His Son, Jesus Christ. . . . God will be true to the picture He painted in Genesis: first warning, then rescue, and then judgment."[51]

Age of Human Government: When the flood recedes, God makes a covenant with Noah to never again destroy the world if humanity follows certain rules.[52] Noah's descendants repopulate the earth. The first legendary warrior, named Nimrod, emerges to found Babel and other early Mesopotamian cities. The people of Babel build a tower to connect themselves with the heavens, but their hubris offends God who destroys the tower and scatters the inhabitants. Abraham, the ancestor of Israel, leaves Mesopotamia to settle in Palestine. Hagee concludes: "They made lofty plans for their one-world religion and their one-world government, but God had other ideas! . . . *Babel and its founder, a man called Nimrod, are pictures of the coming Antichrist and his empire.*"[53]

Age of Promise: God promises Abraham that his descendants will be entitled to the lands of Palestine forever, but they lose faith and are enslaved in Egypt. God afflicts Egypt with a series of ten plagues and catastrophes; after the last plague, when God spares the children of the Israelites from the death of first-born children he has decreed (the first Passover), God helps the Israelite tribes escape Egypt and they enter the wilderness of Sinai under the leadership of Moses.

Age of Law: God reveals his Law to Moses in the wilderness of Sinai and he memorializes it in the first five books of the Bible, the *Torah*. The central event of the *Age of Law* is Moses' receipt of the Ten Commandments, which in Hagee's view are "the keys to personal, social, and national greatness."[54] The Israelites establish a nation but disobey the Law. Their repeated rebellions against God result in the division of the nation, military defeat, and exile and occupation by empires. After Jesus, the Messiah, is killed, Israel's temple is destroyed and the Jews are dispersed, but the disciples of Jesus Christ organize a church.

Age of Grace: God temporarily ends his work through Israel and works instead through the church. However, "division, strife, immorality, greed, and

---

[51] Ibid., 70.
[52] Ibid., 91-3. The covenant is Gen 9:1-16.
[53] Ibid., 101, emphasis original.
[54] Ibid., 162.

apostasy crept swiftly into the early church, and the situation didn't improve much in later years."[55] The antichrist will appear and the tribulation will begin after the rescue of the born-again in the rapture. The tribulation kills multitudes; billions more die in the climactic battle of Armageddon. The survivors—the sheep and the goats—are judged by Jesus when the Age of Grace closes.

Age of the Kingdom: Beginning with the judgment that closes the tribulation, God keeps his promise to Abraham by settling Christians and converted Jews in the nation of Israel, now ruled by Jesus Christ. After a thousand years, the antichrist as Satan emerges from his captivity to lead a rebellion but is permanently defeated. Again, God judges all people, and for the saved, eternity begins.

✝

That there are seven ages, reflecting the seven days of creation and the other uses of the number seven throughout the Bible, persuades dispensationalists that their sevenfold interpretation of biblical history is consistent with the primordial rhythm of judgment and redemption established when God created the world in six days and rested on the seventh. Furthermore, the rhythm culminates in the closing book of the Bible, Revelation, where God battles the forces of evil in a sevenfold battle.

During each of the first five ages that concluded with Jesus' death and especially during the *Age of Law*, prophets warned people of imminent judgment that later occurred as they predicted; Hagee believes that biblical prophecies about the coming judgment at the end of the current, sixth, dispensation and at the end of the seventh, the millennium, will similarly prove to be accurate. Here's Hagee on the subject of prophetic inerrancy:

> The books that form the foundation for other major religions and cults interpret the present or deal with the past, but the Bible, when written, was 25 percent prophecy. From Genesis to Revelation, countless prophecies were given, and most have been *exactly* fulfilled.[56]

The repetition of the dispensationalist regime in each of the ages—revelation, covenant, judgment, defeat of evil, and preservation of a remnant—communicates a dark and pessimistic understanding of humanity's relationship with God. It views God as punitive and authoritarian and people as weak, immoral, and irresponsible. God's treatment of unrepentant humanity is marked by willful and disproportionate violence. God's laws must be followed at the risk of judgment and eternal damnation; the risk of punishment, not the proffer of hope, drives the human spirit. Hope is limited to the conviction that at some uncertain time, but soon, Jesus Christ will descend into the midair and

---

[55] Ibid., 204.

[56] Hagee, *From Daniel to Doomsday*, 3, emphasis original.

gather up the believers to spare them from the global catastrophe that will end this immoral age. God's judgment is cataclysmic, inevitable, and imminent.[57]

Considering how the current age will end, Hagee extends God's condemnation, typical of end-times writers, to his nation:

> *God always judges sin.* This is a message America needs to hear. If God crushed Israel because they became a pagan society, God will crush American for the same reason. . . .
>   God will judge America for our slaughter of unborn children in America's abortion mills and for the official endorsement from the White House to the church house of homosexuality as an alternative lifestyle.[58]

Hagee despairs that increasing instances of cyber-terrorism, the collapse of international economies, the wider availability to terrorists of chemical and biological weapons, all indicate the imminence of a time when God will judge America for its unrepentant sinfulness: "Our national conscience is *dead.* . . . America is a soulless mockery of what she once was. Our society, like ancient Rome's, is headed for *destruction.*"[59]

Death and *destruction.* Is that what the Bible predicts?

---

[57] As I write this, the world grieves victims of a cataclysmic earthquake in Port-au-Prince, Haiti, a nation of descendants of a successful slave rebellion against France not long after the American Revolution against Great Britain. Televangelist Pat Robertson, a candidate for President in 1987, reacted to the news by saying that Haiti suffered this catastrophe because it signed a pact with the devil during their revolution, which ironically was made against the satanic power of slavery and colonialism. Associated Press, "Pat Robertson: Haiti 'Cursed' by Pact With Devil," New York Times, January 13, 2009. Online at: http://www.nytimes.com/aponline/2010/01/13/us/AP-US-Haiti-Pat-Robertson.html

[58] Hagee, *From Daniel to Doomsday*, 8, emphasis original.

[59] Ibid., 86, emphasis added.

Chapter 4

ONE END-TIMES SCENARIO

By the end of the nineteenth century, conservative evangelicals had developed a consensus framework for end-times scenarios and a standard portfolio of related Bible verses that are still used by most end-times writers as their basis. End-times books reflect changing ideas about the identity of God's enemies (such as the recent shift from Soviet communism to militant Islam) and target the social trends that most alarm conservative evangelicals (usually sexual), but the basic ingredients are present in all of them. A good modern example is John Hagee's 1999 book *From Daniel to Doomsday: The Countdown Has Begun*, and what follows is a précis of that book's end-times scenario.

Rapture

As it does in the opening novel in the *Left Behind* series, the rapture occurs suddenly and chaos results: "Empty cars will careen down the highway, their drivers and occupants absent. Homes of believers will stand empty with supper dishes on the dining table, food bubbling on the stove, and water running in the sink."[60]

Russia's attack

Now that the true church is no longer present on earth to restrain Satan, Hagee says, "The wrath of God can now be poured out on the earth."[61] Russia attacks Israel.

End-times writers differ on whether the attack from Russia occurs at the opening of the tribulation, at its conclusion, or at the end of the millennium. Hagee is reluctant "to be dogmatic" about the timing of the attack and writes, "Make no mistake—at some moment in the countdown to doomsday, Russia,

---

[60] Ibid., 92.
[61] Ibid., 100.

together with her Arab allies, will lead a massive attack upon the nation of Israel that probably will involve nuclear weapons."[62] Russia, eager to control Persian Gulf oil on which its enemies in the west depend, will ally with Turkey, Libya, Iran, and Ethiopia, nations "that are constantly calling for holy war to exterminate Israel."[63]

Hagee doesn't address some obvious difficulties in this scenario, if it is to occur soon. Turkey, while predominantly Muslim, is a secular democracy and a member with the United States in NATO, the North Atlantic Treaty Organization, which provides for a common defense. A third of Ethiopia's inhabitants are Muslim, but the majority of its population is Christian. Neither of these nations is preoccupied with Israel as an enemy. Still, Hagee believes that peace negotiations over Palestine are doomed because conflict between Islam and Israel is essentially racial and foreordained by God:

> The enmity that exists between Israel and the Arabs goes all the way back to Abraham, Hagar, and Sarah. The Arab tribes are descended from Ishmael, the son of Abraham's impatience, while the Israelites are descended from Isaac, the son of God's promise.[64]

When Russia and her Muslim allies attack Israel, God reacts in fury. An earthquake shakes mountains and the seas. God sows dissension and the allies turn on one another, exchanging biological, chemical, and nuclear weapons. Perhaps, Hagee speculates, Israel fires her nuclear weapons at Russia, provoking a nuclear exchange between Russia and Israel's chief ally, the United States. Regardless, the invading army will be annihilated, and the dead soldiers will provide a ghastly banquet for birds of prey and wild animals.[65]

The antichrist and the tribulation

The rapture and the attack by Russia signal the beginning of the tribulation: seven years of war, famine, and natural disaster.

The key actor in the tribulation is a figure end-times writers call *the antichrist*, a "global personality whose name will be on everyone's lips."[66] He pretends to be the savior of the world from its troubles, but he is in fact a fraud. There's a tradition in end-times books of suggesting some contemporary person as the antichrist,[67] but Hagee demurs: "I don't know his name and wouldn't hazard a guess, but I believe he is alive at this moment and knows his satanic assignment."[68] He will have a "reputation of being a powerful man of peace .

---

[62] Ibid., 118.

[63] Ibid., 123.

[64] Ibid., 129.

[65] Ibid., 138-150.

[66] Ibid., 161.

[67] Boyer lists many candidates from the end-times literature ranging from the Pope through John F. Kennedy to Henry Kissinger in Chapter 8 of *When Time Shall Be No More*.

[68] Hagee, *From Daniel to Doomsday*, 161.

. . perhaps a Nobel Prize winner"; he has "hypnotic charm and charisma"; he will emerge from somewhere in the lands of the former Roman Empire; he will have made his reputation as an authoritarian leader; and he will offer Israel seven years of his protection following the failed Russian invasion.[69]

Under the antichrist's influence and ultimately his hegemony, the tribulation begins. The antichrist has "a three-point plan for world domination":[70]

"One world economy." The antichrist will implement a single currency where all transactions are monitored and economic transactions are limited to people who carry a mark. Hagee warns that the appropriate technology, and the readiness to use it, is at hand: "American politicians are now talking about implementing a national identity card, ostensibly to cut down on illegal aliens. Our government is putting on a full-court press that ultimately will give them the power to control cash transactions."[71]

"One-world government." Warning about international cooperative efforts since the world wars of the twentieth century to prevent war and improve global human conditions, Hagee provides an unreferenced quote from the first director of the World Health Organization, Brock Chisholm (1896-1971), as symptomatic of Satan's continuing effort to force humanity into a dehumanizing amalgam under a single authority: "'To achieve world government, it is necessary to remove from the minds of men their individualism, loyalty to their families, national patriotism, and religion.'"[72]

"One-world religion." Referring to a thirteenth-century prophecy by Rabbi Maimonides that the Messiah will rebuild the temple and "gather the dispersed remnant," Hagee writes: "After the war of Gog-Magog [the Russian invasion], the hearts of the children of Israel will turn toward the God of Abraham, Isaac, and Jacob. In a surge of reawakening religious interest, they will rebuild the temple."[73]

---

[69] Ibid., 176-7. The arguably premature award in 2009 of the Nobel Peace Prize to President Barack Obama, whom an evangelical fringe have already identified as the antichrist, has fueled their suspicions; for example, Patrice Lewis, "The One won, but for what?," *World Net Daily*, online at: http://www.wnd.com/index.php?fa=PAGE.view&pageId=112466

[70] Ibid., 178.

[71] Ibid., 180. As I edit this in 2010, the Virginia state legislature (with the legislatures of other southern states) is considering legislation to prohibit this use of technology, as if anyone is considering it: "Human microchips seen by some in Virginia House as device of antichrist," New York Times, February 10, 2010. Online at: http://www.washingtonpost.com/wp-dyn/content/article/2010/02/09/AR2010020903796.html

[72] Ibid., 182. Brock Chisholm was a Canadian, a psychiatrist, an internationalist, and a Unitarian, each sufficient by itself for condemnation by the religious right. Hagee doesn't source the quote, but it appears frequently on far-right Internet sites, some of which source it to John A. Stormer's book, *None Dare Call It Treason*, a nonfiction bestseller when it appeared in 1964, the year of ultraconservative Barry Goldwater's unsuccessful run for the presidency. Stormer feared that the United States would lose the Cold War because its government had been infiltrated by Communists. See PublicEye.org, "Goldwater and the True Believers," online at: www.publiceye.org/huntred/Hunt_For_Red_Menace-04.html

[73] Ibid., 183-4. Maimonides is quoted by Hagee, but he doesn't source the quote.

Hagee doesn't acknowledge that rebuilding the temple has huge geo-political consequences. On the Temple Mount in Jerusalem presently sits the Al Aqsa Mosque marking where Mohammed, the Prophet of Islam, departed on his "Night Journey" to heaven. The mosque is the third-holiest site for Sunni Muslims who are majorities in Saudi Arabia, Kuwait, and Jordan, all of them allies of the United States. Hagee is also sanguine about prospects for a new temple on the site in his more recent book about the Mideast crisis, *Jerusalem Countdown*, where he writes: "I believe my generation will live to see [Jesus Christ] sitting on the throne of King David on the Temple Mount in the city of Jerusalem, bringing the Golden Age of Peace to the world. It's coming much sooner than you think!"[74]

Amid the ruins left in the aftermath of the Russian invasion of Israel, Satan's evil influence on human events spreads. "Anarchy will reign as societies break down, the 'haves' rioting against the 'have nots.' . . . People will kill one another on battlefields, in subways, on highways, in cities, in country fields."[75] A meteor strike will cause an earthquake, tidal waves, and months of darkness: "Astronomers predict that Earth's next close brush with a meteor will be in 2126 when the comet Swift-Tuttle comes near, but I believe God could bring a comet any time He chooses to accomplish His purposes."[76]

As the midpoint of the tribulation nears, God places a mark on 144,000 Jews who have converted to Christianity to preserve them from the *great tribulation* that will soon begin; for Hagee, this group will be the Jewish evangelists of whom Jesus speaks in his prophecy of the judgment of the sheep who minister to the evangelists, and the goats who don't.

The great tribulation

At the midpoint of the tribulation, the antichrist goes to Jerusalem. An assistant, the *false prophet*, builds an image of the antichrist in the temple; it seduces people to worship it and is capable of decapitating people who don't. Their appearance inaugurates the great tribulation, the final three-and-a-half years of the seven-year tribulation.

It opens with seven natural disasters that affect everyone except the 144,000 Jewish-Christian evangelists who have been sealed against the tribulation's effects. There's a hail of fire; a meteor strikes the oceans, killing a third of its fishes; a meteor strike poisons the earth's fresh waters; a "veil of thick fog" dims the sun, moons, and stars;[77] stinging locusts emerging from a smoking pit; a demonic cavalry 200 million strong crosses toward Palestine from present-day

---

[74] Hagee, *Jerusalem Countdown*, 228. As a marker for his generation, Hagee was born in 1940. Tim LaHaye writes hopefully that efforts to rebuild the temple may already be underway: *Revelation Unveiled*, 184.

[75] Hagee, *From Daniel to Doomsday*, 184.

[76] Ibid., 189.

[77] Ibid., 212.

Iraq, killing a third of mankind.

The seventh disaster is a series of seven global catastrophes: a plague of sores; the death of all the fish in the sea; rivers turn to blood; the sun increases its heat; darkness covers the earth; the Euphrates River dries up, permitting a 200 million-strong cavalry to ride toward Palestine; an earthquake and giant hailstones destroy the mountains and all the cities.

Armageddon

The antichrist has earthly enemies. He is attacked by armies from Egypt; he's victorious, but troubled by armies from the east who array themselves against the other armies for a battle that begins in the plains of Megiddo, north of Jerusalem.

But Jesus Christ intervenes with *his* army, which includes John Hagee: "I will be in that army, for it is composed of the loyal angels of God and those who were raptured with the Church!" Jesus, armed with a sword in his mouth, speaks and slays the assembled worldly armies "in milliseconds."[78] The antichrist and the false prophet are cast into a lake of fire.

Millennium, judgment, and eternity

Jesus Christ's defeat of the antichrist is an occasion for rejoicing; the Jews of Israel realize that the Messiah has come. But before Jesus Christ's thousand-year reign over Israel begins, Gentiles are judged on how they treated the Jews; not just those who persecuted the 144,000 Jewish-Christian evangelists during the tribulation but also the Roman Catholic Church (for the Spanish Inquisition) and the British Government (for preventing Jewish immigration from Nazi Germany to Palestine) are also condemned.[79]

Then, the millennial kingdom begins. Jesus Christ rules a transformed Israel whose borders now extend to the lands promised to Abraham. A miraculous river flows east and west from the Mount of Olives, near Jerusalem, restoring aquatic life to the Dead Sea. Jerusalem becomes a dazzling city and a global center of worship, a place where all the nations visit to learn the ways of the Lord.

A final war with Satan reminiscent of the Russian invasion that opened the tribulation will occur at the close of the millennium; to prevail, God must destroy the world. A final judgment occurs for the souls waiting in hell, who are cast into the lake of fire. The faithful from all ages escape earth's implosion to live in the New Jerusalem in heaven for eternity.

Thus does God's creation end.

---

[78] Ibid., 234.
[79] Ibid., 240-42.

BIBLICAL SOURCES FOR END-TIMES EVENTS
Chapter 5

John Hagee does a better job than most end-times writers of documenting biblical sources for his scenario of last things, and in the pages that follow I'll list those sources and indicate where they will be discussed in my book. In most cases, I've quoted the relevant biblical passages so the reader can get a sense of how they inform Hagee's scenario. The Bible's prophetic and apocalyptic literature centered on important events in Israel's history, so a chronology will be helpful as we proceed; the reader can find one in Appendix 2.

Rapture

Among other New Testament passages, Hagee identifies this passage in a letter of the Apostle Paul as the basis for his prediction of a rapture:[80]

> Then we who are alive, who are left, will be caught up in the clouds together with [the faithful who have died] to meet the Lord in the air; and so we will be with the Lord forever. (1 Thess 4:17)

Paul wrote his first letter to the Thessalonian Christians about two decades after Jesus' death and addressed, among other things, their concern that faithful members of the congregation have died before Jesus Christ's promised return within their lifetimes to fulfill God's kingdom. A second letter to the Thessalonians, most likely written two decades later, also alludes to a rapture but addresses why Jesus' promised return has been delayed beyond the lifetimes of *all* of the people to whom Jesus made his promise. I'll discuss both letters as part of my review of the Bible's apocalyptic literature in Part Three.

Russia's attack

Hagee's biblical source for the attack by Russia and her allies on Israel is a prophecy by the Old Testament prophet Ezekiel about a warlord named Gog of Magog.[81] Ezekiel was a priest and prophet during the exile of Jews in Babylon following catastrophic military defeats and the destruction of Solomon's temple in Jerusalem in 587 BCE. In his "Gog of Magog" prophecy (Ezek 38-9), the

---

[80] Ibid., 90-91.
[81] Ibid., 121-153.

armies of Gog invade Palestine from the far reaches of the then-known world. In the New King James Version of the Bible used by Hagee, Gog is described as "the prince of Rosh" (38:2 NKJV), a place that Hagee and many, but not all, end-times writers identify as Russia.[82] In other Bibles, notably the KJV and NRSV, the word *rosh* in the original Hebrew is translated as an adjective, *chief,* to modify the word *prince* so that Gog is the *chief prince* rather than the *prince of Rosh.* Ezekiel prophesies that Gog's armies will be joined by armies from Persia, Ethiopia, Put (modern Libya), and Gomar-Bethtogarmar (modern Turkey) (Ezek 38:5-6), all places that are more reliably located by other ancient sources.

Ezekiel describes an earthquake, confusion, and fiery natural phenomena that fall on Gog's armies after God tempts them to attack:

> On that day, when Gog comes against the land of Israel, says the Lord God, my wrath shall be aroused. . . . On that day there shall be a great shaking in the land of Israel; . . . With pestilence and bloodshed I will enter into judgment with him; and I will pour down torrential rains and hailstones, fire and sulfur, upon him and his troops and the many peoples that are with him. (Ezek 38:18-22)

That the United States may be involved in a nuclear exchange with Russia is deduced from the following passage, where Hagee and many other end-times writers interpret "coastlands" as a symbol for America: "I will send fire on Magog and on those who live securely in the coastlands; and they shall know that I am the Lord" (Ezek 39:6).

Ezekiel's prophecy of God's battle with Gog ends with the restoration of Israel to her land, but not without a ghastly banquet enjoyed by birds of prey and wild animals, for Jews an unimaginably unclean vision of the treatment of dead bodies:

> As for you, mortal [Ezekiel], thus says the Lord God: Speak to the birds of every kind and to all the wild animals: Assemble and come, gather from all around to the sacrificial feast that I am preparing for you, a great sacrificial feast on the mountains of Israel, and you shall eat flesh and drink blood. (Ezek 39:17)

The unclean feast ironically inverts a more hopeful prophecy by another

---

[82] Similarly, Lindsey, *The Late Great Planet Earth,* 53-4. Interpreting *Rosh* as a name for Russia was advanced by the nineteenth century commentator Wilhem Gesenius (1786-1842); Lindsey and other modern end-times writers continue to reference his conclusions. The identification also tracks back to Scofield, who writes in his Reference Notes: "That the primary reference is to the northern (European) powers, headed up by Russia, all agree. . . . The reference to Meshech and Tubal (Moscow and Tobolsk) is a clear mark of identification. Russia and the northern powers have been the latest persecutors of dispersed Israel, and it is congruous both with divine justice and with the covenants . . . that destruction should fall at the climax of the last mad attempt to exterminate the remnant of Israel in Jerusalem." Cyrus Scofield, Reference Notes, "Gog" (Ezek 38:2); online at: http://www.searchgodsword.org/com/srn/view.cgi?book=eze&chapter=038

prophet of that time, Isaiah, of a messianic feast among the nations of the world who come to Jerusalem in peace (Isa 25:6-10). We'll discuss the prophecies of Isaiah and Ezekiel in the next part.

The antichrist

Many books of the Bible refer to a monstrous figure who works in opposition to God or Jesus Christ; it is these prophecies and visions that end-times writers use to characterize the person they call the antichrist. However, in the entire Bible the word *antichrist* appears only in the letters of John in the New Testament, and here is how it is used there: "Children, it is the last hour! As you have heard that antichrist is coming, so now many antichrists have come. From this we know that it is the last hour" (1 John 2:18).

The letters of John were written to a church that had undergone a schism where members with irreconcilable beliefs had left. The remaining church members are commended; those who departed are termed *antichrists* because they focused on a spiritual conception of Jesus Christ to the exclusion of his human, healing aspects. We'll review the history and content of John's letters in Part Three.

Hagee draws part of his profile of the antichrist from references to a figure called "the beast" in the Old Testament book of Daniel.[83] The first half of that book is composed of stories about Daniel, a Jew exiled to Babylon who becomes a valued member of the court of King Nebuchadnezzar (605-562 BCE), who had defeated Judah and carried its aristocracy to Babylon. After the book tells stories about Daniel, it has Daniel himself recount dreams about the future rise to power of an evil ruler. Angels interpret the dreams to Daniel, explaining to him that the dreams are symbol-laden accounts of seven years of tyrannical rule that Israel will endure four hundred years in the future, events that indeed occurred during the second century BCE, when the book of Daniel was almost certainly written. We'll discuss the book of Daniel in Part Three.

The antichrist's origin in ten European nations of the former Roman Empire is sourced by Hagee to this passage in Daniel:

> As for the ten horns [of the fourth beast],
> out of this kingdom ten kings shall arise,
>   and another shall arise after them.
> This one shall be different from the former ones,
>   and shall put down three kings. (Daniel 7:24)

The symbolism here isn't transparent and the dispensationalist analysis is complex, often intertwined with Gibbons' account of history in *The Rise and Fall of the Roman Empire*.[84] Hagee doesn't wade into that swamp but says that

---

[83] Hagee, *From Daniel To Doomsday*, 160-190.
[84] For example, this helpfully-named Web site: www.who-is-the-antichrist.info/

the antichrist's predicted origin in Europe is something "we believe."[85]

Hagee finds the biblical basis for the antichrist's bogus reputation as a peacemaker in this passage in Daniel:[86]

> By his cunning
>   he shall make deceit prosper under his hand
> and in his own mind he shall be great.
>   Without warning he shall destroy many
> and shall even rise up against the Prince of princes. (Daniel 8:25)

The careful reader will notice that the word *peace* isn't used in the NRSV translation of the passage, nor is *peace* used in the passage's other modern translations. Hagee primarily uses the New King James Version for biblical references, but that version doesn't use the word *peace*, either. *Peace* does appear, however, in the original King James Version, the basis for the construction of the dispensationalist end-times scenario in the nineteenth century and a legacy Hagee inherits. Here is the passage as translated by the KJV: "And through his policy also he shall cause craft to prosper in his hand; and he shall magnify himself in his heart, and by *peace* shall destroy many: he shall also stand up against the Prince of princes; but he shall be broken without hand" (Dan 8:25 KJV, emphasis added).

Hagee sources the one-world government ruled autocratically by the antichrist to these texts in Daniel:[87]

> There shall be a fourth kingdom on earth
>   that shall be different from all the other kingdoms;
> it shall devour the whole earth,
>   and trample it down, and break it to pieces. (Dan 7:23)

> "The king shall act as he pleases. He shall exalt himself and consider himself greater than any god. . . ." (Dan 11:36)

That the antichrist will establish a one-world economy is sourced by Hagee to this passage in the book of Revelation:[88] "Also it [a second beast] causes all, both small and great, both rich and poor, both free and slave, to be marked on the right hand or the forehead, so that no one can buy or sell who does not have the mark, that is, the name of the beast or the number of its name (Rev 13:16)."

The book of Revelation closes the New Testament and is a series of fantastic visions of worship and conflict that are seen and heard by John, a late first-century Christian prophet and evangelist. John's visionary account of the final battle between God and Satan is addressed to seven churches in what is

---

[85] Hagee, *From Daniel to Doomsday*, 176.
[86] Ibid., 177.
[87] Ibid., 180.
[88] Ibid., 179.

now western Turkey. Some of the churches were complacent about and even participating in civic ceremonies that honored Roman gods, a practice that the book condemns; the other churches, having resisted Rome's state religion, are encouraged to endure the ostracism and persecution they are suffering as a result. The book of Revelation is the subject of this book's fourth part.

Hagee fails to identify a biblical source for his assertion that the antichrist will impose a one-world religion, although he may have thought it so obvious, so central to his beliefs, a source is unnecessary. In the book of Revelation, the beast "was given authority over every tribe and people and language and nation, and all the inhabitants of the earth will worship it" (Rev 13:7-8).

The tribulation

Hagee refers to several Old Testament prophecies in his discussion of why a tribulation must occur in the end-times.[89] The notion of intense troubles soon that will result in a new age of peace and justice, often using the metaphor of "birth pangs," is common in both the Old and New Testament.[90] Typical is this passage from the prophet Zephaniah who, prior to the Babylonian exile, warned of a *day of the Lord*:

The great day of the Lord is near,
    near and hastening fast;
the sound of the day of the Lord is bitter,
    the warrior cries aloud there.
That day will be a day of wrath,
    a day of distress and anguish,
a day of ruin and devastation,
    a day of darkness and gloom,
a day of clouds and thick darkness,
    a day of trumpet blast and battle cry
against the fortified cities
    and against the lofty battlements. (Zeph 1:14-16)

The next part in this book will discuss Old Testament prophecy, the concept of *the day of the Lord*, and the forms of faithlessness and injustice the prophets believed had earned it.

For New Testament passages that appear to substantiate a tribulation, Hagee uses a saying from Jesus in the gospel of Matthew:[91]

"For many will come in my name, saying, 'I am the Messiah!' and they will lead many astray. And you will hear of wars and rumors of wars; see that you are not alarmed; for this must take place, but the end is not yet. For nation

---

[89] Ibid., 156-7.

[90] Among passages that use the birth-pang metaphor are: Isa 26:17-21; Matt 24:8; 1 Thess 5:2-3; and, symbolically, Rev 12:2. Dennis C. Duling, also suggests two sources from the intra-testamental period: 2 Esd 13:31-32 and 2 Baruch 17. *NRSV Study Bible*, 1902, note on Matt 24:6-8.

[91] Hagee, *From Daniel To Doomsday*, 157.

will rise against nation, and kingdom against kingdom, and there will be famines and earthquakes in various places: all this is but the beginning of the birth pangs." (Matt 24:5-8)

The book of Matthew is a gospel, a biography of Jesus in which his teaching is embedded, that was used in the early church to educate people into the Christian faith. Matthew is one of the four gospels in the New Testament, and it was written about four decades after Jesus' death, following the destruction of Jerusalem by besieging Roman armies in 70 CE. Because it is full of Old Testament allusions, it likely had a Jewish-Christian audience. We will consider the book of Matthew in the third part.

That the tribulation is the ultimate in a series of seven-year periods ("weeks of years" in the Bible) is attributed by Hagee to the book of Daniel, where several timetables allude to a seven-year time of trouble and to a particularly heinous event that occurs midway. [92] In one passage, the angel Gabriel speaks to Daniel during his prayers:

> "After the sixty-two weeks [of years], an anointed one shall be cut off and shall have nothing, and the troops of the prince who is to come shall destroy the city and the sanctuary. Its end shall come with a flood, and to the end shall be war. Desolations are decreed. He shall make a strong covenant with many for *one week*, and for *half of the week* he shall make sacrifice and offering cease; and in their place shall be an abomination that desolates, until the decreed end is poured out upon the desolator." (Dan 9:26-27, emphasis added)

This passage has tantalized end-times writers for centuries because of the apparently precise time periods that precede the culminating tribulation. Given some benchmark in history and accepting the prophecy to be literally true (as well as about the future[93]), one should be able to predict when the tribulation begins.

Hagee's source for the war, civil disorder, famine, pestilence, and dangerous wild animals that open the tribulation is one of the most famous images of the book of Revelation: the four horsemen of the apocalypse.[94] The figure of a lamb, who represents the sacrifice of Jesus, opens the first four of seven seals on a scroll bearing a decree from God:

---

[92] Ibid., 32-33.

[93] The book of Daniel and other prophetic and apocalyptic books often talk about the past and present as if it were the future. The book of Daniel almost certainly was written in the second century BCE to address contemporaneous events, as we will see in Part Three. Hagee, however, applies the "Law of Double Reference" popularized by J. Dwight Pentecost, a prolific writer on the end-times and Professor of Bible Exposition Emeritus at Dallas Theological Seminary, to deduce that Daniel speaks of events in modern times, too. The "law" explains that biblical prophecy may be interpreted as having two referents: one more immediate to the prophet's time, another in the future. Ibid., 167.

[94] Ibid., 184-7.

Then I saw the Lamb open one of the seven seals . . . I looked, and there was a white horse! Its rider had a bow; a crown was given to him, and he came out conquering and to conquer.

When he opened the second seal . . . out came another horse, bright red; its rider was permitted to take peace from the earth, so that people would slaughter one another; and he was given a great sword.

When he opened the third seal . . . there was a black horse! Its rider held a pair of scales in his hand, and I heard what seemed to be a voice . . . saying, "A quart of wheat for a day's pay, and three quarts of barley for a day's pay, but do not damage the olive oil and the wine!"

When he opened the fourth seal . . . I looked and there was a pale green horse! Its rider's name was Death, and Hades followed with him; they were given authority over a fourth of the earth, to kill with sword, famine, and pestilence, and by the wild animals of the earth. (Rev 6:1-7)

Hagee also identifies Ezekiel and Matthew as sources for his predictions about particular troubles during the tribulation:[95] "For thus says the Lord God: How much more when I send upon Jerusalem my four deadly acts of judgment, sword, famine, wild animals, and pestilence, to cut off humans and animals from it! (Ezek 14:21); "For nation will rise against nation, and kingdom, and there will be famines and earthquakes in various places: all this is but the beginning of the birth pangs" (Matt 24:5-7).

Revelation and Matthew were written about the same time, at the end of the first century CE, and both used Ezekiel as their source. New Testament writers often used the imagery of Old Testament prophets to associate their teachings with the prophets' messages about God's holiness, Israel's obligation to mercy and justice, and hope for Israel's redemption; the books of Matthew and Revelation are making those associations in these passages. We'll speak often of re-interpretations of prophecy by later biblical writers throughout this book.

Hagee's source for martyrdoms and a meteor strike during the tribulation is a description in the book of Revelation of the results of the Lamb's opening the fifth and sixth seals on the scroll of God's decree.[96] In Matthew, which we will consider in Part Three of this book, Jesus discusses the signs of the apocalypse with his disciples and predicts a time of persecution:

Then they will hand you over to be tortured and will put you to death, and you will be hated by all nations because of my name. . . . And this good news of the kingdom will be proclaimed throughout the world, as a testimony to all the nations; and then the end will come." (Matt 24:9, 14)

The great tribulation

The biblical source identified by John Hagee for the temple's desecration by the antichrist midway during the seven-year tribulation is the passage in

---

[95] Ibid., 187.
[96] Ibid., 188-9.

the book of Daniel, just above:[97] ". . . for *half of the week* [of years] he shall make sacrifice and offering cease; and in their place shall be an abomination that desolates, until the decreed end is poured out upon the desolator" (Dan 9:27). Half a week of years, or three-and-a-half years, is a symbol of evil used commonly in several New Testament books that I will discuss.

Hagee's biblical sources for the arrival of the antichrist at the (rebuilt) temple in Jerusalem include the gospel of Matthew and Paul's second letter to the Thessalonians:[98] "[Jesus said,] 'So when you see the desolating sacrilege standing in the holy place, as was spoken of by the prophet Daniel . . .'" (Matt 24:15); "He opposes and exalts himself above every so-called god or object of worship, so that he takes his seat in the temple of God, declaring himself to be God (2 Thess 2:4)."

Hagee says that the book of Revelation speaks to the erection of an Oz-like image of the antichrist in the temple by his assistant, the false prophet:[99]

> [The second beast] deceived the inhabitants of the earth, telling them to make an image for the beast that had been wounded by the sword and yet lived; and it was allowed to give breath to the image of the beast so that the image of the beast could even speak and cause those who would not worship the image of the beast to be killed. (Rev 13:14-15)

The ability of the antichrist's image to delude people into worship and to kill people by decapitation are sourced by Hagee to the book of Revelation and the second letter to the Thessalonians:[100]

> I also saw the souls of those who had been beheaded for their testimony to Jesus and for the word of God. They had not worshiped the beast or its image and had not received its mark on their foreheads or their hands. (Rev 20:4)

> The coming of the lawless one is apparent in the working of Satan, who uses all power, signs, lying wonders, and every kind of wicked deception for those who are perishing, because they refused to love the truth and so be saved. For this reason God sends them a powerful delusion, leading them to believe what is false, so that all who have not believed the truth but took pleasure in unrighteousness will be condemned. (2 Thess 2:9-12)

The six of seven plagues are found by Hagee in what he calls Revelation's *trumpet judgments*, because they are announced by trumpets (Rev 8:6-9:20).[101] The seventh trumpet judgment announces a sevenfold global catastrophe, which he terms the *vial* or *bowl judgments* because, in Revelation's imagery, the catastrophes are poured out from bowls (Rev 16).[102]

---

[97] Ibid., 204.
[98] Ibid., 197, 204.
[99] Ibid., 198-99.
[100] Ibid., 204, 205.
[101] Ibid., 209-16.
[102] Ibid., 222-4.

Armageddon

Hagee's sources for the order of battle at Armageddon are, among others, these passages from the Old Testament prophets Daniel, Joel, and Zechariah:[103]

> But reports from the east and the north shall alarm him, and he shall go out with great fury to bring ruin and complete destruction to many. He shall pitch his palatial tents between the sea and the beautiful holy mountain. Yet he shall come to his end, with no one to help him. (Dan 11:44-45)

> See, I am about to make Jerusalem a cup of reeling for all the surrounding peoples; it will be against Judah also in the siege against Jerusalem. (Zech 12:2)

> For I will gather all the nations against Jerusalem to battle, and the city shall be taken and the houses looted and the women raped; half the city shall go into exile, but the rest of the people shall not be cut off from the city. (Zech 14:2)

> I will gather all the nations and bring them down to the valley of Jehoshaphat, and I will enter into judgment with them there, on account of my people and my heritage Israel, because they have scattered them among the nations. (Joel 3:2)

We'll consider the book of Joel, who likely prophesied shortly after the conquest of the Middle East in the fourth century BCE by Alexander the Great, with other Old Testament prophets who spoke of a *day of the Lord* in Part Two.

Hagee attributes information about the composition of Jesus' army at Armageddon (which will include him!) to this passage in the brief New Testament book of Jude:[104] "'See, the Lord is coming with ten thousands of his holy ones'" (Jude 14).

Hagee's source for Jesus Christ's assault on the assembled armies is the book of Revelation:[105]

> Then I saw heaven opened, and there was a white horse! Its rider is called Faithful and True, and in righteousness he judges and makes war. His eyes are like a flame of fire, and on his head are many diadems; and he has a name inscribed that no one knows but himself. He is clothed in a robe dipped in blood, and his name is called the Word of God. And the armies of heaven, wearing fine linen, white and pure, were following him on white horses. From his mouth comes a sharp sword with which to strike down the nations, and he will rule them with a rod of iron; he will tread the wine press of the fury of the wrath of God the Almighty. On his robe and his thigh he has a name inscribed, "King of kings and Lord of lords." (Rev 19:11-16)

---

[103] Ibid., 227-33.
[104] Ibid., 234.
[105] Ibid., 234-5.

Millennium, final judgment, and eternity

The reign of Jesus Christ over Israel in a world untroubled by the machinations of Satan for a thousand years is attributed by Hagee to this passage in the book of Revelation:[106] "I also saw the souls of those who had been beheaded for their testimony to Jesus and for the word of God. . . . They came to life and reigned with Christ a thousand years" (Rev 20:4).

For Jesus' judgment of the Gentiles at the end of the tribulation for their treatment of the Jews over history, Hagee uses the passage from the gospel of Matthew (25:31-46) where Jesus contrasts *sheep* that fed the poor and visited the prisoners, with *goats* that didn't.[107] Previously, I contrasted Hagee's interpretation of this passage (as documentation of a judgment that closes the tribulation and opens Jesus' millennial reign) with the interpretation of Senator John Kerry, who viewed it a passage encouraging humanitarian service by the faithful today.

†

My patient reader at this point will feel bludgeoned by these seeming manifestations of an angry and bloodthirsty God. You won't see much in the dispensationalist end-times scenario about Jesus' proclamation to his first century peers of the good news of love, compassion, and forgiveness, which arguably is the organizing theme of the New Testament and, in retrospect for Christians, the foundation of the Old. The reader of end-times books rather comes to understand that the kingdom of God arrives on the heels of a future global catastrophe marked by plague, natural disasters, global warfare, and rivers of blood from which they can be spared if they go to a nearby megachurch and belly up to the Jesus bar.

But the New Testament is filled with passages about Jesus' proclamation two thousand years ago that God's kingdom of healing and reconciliation has arrived. In fact, it's hard to read the gospels without concluding that Jesus astonished the people of Galilee and Jerusalem with the news that their wait for the Messiah and the kingdom of God was *over*.

Jesus wasn't the Messiah everyone was expecting, especially after he ended up dead from a tortuous and humiliating Roman punishment. But during his ministry he healed the sick, fed the hungry, cast out demons, and raised the dead, overcoming all the barriers that separate people from one another and from the God who loves them. These were signs in those ancient times that the prophesied day of the Lord had arrived and that the king of an independent Israel, the Messiah, had come. But the arrival that Jesus announced was a reign without an earthly ruler and a kingdom without borders.

---

[106] Ibid., 236.
[107] Ibid., 240-41.

The gospel of Matthew recalls that "Jesus went throughout Galilee, teaching in their synagogues and proclaiming the good news of the kingdom and curing every disease and every sickness among the people" (Matt 4:23). When Jesus commissioned his disciples to preach his message, he urged them to bring the good news about the nearness of the kingdom to people who are poor, sick, or despised—even to the dead: "As you go, proclaim the good news, 'The kingdom of God has come near.' Cure the sick, raise the dead, cleanse the lepers, cast out demons" (Matt 10:7-8). In one of the earliest passages in the gospels,[108] some followers of John the Baptist asks if Jesus is the Messiah—"are you the one who is to come?"—and Jesus replies with his usual indirection: "Go and tell John what you hear and see: the blind receive their sight, the lame walk, the lepers are cleansed, the deaf hear, the dead are raised, and the poor have good news brought to them" (Matt 11:2-6).

The gospels and letters of the early churches abundantly attest that Jesus' resurrection following his death demonstrated to his followers that the kingdom had arrived and that God would ultimately be victorious over the evil of this world. The reign of God that Jesus announced was characterized by sharing, forgiveness, and healing, and it was manifest when the kingdom came to the poor, the meek, and people who make peace. In contrast, dispensationalists describe a *future* kingdom that is separated from us by military and natural catastrophes characterized by unparalleled, and unpitied, suffering and death.

Some biblical passages, particularly in the book of Revelation, do seem to prophesy horrible events. Gospel accounts of the nonviolent victory of forgiveness are difficult to reconcile with accounts of God-inflicted catastrophes such as the ones I've just recounted.

Jesus lived in a time when people believed that the crises they endured were worldly counterparts of a hidden cosmic struggle between God and Satan. Apocalyptic literature and the thinking behind it parted the curtain that hid that struggle from mortals and let them know how their troubles related to God's battle. Indeed, *apokalypsis* is the Greek word for *lifting the veil*. The authors of apocalyptic literature in the Bible drew aside the veil to reveal the greater, trans-historical meaning of current events to their contemporaries. The struggle against injustice and oppression was the worldly counterpart of God's titanic struggle in heaven, one that God would extend to the earth with the incarnation of Jesus as Christ, and win.

Jesus himself taught using apocalyptic metaphors, and his resurrection was an apocalyptic event revealing that God, in at least this one important instance, had prevailed not just in heaven but on earth. Having encountered the resurrected Jesus Christ on earth, the apostles urged their followers to minister to others using what he had taught, sharing, worshipping, and healing

---

[108] The passage has its parallel in Luke 7:18-23, indicating their common source in an older, lost collection of sayings that scholars call "Q." This source will be discussed more in Part Three.

and doing so with patience and courage as time spun forward toward God's victory in the fulfillment of time.

The lurid predictions of end-times writers about a violent future, which usually are based on visionary descriptions of catastrophes that have already occurred in Israel's history, also form a veil that must be pulled aside for us to appreciate the good news. When the Bible's apocalyptic passages are considered in their ancient literary and historical contexts, they reveal the certain and ultimate victory of the kingdom of justice and reconciliation that Jesus proclaimed during his ministry and that God opened to the world through Jesus' resurrection. They also give us some insight into how we should live today.

For too long, dispensationalists have twisted the Bible's apocalyptic literature into bloodthirsty and scary science fiction. Gaining a new appreciation of the apocalyptic passages of the Bible is the aim of this book. In the next part, I will discuss the message of the Old Testament prophets about a reckoning they called "the day of the Lord." In the two parts that follow, I will review the apocalyptic literature of the book of Daniel written 170 years before Jesus' birth, and apocalyptic themes in writings of the early church in the century following his death. I will devote the fourth part to the book of Revelation, which was written near the end of that first century CE and is the most fantastic and troubling of the Bible's books. In the fifth and final part, I will discuss how two common Christian practices, table fellowship and recitation of the Lord's Prayer, are rooted in the prophetic and apocalyptic thinking that formed the New Testament and make apocalyptic faith still relevant two thousand years later.

Part Two
PROPHECY

[King] Zedekiah rebelled against the king of Babylon. And in the ninth year of his reign . . . King Nebuchadnezzar of Babylon came with all his army against Jerusalem, and laid siege to it; they built siegeworks against it all around. So the city was besieged until the eleventh year of King Zedekiah. On the ninth day of the fourth month the famine became so severe in the city that there was no food for the people of the land. . . .

In the fifth month, on the seventh day of the month . . . Nebuzaradan, the captain of the bodyguard, a servant of the king of Babylon, came to Jerusalem. He burned the house of the Lord, the king's house, and all the houses of Jerusalem; every great house he burned down. . . Nebuzaradan the captain of the guard carried into exile the rest of the people who were left in the city and the deserters who had defected to the king of Babylon—all the rest of the population. But the captain of the guard left some of the poorest people of the land to be the vinedressers and tillers of the soil.

—2 Kings 25:1-12, describing the fall of Jerusalem to Babylon in 587 BCE.

Chapter 6
PROPHECY IN ISRAEL

End-time scenarios like those of John Hagee and the *Left Behind* series rip a highly selective suite of passages from their contexts in the Bible to build the case for rapture, tribulation, millennium, and judgment. What these passages have in common is catastrophe: Old Testament prophecies that interpreted the meaning of Israel's ruin by Babylon in the sixth century BCE; books of re-assuring visions written in reaction to vicious imperial persecutions in the centuries before and after Jesus' life; Jesus' observations on the conflicts among Jews centered on a temple occupied by Roman troops; letters written by first-century evangelists to churches that struggled with schism, ostracism, and sometimes persecution under a corrupt, sycophantic, and violent empire; and New Testament literature finalized after Rome's brutal siege of Jerusalem and the destruction of the second temple in 70 CE.

That these selected passages might predict events two or three thousand years later is a theory that doesn't bear up well under scrutiny. Rather, as this and later chapters will reveal, prophets, visionaries, and apostles had the immediate circumstances of their *own* communities in mind. Prophets warned their contemporaries about consequences for faithlessness and injustice that would occur soon, not twenty or thirty centuries later. Many first-century Christians believed that Jesus would return as the Messiah within their lifetimes, not fifty generations later. Almost always, biblical prophecies urged repentance and perseverance when catastrophe loomed and offered hope to people confronted with insuperable injustice. These messages were preserved in the Bible not as tea leaves to be read by future generations about how the world will end; they are there because of their continuing relevance to the inevitable challenges confronting people of faith.

Beyond wrongly interpreting the metaphors of prophets and visionaries as predictions of events in the twenty-first century, end-times writers make an overarching assumption that these supposed events are linked as episodes in a complex scenario.

Hal Lindsey, mistaken predictor in the 1970s of the world's end a decade later, justifies the dispensationalist scenario in a more recent book:

> Beginning 3400 years ago and continuing into the next 1400 years, the Hebrew prophets predicted a precise sequence of events would fit together. All the elements of this predicted pattern would lead to a cataclysmic war of such magnitude that it will almost end life on this planet.
>
> Even though different prophets at different times predicted the various components of these events, they can be easily identified and joined together because they pertain to the great, final conflict which begins in the Middle East and draws all nations into it.[1]

The premises of dispensationalist theology—that God has a derailed plan for human history, that the Bible predicts certain events in the future, and that God's relationship with humanity is marked by violent judgment that a faithful remnant can escape—require end-times writers to use what limited material in the Bible may be available. Their approach omits broad swaths of the Bible and the literature and history of God's people that are recorded in it. Moreover, dispensationalist arguments often depend on misinterpretations of dated translations, require us to suspend our God-given critical judgment, or ask us to ignore relevant historical and archaeological evidence. Finally, and most importantly, end-times writers strip prophecy's words away from its poetry, which communicates emotions that are more significant than any wisps of facts a passage of prophecy may contain. Yes, prophecy often threatens catastrophe and apocalyptic writing frequently describes one, but prophets spoke of judgment to urge Israel toward a more just society, and New Testament writers wrote apocalyptically to urge perseverance in Jesus' spirit of compassion and sharing despite the immoral empire that engulfed them. Advocacy for justice, peace, and love is absent from the dispensationalist writings about the end-times; their preoccupation is with catastrophe, and there's cold-bloodedness in their speculations, to boot.

The next three parts of my book will look at the books of the Bible where the passages most commonly used by end-times writers are found. The part that has now begun will look at the Old Testament books of Isaiah, Zephaniah, Ezekiel, Joel, and Zechariah. The part that follows, Part Three, will review the Old Testament book of Daniel and the New Testament writings of the Letters to the Thessalonians, the Letters of John, and the gospel of Matthew. Part Four will be devoted to the book of Revelation.

A reader already familiar with the Bible will observe that I discuss the

---

[1] Lindsey, *The Everlasting Hatred*, 227.

books out of their order in the Bible, and that Part Three combines a discussion of an Old Testament book, Daniel, with discussions of books from the New. I approach this study by taking these books in the order that most scholars believe they were written, which is different from their order in the Bible, and by grouping them to express the development of prophetic and apocalyptic thought and literature.[2]

The passages I have selected were spoken and written across a thousand years of history in a variety of literary styles that reflect the diverse ways ancient peoples expressed their religious beliefs. Their literature responded to historical conditions that changed with the ebb and flow of ancient empires that extended then withdrew their power over the tiny, largely defenseless terrain Israel and her neighbors inhabited at their crossroads. Israel's government—endowing power, justice, and worship in a cooperative but sometimes competing mix of priest, king, and prophet—evolved from tribal confederacy, through unified kingdom, through division, enslavement, and exile, through vassal state dependent on empires for security, and finally to involuntary dispersion among the nations of the world.

The Bible contains the stories, poems, laments, rants, prayers, raves, cries, hopes, and songs of a people who struggled to stay faithful while enduring one catastrophe after another, and who only wished for peace to enjoy together (and with God) the fruits of their vineyards and wheat fields. End-times writers trivialize these wonderfully rich texts by casting them as predictive rather than prophetic, soothsaying rather that faith-building, fortune-telling rather than hope-filling, and awful rather than awesome. I mean to correct that in the chapters that follow.

We begin my assessment of the Bible's prophetic and apocalyptic literature with the prophets.

✝

Many ancient peoples had individuals who served as intermediaries between a people and their gods. Biblical theologian David Petersen identifies four Hebrew words used in the Old Testament to describe individuals who occupied these intermediary roles in Israel, and listing them illustrates the range of their activities and roles:[3]

Nabi, typically translated *prophet*, is the term most frequently used for *prophet* in the Old Testament and means *divine intermediary*; it has a root meaning in Hebrew of "someone called to a certain task."

Hozeh is used interchangeably with *nabi* in the book of the prophet Isaiah and can be translated as *seer*—a person who sees and hears revelations and

---

[2] A chronology of Israel's history and the creation of the books of the Bible may be found in Appendix 2.

[3] Petersen, *The Prophetic Literature*, 5-6.

reports them to an audience.

Roeh, strictly translated as *diviner*, is a person who can learn information by using spiritual methods of inquiry. This word is used to describe Samuel, the prophetic figure who ushered in the kingships of Saul and David.

'Is ha'elohim, literally translated *man of God* or *holy man*, is used to describe the early prophets Elijah and Elisha. Petersen writes: "Unlike visionaries, who occasionally engage in trance or possession behavior, the holy man personifies the deity in the midst of the profane world."[4] The holy man can also use divinely-given spiritual powers to make things physically happen.

Using one of these four Hebrew words, the Old Testament refers to many of Israel's earliest leaders as *prophets*, beginning with the legendary patriarch Abraham (Gen 20:7) and including Moses (Deut 34:10), who led the Israelite tribes out of slavery in Egypt. *Prophet* is also used to describe the judge, Deborah (Judg 4:4), who famously defended the Israelite tribes against overwhelming enemy forces at the battle of Har Megiddo, the location of the apocalyptic battle of Armageddon in the book of Revelation.

We don't have collections of oracles in classical forms from these early leaders; however, they certainly acted as intermediaries between people and God. Abraham, grandfather of twelve sons who become the tribes of Israel, is credited with developing the first human relationship with the one God of Israel. Moses received the Law from the one God and interpreted it to the Israelite tribes as they wandered in the desert, awaiting their opportunity to enter Palestine. Deborah was among the many charismatic leaders who emerged from the confederation of Israel's tribes and acted in ways that revealed the nature of God's stewardship of the nation.

As Israel's judges were replaced by more formal systems of authority led by kings and priests, a narrower prophetic role emerged, one that stood apart from political and religious power but was still essential because it legitimized priests and kings before the ultimate power, the one God. Elijah and Elisha represent early models: they were called to warn kings and priests whose power was presumptuous because they substituted their authority for God's. The prophets warned that the consequences would be severe if leaders failed to rule with justice and humility.

Aside from these outstanding ancient prophets named in the law and history books of the Bible, there's also evidence in the Bible of swarms of common prophets whose individual lives weren't so memorable.

> After that [Samuel says to Saul], you shall come to Gibeath-elohim, at the place where the Philistine garrison is; there, as you come to the town, you will meet a band of prophets coming down from the shrine with harp, tambourine, flute, and lyre playing in front of them; they will be in a prophetic frenzy. (1 Samuel 10:5)

---

[4] Ibid., 6.

These roving bands of prophets engaged in magic or other idolatrous practices; Amos, the first classical prophet, will deny he's a prophet as a result (Amos 7:14). Other prophets joined the payroll,[5] providing sycophantic support to the king as members of a fawning court.

Certain prophets emerged from the background noise of these more mundane groups when their oracles were acutely relevant to understanding the consequences of political or religious decisions made by the kings and priests of Israel. Early prophets condemned idolatry, injustice, empty religiosity, oppression of the poor, inhospitality to travelers, insensitivity to widows and orphans, and other manifestations of the accumulation of wealth, power, and self-satisfaction by Israel's elites. They warned of military defeat and humiliation if the kingdoms did not repent. Their warnings sometimes came at the price of personal humiliation, as in the case of Jeremiah, who prophesied Judah's defeat by and exile to Babylon:

> [Jeremiah said,] Thus says the Lord, This city shall surely be handed over to the army of the king of Babylon and be taken. Then the officials said to the king, "This man ought to be put to death, because he is discouraging the soldiers who are left in this city, and all the people, by speaking such words to them. For this man is not seeking the welfare of this people, but their harm." . . . So they took Jeremiah and threw him into the cistern of Malchiah, the king's son, which was in the court of the guard, letting Jeremiah down by ropes. Now there was no water in the cistern, but only mud, and Jeremiah sank in the mud. (Jer 38:3-6)

The utterances of these *classical* prophets, so named because their prophecies were organized into books named after them, were remembered and written down after they were fulfilled by later events, particularly when Babylon defeated the kingdoms of Israel and Judah, destroyed the Jerusalem temple in the sixth century BCE, and took Judah's elites into exile. As a result of that huge catastrophe in Israel's history, what the prophets had condemned and the forms of repentance they had urged became extremely important and the record of their prophecies entered their holy scriptures. Future prophets would continue to warn of a *day of the Lord*, a reckoning colored by the drama of natural catastrophe and recalled the disaster that befell Jerusalem, to condemn Israel's continuing problems with faithlessness and injustice.

What all prophets had in common was a mission from God to remind the Jews of God's authority and will. What God willed was purity and justice, as they had been codified in the political, religious, and moral codes in the Law. In prophetic terms, submitting to God's Law represented a choice for *life* under the beneficence and protection of God, as opposed to a choice to perpetuate faithlessness and injustice, a choice for a separation from God, or *death*. In

---

[5] The Reverend Dr. G. David Hawley has reminded me of the term, "prophet on a payroll," used by the late Professor Harold Nebelsick of Louisville Presbyterian Theological Seminary, our *alma mater*.

his reflection on prophecy in ancient Israel, Norman Podhoretz identifies this speech of Moses as the *vade mecum* of the prophetic message:[6]

> Surely, this commandment that I am commanding you today is not too hard for you, nor is it too far away. . . . No, the word is very near to you; it is in your mouth and in your heart for you to observe.
>
> See, I have set before you today life and prosperity, death and adversity. If you obey the commandments of the Lord your God that I am commanding you today, by loving the Lord your God, walking in his ways, and observing his commandments, decrees, and ordinances, then you shall live and become numerous, and the Lord your God will bless you in the land that you are entering to possess. But if your heart turns away and you do not hear, but are led astray to bow down to other gods and serve them, I declare to you today that you shall perish; you shall not live long in the land that you are crossing the Jordan to enter and possess. I call heaven and earth to witness against you today that I have set before you life and death, blessings and curses. Choose life so that you and your descendants may live. (Deut 30:11-19)

As we review the prophetic and apocalyptic writings of the Old and New Testament, we will see again and again the choice presented by prophets between justice and life on the one hand and injustice and death on the other. God's message assures security and plenty, but it is ignored at the cost of separation from God—*death*. The duty of faithful people is to love God, remain pure, and be just and compassionate to the poor; their reward is—*life*. Apocalyptic thinking would reframe the choice as judgment: refusal to embrace God's love results in God's condemnation to a place of separation, in the book of Revelation *a lake of fire*, while a choice for life is salvation from that separation. Jesus will affirm the choice of life, which to him was the love of God and of one's neighbors, but at the risk of his life on earth.

✝

The first book of the prophets in the Bible is Isaiah, followed by the books of Jeremiah, Ezekiel, Daniel, and the *Book of Twelve* that includes the briefer books of Amos, Joel, Zechariah, and Zephaniah, among others. Except for Daniel and Joel, whose books were written much later, the classical prophets were active in the eighth, seventh, and sixth centuries BCE. The legacy of the classical prophets, originally, was oral: preserved for us are utterances and oracles spoken by them (or their students) then remembered by their followers. Their sayings (with some historical and biographical information, but not much) were later written down and collected into books. (Appendix 1 provides a time line for key historical events and the writing of biblical books.)

The classical prophets condemned idolatry, but that term doesn't do justice to the scope of their concerns. Idolatry for the classical prophets was broader and

---

[6] Podhoretz, *The Prophets*, 38.

more insidious than the worship of idols, such as the golden calf that famously greeted Moses when he descended Mount Sinai with God's commandments (Ex 32). Among the classical prophets idolatry more often entailed faith in anything less than God, particularly the substitution of worship for the justice, compassion, and mercy that God demanded toward the poor and dispossessed. As a consequence of idolatry, the prophets warned, nearby empires would militarily defeat Israel and destroy her system of worship—consequences that indeed befell first the Northern Kingdom of Israel in the eighth century BCE, and Judah in the sixth.

The most egregious form of idolatry was the arrogance and hypocrisy of elaborate religious rituals despite continuing oppression of the poor. The specific injustice was the failure to relieve debts every seven years as required by the Sabbatical Law (Deut 15:1-11). Furthermore, in the prophetic view, justice was subverted every seven *weeks* of years plus one, or 50 years, when the Jubilee Law was ignored; it provided for *liberty*, which was understood in those times to be freedom for indentured slaves, the cancellation of debts, and the return of ancestral lands:

> You shall count off seven weeks of years, seven times seven years, so that the period of seven weeks of years gives forty-nine years. Then you shall have the trumpet sounded loud; on the tenth day of the seventh month—on the day of atonement—you shall have the trumpet sounded throughout all your land. And you shall hallow the fiftieth year and you shall proclaim liberty throughout the land to all its inhabitants. It shall be a jubilee for you: you shall return, every one of you, to your property and every one of you to your family. (Lev 25:8-10)

The Sabbatical and Jubilee laws reflected God's early purposes for periodically restoring economic security and social justice in Israel to relieve the inevitable oppression of the peasantry. Petersen writes: Israelite prophets during the Neo-Assyrian period seem concerned about a particular form of social and economic development in the eighth century, a style of life that stood in tension with the realization of basic norms. It was increasingly difficult to provide for economic justice as larger estates were being created. People's land was being taken away, high interest rates made it difficult to retain financial independence, and debt slavery was rampant. When addressing these issues, the prophets were indicting social structures as well as the behavior of individuals.[7]

The Sabbatical and Jubilee Laws were never implemented and they were honored only once in the breach, by the governor Nehemiah after the Babylonian exile ended and Jewish customs were revived in Judah (Neh 5:6-13). However, righting the injustice of incapacitating debt and landlessness was critically important not only to the classical prophets but also to Daniel, when apocalyptic thinking exploded in the second century BCE, and to Jesus in the first century CE, who urged his followers to forgive sins, trespasses, and

---

[7] Petersen, *The Prophetic Literature*, 40.

most importantly *debts*. Common among these centuries of prophecy and apocalypse is the number seven: *seven years* and *seven weeks of years* define the Sabbath and Jubilee Laws, measure the prophecies of the book of Daniel, and organize the book of Revelation. And for good reason: when seven things occur in the Bible, we are reminded of the seven days when God organized the world, and how God decreed that its order was complete, and good (Gen 1:31).

It fell to prophets to condemn kingdoms that invested in religious celebrations but ignored rampant poverty and homelessness. Here is the prophet Amos, speaking to the Northern Kingdom of Israel on the eve of its destruction by the Assyrian Empire in the eighth century BCE:

> I hate, I despise your festivals,
>   and I take no delight in your solemn assemblies.
> Even though you offer me your burnt offerings and grain offerings,
>   I will not accept them;
> and the offerings of well-being of your fatted animals,
>   I will not look upon.
> Take away from me the noise of your songs;
>   I will not listen to the melody of your harps.
> But let justice roll down like waters,
>   and righteousness like an ever-flowing stream. (Amos 5:21-24)

Here is the prophet Micah, addressing Judah about the same time as Amos was speaking to the Northern Kingdom:

> "With what shall I come before the Lord,
>   and bow myself before God on high?
> Shall I come before him with burnt offerings,
>   with calves a year old? . . ."
> He has told you, O mortal, what is good;
>   and what does the Lord require of you
> but to do justice, and to love kindness,
>   and to walk humbly with your God? (Mic 6:6-8)

Prophetic threats of worldly consequences for persistent injustice usually identified the forms of faithlessness that prompted them, as Amos and Micah did in these two excerpts. The goal of the classical prophets is repentance; they urge their listeners to choose life (justice, purity, mercy, and repentance) over death (worship absent justice).

Even when doom was prophesied, hopeful assurances about the remnant that would survive usually accompanied the warning. End-times writers often interpret the prophets' assurance of the preservation of a remnant as documentation of the rapture, when people who have a church-approved relationship with Jesus escape the earth to safety when the tribulation begins. But the prophets didn't predict a rapture; they prophesied—spoke to people on God's behalf—that imminent judgment should not foreclose hope, that repentance could forestall consequence, and that *life* was an urgent choice to avoid catastrophe.

ISAIAH:

Chapter 7
ISAIAH:
THE CITY OF CHAOS

The book of Isaiah is a collection of prophecies spoken or written over three centuries, roughly the eighth through the sixth centuries BCE, before, during, and after the Babylonian exile of Judah, the southern kingdom of Israel. The oldest prophecies are by the historical Isaiah of Jerusalem, for whom the book is named; the rest were written or spoken later by his students and others who worked within the great prophetic tradition he established. This isn't unusual for the record of prophecy we have in the Bible; Petersen notes that the imagery created by a classical prophet had "remarkable generative properties" and "an almost inherent capacity to elicit elucidation at a later time."[8] This generative capacity extends into our modern times: the tropes of Israel's prophets are recognizable in a speech of Martin Luther King, Jr., that we will encounter in a future chapter. It must also be said that prophecy's generative properties inspire dispensationalist end-times writers to imagine obscenely violent variations on ancient metaphors of judgment.

The book of Isaiah rarely provides details useful in the scenarios of end-times prognosticators.[9] However, Isaiah is worth reviewing, for several reasons.

It introduces us to a defining period in the history of Israel. The two

---

[8] Ibid., 4-5.

[9] Sometimes I wonder why passages from the book of Isaiah figure so rarely in dispensationalist end-times scenarios. Is it because the classical prophets (except Daniel and Joel, two of their favorites and who likely wrote much later than the classical period) focused primarily on injustice and empty religiosity? Would it be possible to assemble from the prophecies of Isaiah and other classical prophets a scenario that warns of the imminent punishment of people who are responsible for or indifferent to poverty, oppression, and war, and promises the rescue and resurrection of their victims? But then I realize that such a scenario would do just as much violence to Jesus' message about the kingdom of God as the dispensationalist scheme, and I abandon the project.

kingdoms of the Jews, Judah and the Northern Kingdom, had joined fateful alliances with empires to the north and south that ultimately doomed their independence. Invading armies destroyed first the Northern Kingdom in 721 BCE, then Jerusalem and its temple in 587 BCE. The priestly class and other aristocrats were taken from Jerusalem to Babylon (following the custom of the times); those who remained behind in Judah, mostly peasants, were impoverished. For all practical purposes, the Jewish nation had been destroyed, apparently betraying God's promises. Still, its prophets urged repentance, perseverance, and hope. Seventy years after the exile of Judah and in fulfillment of Jeremiah's prophecy about its duration, Cyrus of Persia, the conqueror of Babylon, permitted exiled Jews to return to Jerusalem and rebuild the temple. Isaiah and the prophets in his tradition interpreted the meaning of this cataclysm before, during, and after the exile, and their words provided comfort and hope as the Jews suffered through Israel's destruction, endured exile in Babylon, and celebrated their return to Jerusalem.

Another reason an appreciation of the book of Isaiah is helpful to an understanding of apocalyptic passages of the Bible is the broad range of literary forms its sixty-six chapters include. Here we can observe parallelism, a common form in Hebrew prophecy where the same idea is expressed twice in different yet complementary ways to fully develop an idea. We can see other examples of poetic forms used throughout prophecy and continuing into the writing of apocalyptic and New Testament writers, where the hymns of people, the laments of priests, and the judgments of courts are used to frame prophetic observations by borrowing mundane settings to enhance their messages.

A third reason that an appreciation of Isaiah is helpful is its relevance to traditions about Jesus. The gospel of Matthew, in particular, recounts (and sometimes shapes) events in Jesus' life and ministry that fulfill the prophecies of Isaiah, the birth and crucifixion narratives being examples. By referring to the book of Isaiah, the author of Matthew (and the book of Revelation, which also frequently alludes to Isaiah) appropriates the themes and messages of the Isaiah tradition to explain to his readers and listeners the significance in Israel's history of Jesus' life and message. We will identify some of Isaiah's themes in the next section, and look more carefully at how Matthew appropriates their meanings in Chapter 15.

While the book of Isaiah assembles prophecies uttered across three centuries of tumultuous Jewish history, certain themes pervade it. First, God is on God, he is the God of all nations, and his name is hallowed:

"Holy, Holy, Holy is the Lord of hosts;
    the whole earth is full of his glory." (Isa 6:3)

A second theme is the centrality of Israel in God's plans for the earth, focusing on Jerusalem (which Isaiah calls *Zion*) as God's home. Among all the nations, God has a covenant with Israel that demands Israel to honor God's holiness and be just to the poor. If faithlessness and injustice are commonplace in Israel, then Israel's religious practices are abhorrent to God and Israel must make the prophetic choice: choose life through justice and mercy to the poor, or choose death by persisting in worship without them:

> What to me is the multitude of your sacrifices?
>   says the Lord;
> I have had enough of burnt offerings of rams
>   and the fat of fed beasts;
> I do not delight in the blood of bulls,
>   or of lambs, or of goats. . . .
> Wash yourselves; make yourselves clean;
>   remove the evil of your doings
> from before my eyes;
>   cease to do evil,
> learn to do good;
>   seek justice,
> rescue the oppressed,
>   defend the orphan,
> plead for the widow. . . .
>   If you are willing and obedient,
> you shall eat the good of the land;
>   but if you refuse and rebel,
> you shall be devoured by the sword. (Isa 1:11-20)

A third major theme is God's intent to restore Israel to its status as a "light to the nations" with the promise of a provident, faithful, and just king in a line of descent from David, the shepherd boy who was the second king of a united Israel (c. 1040-970 BCE). Although military defeat, destruction of the temple, and exile to a foreign land eventually will be the consequences of Israel's faithlessness and injustice, there's also a promise that after the exile, a delivering king like David will come to make things right:

> For a child has been born for us,
>   a son given to us;
> authority rests upon his shoulders;
>   and he is named
> Wonderful Counselor, Mighty God,
>   Everlasting Father, Prince of Peace. (Isaiah 9:6)

This passage should be familiar, even if you haven't read much of the Bible but you've attended church at Christmas time or listened to highlights of Handel's oratorio, *Messiah*. The passage has the form of other royal hymns in the book of Psalms, like this one:

> The kings of the earth set themselves,
>   and the rulers take counsel together,
>   against the Lord and his *anointed*. . . .
> I will tell of the decree of the Lord:
> He said to me, "you are my son;
>   today I have begotten you." (Ps 2:2, 7, emphasis mine)

Psalm 2 was sung to celebrate the coronation of a king in a ceremony called in Israel an *anointment*, because during it, priests applied oil as a symbol of the blessing that has conferred the person's status. For example, the prophet Samuel anointed Saul, Israel's first king: "Samuel took a vial of oil and poured it on his head, and kissed him; he said, 'The Lord has anointed you ruler over his people Israel. You shall reign over the people of the Lord and you will save them from the hand of their enemies all around'" (1 Samuel 10:1). Saul's protégé, then rival, then successor David was similarly anointed by the prophet Samuel: "Then Samuel took the horn of oil, and anointed him in the presence of his brothers; and the spirit of the Lord came mightily upon David from that day forward" (I Sam 16:13).

While Isaiah's early messianic hopes are focused on a Davidic king, later prophecies in the book of Isaiah made after the exile reinterpret them. Petersen notes that the "you" to whom "an everlasting covenant" is made is plural, suggesting that it is the *people of Israel* who will be anointed as a holy nation:[10]

> Incline your ear, and come to me;
>   listen, so that *you* may live.
> I will make with *you* an everlasting covenant,
>   my steadfast, sure love for David. (Isa 55:3, emphasis added)

The Anointed One

David is the prototype for an *anointed one*; at least at first, people considered him humble, brave, righteous, and just, and his reign was one of the few periods in Israel's history when her borders extended to the lands promised by God to Abraham. The Hebrew word for *anointed* is *moshiach*, rendered in English *messiah*; the Old Testament never uses *messiah* as a noun—*the anointed*—only as an adjective—*the anointed <u>one</u>*. After Babylon's defeat of Judah ended traditional kingship in Israel, power was shared between a governor installed by the empire that ruled Israel and the chief priest; it was usually the priest who was *the anointed one*, but here is Zechariah prophesying about the two men most responsible for rebuilding the temple after the return of the exiles from Babylon to Jerusalem, Joshua, the chief priest, and Zerubbabel, Judah's appointed governor:

> Then I said to [the angel], "What are these two olive trees on the right and the left of the lampstand?" And a second time I said to him, "What are these two branches of the olive trees, which pour out the oil through the two golden pipes?" He said to me, "Do you not know what these are?" I said, "No, my lord." Then he said, "These are the two anointed ones who stand by the Lord of the whole earth." (Zech 4:11-14)

The image of the two olive trees and the lampstands that illuminate them will figure significantly in the New Testament book of Revelation, which recalls

---

[10] Petersen, The Prophetic Literature, 94.

this historical imagery to describe the circumstances of the persecuted churches for whom Revelation was written; they are lights to the world that illuminate God's reign (1:12). The books of Zechariah and Revelation use the metaphor of light to reinterpret the fulfillment of messianic hope as a holy people in a restored Jerusalem, or in New Testament terms, the faithful perseverance of the early church awaiting the new Jerusalem presently descending from Heaven.

Classical prophets after Isaiah will point to a king like David as the future redeemer of Israel, although they won't necessarily describe the redeemer as *an anointed one*. Some Jewish apocalyptic writings around the time of Jesus will describe a future redeemer who is not called *an anointed one*; for example, in Chapter 12 we will learn more about a kinglike redeemer that the book of Daniel calls, not *anointed one*, but *one like a son of man*. Increasingly, speakers of prophecy and writers of apocalypse will place less emphasis on a redeeming king and more emphasis on the future direct rule of God over the perfect kingdom. D. S. Russell, for example, lists Jewish apocalypses written around the time of Jesus that dispense entirely with the notion of a future redeeming king, neither *anointed one* nor *one like a son of man*.[11]

Still, some Jewish apocalyptic writings and, significantly for us, the New Testament writings use *anointed one* and *one like a son of man* to refer to an ideal king in David's line who will establish the millennial kingdom after God sets things right. In fact, the New Testament (and Greek versions of the Old Testament) render the Hebrew word *messiah* as *khristos*, or Christ. The book of Revelation wades into the controversy by offering a compromise, an interim thousand-year reign by the *khristos* pending a final resolution of the battle between good and evil when existence vaporizes into eternity.

To sum up, *anointed one* (*messiah* in Hebrew and *khristos* in Greek) is used in the Bible to describe blessed priests and kings of the past (for example, David); leaders specially blessed by God throughout Israel's history (the chief priest, but also Jesus during his ministry); and an ideal future king for whom people hope (for Israel, a king in David's line, and for Christians, Jesus Christ in the millennium). Here we encounter the fluidity of past, present, and future typical of biblical prophecy; we will encounter a similar fluidity again in other prophetic books and apocalyptic writings. The shifting perspective in time in prophetic and apocalyptic writings permits end-times writers to dip in and out of it at will to build their future chronologies, but it has a larger meaning: the events of the past and our hopes for the future must influence our perception today of God's present reign on earth.

✝

---

[11] Russell, *The Method and Message of Jewish Apocalyptic*, 309.

Isaiah celebrates the arrival of *the anointed one* as the beginning of a permanent reign of peace and justice:

> His authority shall grow continually,
>   and there shall be endless peace
> for the throne of David and his kingdom.
>   He will establish and uphold it
> with justice and righteousness
>   from this time onward and forevermore. (Isaiah 9:7)

The era when the anointed one will rule is also a time of remarkable peace, not only among nations but the entire creation:

> The wolf shall live with the lamb,
>   the leopard shall lie down with the kid,
> the calf and the lion and the fatling together,
>   and a little child shall lead them. (Isa 11:6)

Eight hundred years later when the gospels about Jesus' ministry were written, Matthew would take great pains to trace Jesus' lineage to David (Matt 1:1-17), and the gospel of Luke would incorporate Isaiah's prophesies about *the anointed one* into its story of the birth of Jesus, viewing the birth as a harbinger of worldwide peace and justice that arrives with God's reign:

> The angel said to her, "Do not be afraid, Mary, for you have found favor with God. And now, you will conceive in your womb and bear a son [Isa 7:14], and you will name him Jesus. He will be great, and will be called the Son of the Most High, and the Lord God will give to him the throne of his ancestor David. He will reign over the house of Jacob forever, and of his kingdom there will be no end [cf. Isa 9:7]."
> The angel said, "Don't be afraid [cf. Isa 6:5]; for see—I am bringing you good news of great joy for all the people: to you is born this day in the city of David a Savior [cf. Isa 43:3], who is the Messiah, the Lord. This will be a sign for you: you will find a child wrapped in bands of cloth and lying in a manger [cf. Isa 7:14]." (Luke 1:30-33; 2:10-12)

When we review the gospel of Matthew in Chapter 15, we'll see many other examples where Old Testament prophecy is reinterpreted or recalled. Matthew will frequently announce that an event or saying *fulfilled* a prophecy, but his reference to prophecy is not simply to document that what a prophet had predicted had come true (if the prophecy was a prediction in the first place). More importantly, the prophetic passage is recalled to apply the rich web of meaning associated with the original prophecy to the more immediate event. Hence, when Isaiah's prophecies about a future *anointed one* are recalled in Jesus' birth stories, Isaiah's prophecy that a reign of peace and justice would come with *the anointed one* is also recalled.

While the book of Isaiah is filled with hopeful promises for the righteous, he also casts the future Davidic king as someone who will assess consequences for those who fail to make the prophetic choice of faithfulness and justice:

He shall not judge by what his eyes see,
    or decide by what his ears hear;
but with righteousness he shall judge the poor,
    and decide with equity for the meek of the earth;
he shall strike the earth with *the rod of his mouth*,
    and with *the breath of his lips* he shall kill the wicked.
Righteousness shall be the belt around his waist,
    and faithfulness the belt around his loins. (Isa 11:3-5, emphasis added)

"The rod of his mouth" and the "breath of his lips" are metaphorical variations on the spoken word of God; "kill the wicked" is an expression of the consequences of the prophetic choice of death, a turning away from God's word. When we review the book of Revelation, the same metaphor for the spoken word of God will be deployed as the instrument of judgment against those who don't choose life when Jesus Christ leads the charge against the armies of the beast at Armageddon with a sword in his mouth (Rev 19:11-16).

Isaiah prophesied that the victorious *anointed one* will found the perfect kingdom, accomplishing God's desire that Israel become the world's standard for righteousness. Once the nations repent by conforming to that standard, choosing life over death, war will end and the world will return to the healthy business of feeding and nurturing its inhabitants:

In days to come
    the mountain of the Lord's house
shall be established as the highest of the mountains,
    and shall be raised above the hills;
all the nations shall stream to it. (Isa 2:2)

God will invite the nations of the world to a banquet to celebrate the outbreak of peace:

On this mountain the Lord of hosts will make for all peoples
    a feast of rich food, a feast of well-aged wines,
of rich food filled with marrow,
    of well-aged wines strained and clear.
And he will destroy on this mountain
    the shroud that is cast over all peoples,
    the sheet that is spread over all nations;
    he will swallow up death forever. (Isa 25:6-7)

For the new age, God decrees peace:

For out of Zion shall go forth instruction,
    and the word of the Lord from Jerusalem.
He shall judge between the nations,
    and shall arbitrate for many peoples;
they shall beat their swords into plowshares,
    and their spears into pruning hooks;
nation shall not lift up sword against nation,
    neither shall they learn war any more. (Isa 2:3-4)

The latter two lines are written on a wall and paraphrased on a statue outside the New York headquarters of the United Nations, a place created after the horrors of World War II where, its organizers hoped, the world's leaders could meet to create a more peaceful and prosperous world. Premillennial dispensationalists, however, restrict the applicability of this passage to God's future thousand-year rule through Jesus Christ; it is only then, after the tribulation and Jesus' victory over the antichrist, that war will end. For dispensationalists, mankind's efforts today to forge peace out of conflict at places like the United Nations are hubris, and doomed. Writing in *Good News*, a periodical published by the United Church of God, evangelist Mario Seigle writes:

> The statue in front of the United Nations building is . . . symbolic of what is wrong with humanity. Instead of applying the true meaning of the verse paraphrased from Isaiah, human leaders take it as a present reality. On their own they believe they can forge swords into plows.[12]

Isaiah's prophecies about the *anointed one*, if in fact they are predictions, tell us that the reign of God and an era of peace and justice will begin with the birth of a messiah who, for Christians, is Jesus Christ. But Jesus is dead, and he founded no kingdom like David's. When does God's reign begin? When is peace and justice proclaimed? When is the mountaintop feast? Is peace possible only after this era catastrophically ends?

Prophecy as poetry

One of the moments in music that most moves me is this part of the libretto of Handel's *Messiah*, which uses the King James Version of a passage we have already visited, Isaiah 9:6:

> For unto us a child is born, unto us a son is given, and the government shall be upon His shoulder; and His name shall be called Wonderful, Counsellor, the mighty God, the Everlasting Father, the Prince of Peace.[13]

By listing honorifics associated with *the anointed one* and repeating the musical motif, Handel builds lyrical tension that is only resolved in "Prince of Peace."

And I've always been inspired to support peacemaking by the poetry of another passage, quoted just above, which similarly repeats a theme but in a parallel fashion:

> They shall beat their swords into plowshares,
>   and their spears into pruning hooks;
> nation shall not lift up sword against nation,
>   neither shall they learn war any more. (Isa 2:4)

---

[12] Online at: www.gnmagazine.org/issues/gn06/learnwaranymore.htm
[13] Online at: http://gfhandel.org/messiahlibretto.htm.

These two passages are sufficient to introduce the poetic forms of classical prophecy. While some passages in the classical prophets are in prose form, particularly biographical or historical material, accounts of visions in Zechariah and Ezekiel, and Jeremiah's jeremiads, most oracles are lyrical and the poetry has a distinctive Hebrew form. Petersen identifies and discusses three of that form's aspects: Parallelism, Figures of Speech, and Forms of Prophetic Speech.[14]

Parallelism

As any participant in a responsive reading in a church will recognize, ancient Hebrew poetry is marked by a call-and-response form that scholars call parallelism. Here are two examples from passages in Isaiah that we have just visited:

> For unto us a child is born,
>> Unto us a child is given.

and

> They shall beat their swords into plowshares,
>> and their spears into pruning hooks.

Petersen defines parallelism in Hebrew poetry as "several poetic lines of roughly comparable length that stand in a semantic relationship."[15] A second line restates the thought in the first (as in the examples above), but in ways that enliven its imagery or expand its meaning. In the first example, the two lines are practically the same but subtly different: the evocative image in the first line is a child newly born, suggesting in its context that the hope of Israel is like the joyful expectation of new parents; that meaning is then expanded by the second line, where the parents' joyful hopefulness is identified as a special gift from God. In the second example, the prophet's message is reinforced by the repetition of the same phrase using different implements of war and agriculture, contrasting the implements of death with the implements of life.

Figures of speech

One early passage in Isaiah that anticipates the fall of Jerusalem (which the prophet calls *daughter of Zion*) is this:

> Your country lies desolate,
>> your cities are burned with fire;
> in your very presence aliens devour your land;
>> it is desolate, as overthrown by foreigners.
> And daughter of Zion is left
>> like a booth in a vineyard,
> like a shelter in a cucumber field,

---

[14] Petersen, *The Prophetic Literature*, 25-30.
[15] Ibid., 25.

like a besieged city. (Isa 1:7-8)   ,

Here, Isaiah is using a common figure of speech, *simile* (*like* a booth, *like* a shelter). Later in the same, opening chapter, Isaiah will draw again on *daughter of Zion*, the figure of speech he uses for Jerusalem, but this time as a *metaphor* to condemn Jerusalem's idolatry:

> How the faithful city
>> has become a whore!
>> She that was full of justice,
> righteousness lodged in her—
>> but now murderers! (Isa 1:21)

A prophet's liberty to associate images and words in poetic speech means that what prophets say cannot be taken literally to describe the historical or geographical realities of their times. Isaiah didn't condemn Jerusalem for prostitution and murder; however, by making its faithlessness and injustice equivalent to those crimes, his condemnation of Jerusalem's injustice is impossible for his listeners to ignore. The prophet doesn't record events, he calls attention to intolerable circumstances in poetic ways to move people to correct them. In a warning that also pertains to end-times writers who use metaphors as facts about future events, Petersen writes:

> Poets do not provide reports or chronicles. They offer images calculated to achieve a particular emotional effect or rhetorical response. Hence, when reading prophetic poetry, one should in the first instance attend to the text as poetry and not immediately view the poem as data by means of which to reconstruct the social or economic history of the period during which the prophet lived.[16]

Forms of prophetic speech

The form of speech a classical prophet uses, such as a lament or a hymn, enhances his speech by appropriating the setting where the form is usually heard. Petersen suggests several common forms the prophets use and gives some examples:[17]

Judgment oracle: the prophet speaks an indictment, then a punishment, like a judge in a court of law; the passage is often preceded by, "Thus says the Lord." Here, Isaiah again uses his metaphor of Jerusalem as a prostitute:

> The Lord said:
>> Because the daughters of Zion are haughty
>>> and walk with outstretched necks,
>>> glancing wantonly with their eyes,
>>> mincing along as they go,
>>> tinkling with their feet;

---

[16] Ibid., 28.
[17] Ibid., 28.

the Lord will afflict with scabs
>   the heads of the daughters of Zion,
and the Lord will lay bare their [foreheads]. (Isa 3:16-17)

Woe oracle: the prophet uses a form that in ordinary speech refers to someone who has died; it's an attention-getter when the prophet confers woe on someone who hasn't. In Petersen's words, "The woe oracle [offers] the connotation that the party is as good as dead."[18] It usually begins with the Hebrew word *hoy*, variously translated as "Alas," "Ah," "Oh," or "Woe."

Ah, you who make iniquitous decrees,
>   who write oppressive statutes
to turn aside the needy from justice
>   and to rob the poor of my people of their right. (Isa 10:1-2)

Jesus of Nazareth will speak a series of seven *woe* oracles in his stunning condemnation of Pharisees and scribes at the temple in Jerusalem in the days preceding his arrest and execution (Matt 23:13-36), establishing himself in the long line of prophets who challenged Israel's faithlessness and injustice using an oracle in the form of a *woe*.

Lament: the prophet uses a form from funeral liturgies to conjure the dynamic of confession and salvation of an Israelite funeral service, but applies the form to the nation's faithlessness and injustice. By using the form of the lament, he implicitly assures people that with their repentance, they will be redeemed.

Petersen identifies "a series of standard features [of the lament]: invocation, call for help, expressions of trust, vows to sacrifice or pray," as in this example:

My soul yearns for you in the night,
>   my spirit within me earnestly seeks you.
For when your judgments are in the earth,
>   the inhabitants of the world learn righteousness.
If favor is shown to the wicked,
>   they do not learn righteousness;
in the land of uprightness they deal perversely
>   and do not see the majesty of the Lord. . . .
O Lord, you will ordain peace for us,
>   for indeed, all that we have done, you have done for us. (Isa 26:9-12)

Petersen observes:

There is strong evidence that, during the lament ceremony, a priest would have offered an oracle affirming that the worshiper had been heard and that his or her concerns were being addressed. These oracles of salvation . . . would have been spoken after the people had described their plight and asked for help. Then, after the proclamation of such an oracle, the individual would have continued with the final portion of the lament, acknowledging that the

---

[18] Ibid., 29.

prayer had been heard.[19]

Hymn: the prophet "attests to the character of the deity who, despite judging the people, remains worthy of veneration and worship."[20] Typically, the hymn begins with an imperative "praise" or "sing" as in this example:

> Sing praises to the Lord, for he has done gloriously;
>> let this be known in all the earth.
> Shout aloud and sing for joy, O Royal Zion,
>> for great in your midst is the Holy One of Israel. (Isa 12:5-6)

Reviewing these forms and others, Petersen argues that there are two features distinguishing prophetic poetry from other poetry in the Hebrew Bible: "its character as speech from the divine to the human world, and its tendency to set the world of human affairs in a broader context."[21] The parallelism of Hebrew poetry, in particular, allows the prophet to broaden a comment on current events to wider historical, geographical, or cosmic contexts. For example, Isaiah's warning about the threat of the Assyrians gains wider applicability to a variety of situations, both past, present, and future, in this passage that uses parallelism and the simile of attacking lions:

> He will raise a signal for a nation far away,
>> and whistle for a people at the ends of the earth;
> Here they come, swiftly, speedily! . . .
> Their roaring is like a lion,
>> like young lions they roar;
> They growl and seize their prey,
>> they carry it off, and no one can rescue.
> They will roar over it on that day,
>> like the roaring of the sea.
> And if one look to the land—
>> only darkness and distress;
> and the light grows dark with clouds. (Isa 5:26-30)

The suffering servant

Isaiah includes four unique passages called *servant songs* that are hymns by Israel about its role in the salvation of the world and the suffering it endures in exile. The gospels frequently allude to these songs when narrating Jesus' trial and execution, perhaps using Isaiah to shape their narratives, as in Matthew:

---

[19] Ibid., 108.

[20] Ibid., 30.

[21] Ibid., 32.

Matthew	Isaiah
But [Jesus] gave [Pilate, the Roman procurator] no answer, not even to a single charge, so that the governor was greatly amazed. (27:14)	Just as there were many who were astonished at him . . . , so he shall startle many nations. (52:14-15)
While [Pilate] was sitting on the judgment seat, his wife sent word to him, "Have nothing to do with that innocent man, for today I have suffered a great deal because of a dream about him." (27:19)	By a perversion of justice he was taken away. (53:8)
After flogging Jesus, [Pilate] handed him over to be crucified. (27:26)	I gave my back to those who struck me. (50:6)
[Roman soldiers] spat on him. (27:30)	I did not hide my face from insult and spitting. (50:6)
Then two bandits were crucified with him, one on his right and one on his left. (27:38)	Because he poured out himself to death, and was numbered with the transgressors; yet he bore the sins of many, and made intercession for the transgressors. (53:12)

Christian tradition, especially in worship, has appropriated other passages from Isaiah's servant songs as characteristics of Jesus' role in history, particularly his suffering as a sacrifice for the sins of humanity:

Surely he has borne our infirmities
    and carried our diseases;
yet we accounted him stricken,
    struck down by God, and afflicted.
But he was wounded for our transgressions,
    crushed for our iniquities;
upon him was the punishment that made us whole,
    and by his bruises we are healed.
All we like sheep have gone astray;
    we have all turned to our own way,
and the Lord has laid on him the iniquity of us all. (Isa 53:4-6)

The four servant songs are in the middle part of the book of Isaiah that generally but not exclusively speaks to the conditions of Jewish exiles in Babylon (the first part speaks to the conditions that preceded it, while the last celebrates Israel's reunion in Jerusalem when the exile ends).

In the first servant song (42:1-9), God acknowledges "my servant, whom I uphold, my chosen, in whom my soul delights." In the immediately preceding section, the servant is clearly Israel:

But you, Israel, my servant,
    Jacob, whom I have chosen,
        the offspring of Abraham, my friend;
Do not fear, for I am with you,
    do not be afraid, for I am your God. (Isa 41:8-10)

In the second song (49:1-6), the servant celebrates his (the nation's) purposes for God: to be "a light to the nations, that my salvation may reach to the end of the earth" (Isa 49:6). This is astonishing to a nation whose leadership has been exiled to a foreign empire and whose symbol of national identity, the temple in Jerusalem, has been destroyed.

In the third song (50:4-11), the servant (who may also be speaking as the prophet) must suffer despite listening to God's word and encouraging the nation to endure:

The Lord God has given me the tongue of a teacher,
that I may know how to sustain the weary with a word. (Isa 50:4)

In the last song (52:13-53:12) the prophet, speaking for God, promises that "my servant shall prosper; he shall be exalted and lifted up" (Isa 52:13). Israel's exaltation surprises nations and kings, who sing, "Who has believed what we have heard? . . . He was despised, and we held him of no account. . . . But he was wounded for our transgressions. . . . Through him the will of the Lord will prosper" (Isa 53:1-10).

Remarkably, the songs of the servant have ended with the grateful song of the world's nations. One of Isaiah's great themes, the hope for an *anointed one*, is absent here, but the other two themes, of God's holiness and Israel's nonviolent role in the salvation of the world, are announced to a nation that is presently separated from its homeland.

Isaiah's apocalypse

In a departure from the usual forms of prophetic speech used by Isaiah, prophecies in chapters 24-27 bear the distinctive trappings of a later literary form, the apocalypse. Isaiah usually speaks in more worldly metaphors about the prophetic choice that people need to make, but these passages push that conflict and its resolution into a mythical place and an indefinite future, and they resemble the literature that will flourish in the period when Jesus lived, when the Greek and Roman empires extended their powers over Palestine and Israel's hopes for worldly forms of independence and security receded.

Typical of later apocalypses, God's anger is not just focused on Israel, but is global:

The earth dries up and withers,
    the world languishes and withers;
    the heavens languish together with the earth. . . .
The city of chaos is broken down,
    every house is shut up so that no one can enter. . . .
For thus it shall be on the earth
    and among the nations,
as when the olive tree is beaten,
    as at the gleaning when the grape harvest is ended. (Isa 24:4-13)

Isaiah uses the metaphor of *earthquake*, a common constituent of apocalyptic visions, to describe how heaven's and earth's foundations will be undone:

For the windows of heaven are opened,
   and the foundations of the earth tremble.
The earth is utterly broken,
   the earth torn asunder,
   the earth is violently shaken.
The earth staggers like a drunkard,
   it sways like a hut;
its transgression lies heavy upon it,
   and it falls, and will not rise again (Isa 24:18-20)

An earthquake is used by many biblical writers to signify God's manifestation in nature; through an earthquake, God's omnipotence is clear not just to Israel, but to all the nations, and all of creation.

Earthquakes reveal God as a divine warrior in psalms attributed to King David:

Then the earth reeled and rocked;
   the foundations also of the mountains trembled
   and quaked, because he was angry. (Ps 18:7)

And Isaiah elsewhere prophesies:

Therefore the anger of the Lord was kindled against his people,
   and he stretched out his hand against them and struck them;
   the mountains quaked. . . . (Isa 5:25)

Appropriating earlier prophecies of *earthquake*, the later prophet Zechariah makes it an apocalyptic metaphor for the day of the Lord:

On that day. . . the Mount of Olives shall be split in two from east to west by a wide valley. . . And you shall flee by the valley of the Lord's mountain, for the valley between the mountains shall reach to Azal; and you shall flee as you fled from the earthquake in the days of King Uzziah of Judah. Then the Lord my God will come, and all the holy ones with him. (Zech 14:4-5)

In the New Testament, an earthquake will enter both the crucifixion and resurrection stories in the gospel of Matthew (27:54 and 28:2); these earthquakes recall the prophecies of Elijah, Isaiah, and Zechariah about the day of the Lord and bring their prophecies to bear on the events of Jesus' death and resurrection. As many as *five* earthquakes are envisioned in the book of Revelation as God engages the forces of darkness (Rev 6:12, 8:5, 11:13, 11:19, and 16:18). *Earthquake*, then, is a sign of the presence on earth of the powerful and holy God, creator of the world: in the past, with Elijah and Isaiah, in the present Christian era with Jesus, and in the future, as time is fulfilled.

In other passages of his apocalypse that also anticipate the book of Revelation, Isaiah describes a cosmic struggle between God and an icon of evil, a beast that we'll encounter there:

"On that day the Lord with his cruel and great and strong sword will punish Leviathan the fleeing serpent, Leviathan the twisting serpent, and he will kill the dragon that is in the sea" (Isa 27:1).

In Isaiah's apocalypse we find also the first and perhaps oldest Old Testament reference to the resurrection of the dead:

> Your dead shall live, their corpses shall rise.
> O dwellers in the dust, awake and sing for joy!
> For your dew is a radiant dew,
> and the earth will give birth to those long dead. (Isa 26:19)

Resurrection is a departure from classical prophecy. As we have seen and as D. S. Russell has written, prophetic hope in Israel was "expressed, not in terms of individual destiny, but rather in terms of God's dealings with the nation."[22] The fruits of a prosperous nation at peace with her neighbors would be enjoyed by the people who will live reunited in those times. But what of the righteous people who have died, particularly as martyrs? Justice for them demanded their individual membership in the messianic kingdom, too; bodily participation required their restoration to life. Justice for martyrs, especially those killed resisting the violent repression of Judaism by Antiochus IV Epiphanes in the second century BCE, will drive apocalyptic writing to embrace resurrection as God's ultimate instrument of justice.

As Isaiah's apocalypse closes, God establishes a New Jerusalem for resurrected martyrs and the righteous remnant of the day of the Lord:

> We have a strong city;
> he sets up victory
> like walls and bulwarks.
> Open the gates,
> so that the righteous nation that keeps faith
> may enter in. (Isaiah 26:1-2)

These apocalyptic notions—a cosmic battle between good and evil, a catastrophe that affects the entire earth, a day of judgment, resurrection of the dead, a New Jerusalem—are not typical of Isaiah, although they will be typical of apocalyptic writing and thinking that flourishes in Judaism in centuries closer to Jesus' life. Regardless of when it may have been written, Isaiah's apocalypse recapitulates themes of his more traditional prophecies, but in a different form. The leaders of Israel, a people chosen by God to demonstrate their greatness as a righteous nation, have tolerated idolatry, perpetuated injustice, and been indifferent to the needs of the poor. Therefore, judgment is imminent. However, God is still Israel's God and Israel should continue to work repentantly for the restoration of a just government, an end to oppression and poverty, and a world at peace.

---

[22] Russell, *The Method and Message of Jewish Apocalyptic*, 366.

✝

The sweep of Isaiah's prophecies reflects centuries of radical change for Judah: invasion, military defeat, exile, and return to Jerusalem. The verb tenses Isaiah uses in his prophecies change from future, to present, and to past as the prophet describes the succession of catastrophe, loss, hope, and restoration that Israel endures. For example, the last passage I've quoted is in the *present* tense ("we have a strong city"); the one preceding that is in the *future* tense ("your dead shall live"); and here's a prophecy that's in the *past* tense:

> Like a woman with child,
>> who writhes and cries out in her pangs
>> when she is near her time,
> so *were* we because of you, O lord;
>> we *were* with child, we writhed
>> but we *gave* birth only to wind. (Isa 26:17-18, emphasis added)

Were? *Gave*? End-times writers interpret passages that use the *birth pangs* metaphor to predict a *future* tribulation, but here it is clearly an event in the *past*. Isaiah is a compendium of prophecies made before, during, and after the destruction of the first temple and the exile of Judah's elites to Babylon, so some confusion of tenses in Isaiah can be ascribed to the mix of prophecies he or succeeding prophets uttered at different times, looking forward, looking at the present, and looking back. Isaiah's most apocalyptic passages, where we might expect the future tense to predominate, occur in chapters 24-27, yet this is where the passage above that uses the past tense is located. When we observe how the verb tenses even in Isaiah's most apocalyptic passages are mixed, we can conclude that apocalyptic writing may not always focus on the *future*, as end-times writers believe, but chiefly interprets the *past* to understand the significance of the *present* and the urgency of repentance.

The fluidity of time manifested by the flexibility of verb tense is observable throughout Isaiah and classical prophecy. Hence, I would add a corollary to Petersen's warning against interpreting the poetic words of prophecy as information: one must understand that prophecy may be interpreting things that have already happened or were happening contemporaneously, regardless of the verb tense the prophet uses. When considering the biblical sources of the scenarios of end-times writers, it is essential to understand that prophets use the future tense, in particular, not to predict future events, but to interpret contemporary events in terms of a hopeful vision of the future: worldwide recognition of God's sovereign power, the nation's hopes for peace and prosperity, and the nation's obligation to repent.

Whether he spoke in the literary style of apocalypse or prophecy, Isaiah was not interested in his future acknowledgment as an accurate predictor of the Babylonian exile (or, for that matter, the birth of Jesus as the successor of David). His purposes were to condemn contemporary religiosity and injustice and to encourage Israel to choose life: to be a "light to the nations" so people in every nation could learn to live in peace and bring justice to the poor:

> I am the Lord, I have called you in righteousness,
>> I have taken you by the hand and kept you;
> I have given you as a covenant to the people,
>> a light to the nations,
>> to open the eyes that are blind,
> to bring out the prisoners from the dungeon,
>> from the prison those who sit in darkness. (Isa 42:6-7)

Isaiah's prophecies, including his apocalypse, contrast righteous ways with idolatrous and oppressive ways, and he contrasts them using the prophetic choice between life and death. But like the books of Amos and Micah, the book of Isaiah is vague about the catastrophe that will befall Judah when it is destroyed by Babylonian armies in the sixth century BCE. Therefore, end-times writers rarely mine these, the oldest and greatest books of classical prophecy, respectively, for details in their end-times scenarios. Later prophets, however, provide more florid descriptions, and to them we now turn.

Chapter 8
ZEPHANIAH:
DAY OF WRATH

An ancient hymn we still hear, but not in church, is the *Dies Irae*, a thirteenth-century dirge based on the prophecies of the prophet Zephaniah and originally sung in Latin plainsong for funerals:

Day of wrath! O day of mourning!
See fulfilled the prophets' warning,
Heaven and earth in ashes burning![23]

The *Dies Irae* is rarely sung in churches today; it was removed from the Roman Requiem Mass by the Vatican II reforms. We are more likely to know the *Dies Irae* from horror movies. The medieval tune evokes primitive feelings of dread at impending and inevitable doom, so it's not surprising that movie scores use it to set edgy moods. For example, it opens the movie version of Stephen King's "The Shining" when the family Volkswagen climbs to the haunted mountain hotel where the character played by Jack Nicholson will lose his mind and attempt to kill his family.[24] Classical music aficionados may also know the *Dies Irae* from the breathtaking fifth movement of Berlioz's "Fantastic Symphony," which narrates a hanging and enunciates the musical theme with a chilling combination of tuba and bells.

Zephaniah is the prototypical prophet of doom. He prophesied dreadful things when times were peaceful and prosperous in Judah during the reign of Josiah (640-609 BCE), a king interested in restoring Israel to its glory days under David. Zephaniah's warning of catastrophic consequences from God's

---

[23] "Dies Irae," Wikisource. Online at: http://en.wikisource.org/wiki/Dies_Irae.

[24] Other movie soundtracks that use the *Dies Irae* include "Sweeney Todd," "The Nightmare Before Christmas" (sung by ghouls as they wrap shrunken heads as Christmas presents), "It's a Wonderful Life" (as the suicidal George runs to the bridge), "The Blue Max," and "Return of Dracula."

anger were prescient; shortly after Josiah's reign ended, the armies of Babylon swept down, exiled the Israelite's elites to Babylon, and destroyed Jerusalem and the temple.

Like other prophets, Zephaniah describes the coming cataclysm as *judgment day* or the *day of the Lord*, although in history the "day" rolled out over decades of military and diplomatic maneuvers. End-times writers frequently use details in Zephaniah's prophecies about that metaphorical day for their end-times scenarios, extracting the details from their prophetic contexts of faithlessness and redemption, exile and reunion, and death and life.

A brief book, Zephaniah opens by warning Judah of God's wrath over faithlessness and injustice. By using the Creation Epic (Gen 1:1-2:3) as his opening metaphor and repeating the verb "sweep away," he emphasizes the totality of the judgment he announces:

> I will utterly sweep away everything
>   from the face of the earth, says the Lord.
> I will sweep away humans and animals;
>   I will sweep away the birds of the air
>   and the fish of the sea....
> I will cut off from this place every remnant of Baal
>   and the name of the idolatrous priests; ...
> those who have turned back from following the Lord,
>   who have not sought the Lord or inquired of him. (Zeph 1:2-6)

Zephaniah prophesies a time of reckoning when a cataclysm will occur:

> The great day of the Lord is near,
>   near and hastening fast;
> the sound of the day of the Lord is bitter,
>   the warrior cries aloud here.
> That day will be a day of wrath,
>   a day of distress and anguish,
> a day of ruin and devastation,
>   a day of darkness and gloom. (Zeph 1:14-18)[25]

A city, presumably Jerusalem, is the target of God's wrath. Zephaniah's condemnation of Jerusalem is a "woe oracle," opening with "Ah," an expression used when the dead are mentioned:

---

[25] As I typed these words of Zephaniah into an early draft, television images of the devastation of New Orleans's poorest neighborhoods by Hurricane Katrina were in my room. There on the television was the vast storm in its grays, greens, and blacks as it approached, the darkness of the city as the storm blew through, the roof of the huge stadium sheltering the city's humblest people torn open by the wind, the Coast Guard helicopters churning the air above rooftops where whole families perched, the fear on people's faces as they watched the fouled waters rise to surround them in the merciless sunshine, the bellowing of a strong man—"the warrior cries aloud here"—as he is lifted to the belly of the orange whirling rescue machine in the sky.

Ah, soiled, defiled,
    oppressing city! . . .
The officials within it
    are roaring lions;
Its judges are evening wolves
    that leave nothing until the morning.
Its prophets are reckless,
    faithless persons;
its priests have profaned what is sacred,
    they have done violence to the law. (Zeph 3:1-4)

In contrast to the officials, judges, prophets, and priests the prophet condemns, it is the "humble of the land"—peasants who await the forgiveness of debts in the Sabbatical year and the return of ancestral lands in the Jubilee—to whom Zephaniah offers the prophetic choice:

Seek the Lord, all you humble of the land,
    who do his commands;
seek righteousness, seek humility;
    perhaps you may be hidden
    on the day of the Lord's wrath. (Zeph 2:3)

Although the destruction of the world is imminent, the survival of a remnant is promised:

I will leave in the midst of you
    a people humble and lowly.
They shall seek refuge in the name of the Lord—
    the remnant of Israel;
they shall do no wrong
    and utter no lies,
nor shall the deceitful tongue
    be found in their mouths.
Then they will pasture and lie down,
    and no one shall make them afraid. (Zeph 3:12-13)

Like Berlioz's score of the *Dies Irae* movement of his symphony, Zephaniah ends on a hopeful note: a hymn that foreshadows the good news preached by Jesus of Nazareth and his healing ministry to people whose disabilities and poverty separated them from the worshipping community of his time:

Sing aloud, O daughter Zion;
    shout, O Israel!
Rejoice and exult with all your heart,
    O daughter Jerusalem! . . .
I will remove disaster from you,
    so that you will not bear reproach for it.
I will deal with all your oppressors
    at that time.
And I will save the lame
    and gather the outcast,

and I will change their shame into praise
 and renown in all the earth. (Zephaniah 3:14-20)

Several other classical prophets wrote about the *day of the Lord* but described it in different ways. Here's Ezekiel:

Your doom has come to you,
 O inhabitants of the land.
The time has come, the day is near—
 of tumult, not of reveling on the mountains. (Ezek 7:7)

Here's Joel, who came later and whose prophecies were prompted by a natural disaster, swarming locusts that darken the skies and destroy Israel's crops:

Let all the inhabitants of the land tremble,
 for the day of the Lord is coming, it is near—
a day of darkness and gloom,
 a day of clouds and thick darkness! (Joel 2:1-2)

And Amos, in a woe oracle ("Alas"):

Alas for you who desire the day of the Lord!
 Why do you want the day of the Lord?
It is darkness, not light;
 as if someone fled from a lion,
 and was met by a bear;
or went into the house and rested a hand against the wall,
 and was bitten by a snake. (Amos 5:18-19)

The verb tenses in these prophesies usually set the *day of the Lord* in the future, but it is always imminent and related to a current crisis in Israel's faithlessness. The instrument of judgment is from the full range of natural and military catastrophes. Judgment may be against Israel, or the nations that oppress Israel, or both. A repentant remnant is promised security and happiness in a changed world:

Prophet	God's Weapon	Israel's Provocation	Repentance demanded	Judgment Target	Result
Amos 5:18-20	Darkness	Sacrificial practice absent justice	Justice and righteousness	Primarily Israel, but also sinners in other nations	A remnant is saved and nurtured; the Davidic line of kings is restored.
Ezekiel 7:5-9	Wrath	Idolatry	Restoration of the temple	Israel	Israel's chosen status as a nation is affirmed, and a remnant is preserved.
Zephaniah 1:14-18	Fire	Corruption of Jewish sacrificial practices	Righteousness and humility	All the nations of the world, starting with Judah	A remnant of humble people (Jews and Gentiles alike) is spared.
Joel 2:1-2	Locusts	Absence of repentance	Lamentation at the temple.	Both foreign nations and Judah.	Foreign oppressors are humiliated, but repentant Judah is spared and nurtured.

While there are differences in the instruments of judgment and the reasons that judgment is rendered, there are similarities among the prophets' descriptions of the day of the Lord. It is provoked by Israel's faithlessness. The targeted behaviors vary, but they boil down to idolatry in its broadest sense: Israel and Judah are rebuked for placing their faith in military alliances and not with God, for indifference to the needs of the poor and oppressed, for participation in pagan religious practices, or for abandoning the habits of purity. All these are idolatry, and they are condemned, in Moses' original prophetic formulation, as the choice of death.

Also similar among the prophets' characterization of the *day of the Lord* is the kind of kingdom established by the Lord after that terrible day. The kingdom established by the Lord will be an earthly kingdom that *continues* time, not a cosmic one that *concludes* it. A remnant is preserved and the nation resumes life, secure and prosperous. The line of hereditary kings that started with David is restored, and Israel is esteemed first among the nations for its righteousness and the power of its God.

Two fascinating chapters of the book of Ezekiel describe a battle between God and the exotic warlord Gog of Magog and his worldwide alliance of armies. Twentieth-century end-times writers typically identified Magog as Russia, mirroring the preoccupations of conservatives of that time with the Bolshevik revolution and America's cold war with the Soviet Union. More recent interpretations by Hal Lindsey, John Hagee, and their peers in the end-times publishing business reflect the emergence of militant Islam as the twenty-first century incarnation of Magog. Lindsey provides some continuity by identifying Gog's invading army as former Soviet republics whose ethnicity is primarily Muslim, led by Iran and equipped by Russia:

> Russia is not predicted [by Ezekiel] as a world conqueror, but rather a dangerous regional power with vast arsenals of deadly weapons. They will lead a confederacy of nations, which today are all Muslim, equipping them with weapons.
> Persia, or Iran is the first confederate named. It is no coincident [*sic*] they have signed a treaty with Russia binding it to fight alongside the Iranians if the West attacks. Russia has supplied the Muslim nations with the most lethal weapons known to man.
> The last war will begin with a coordinated attack against Israel by the Iranian led Muslim forces joined by Russia.[26]

Ezekiel wrote and spoke during Israel's exile in Babylon in the sixth century BCE, and his prophecies focus on the same issues that concerned Isaiah: the meaning to Israel of the destruction of its temple and the exile of its leadership from the lands promised to Abraham's descendants by God. Ezekiel's warnings and encouragement are made not just to his fellow exiles, but also to the Jews

---

[26] Hal Lindsey, *The Everlasting Hatred*, 235.

who remain in poverty back in Jerusalem, ruled by a puppet king installed by the Babylonian emperor.

While Isaiah and Ezekiel focus on similar issues for Israel's faith, Ezekiel's prophecies differ from Isaiah's in their stridency, and his metaphors are more visionary and allegorical. Ezekiel has more of an interest in worship, understandably, because the biographical information that opens his book says he was trained as a priest (1:3). Both Isaiah and Ezekiel condemn Israel's faithlessness and idolatry, but Ezekiel's metaphors are sometimes so obscure that an early church commentator, Jerome, reported that Jewish rabbis forbade people younger than thirty to read the first and last chapters of his book.[27]

Ezekiel prophesies that God's judgment had condemned Israel and Judah to exile for her alliances with Egypt and Babylon, relationships that were outside the marriage-like covenant of God and Israel. In a passage that may provide another reason why earlier rabbis kept his work behind the counter, Ezekiel uses a marital metaphor to denounce Israel as a woman who, having been nurtured to lovely adulthood by God, abandons it:

> But you trusted in your beauty, and played the whore because of your fame, and lavished your whorings on any passer-by. You took some of your garments, and made for yourself colorful shrines, and on them played the whore . . . .
>
> Therefore, O whore, hear the word of the Lord: Thus says the Lord God, Because your lust was poured out and your nakedness uncovered in your whoring with your lovers, and because of all your abominable idols, and because of the blood of your children that you gave to them, therefore, I will gather all your lovers . . . from all around and will uncover your nakedness to them, so that they may see all your nakedness. . . . I will deliver you into their hands, and they shall throw down your platform and break down your lofty places; they shall strip you of your clothes and take your beautiful objects and leave you naked and bare. . . . So I will satisfy my fury on you, and my jealousy shall turn away from you; I will be calm, and will be angry no longer. (Ezek 16:15-16; 35-42)

Ezekiel follows this oracle with a discussion of whether the judgment against Israel that began with the exile to Babylon will continue into future generations: the people in exile have asked, will the sins of the fathers be visited on the sons? Ezekiel asks them:

> What do you mean by repeating this proverb concerning the land of Israel, "The parents have eaten sour grapes, and the children's teeth are set on edge"? As I live, says the Lord God, this proverb shall no more be used by you in Israel. Know that all lives are mine; the life of the parent as well as the life of the child is mine; *it is only the person who sins that shall die.* (Ezek 18:1-4, emphasis added)

---

[27] Robert R. Wilson, "Ezekiel," in Actemeier and Mays, eds., *Interpreting the Prophets,* 158.

The prophetic choice between death and life is available to the new generation. In the passages that follow, Ezekiel contrasts a person who makes the prophetic choice for death ("it is only the person who sins that shall die") and the one who makes the choice for life:

> If a man is righteous and does what is lawful and right—if he does not eat upon the mountains or lift up his eyes to the idols of the house of Israel, does not defile his neighbor's wife or approach a woman during her menstrual period, does not oppress anyone, but restores to the debtor his pledge, commits no robbery, gives his bread to the hungry and covers the naked with a garment, does not take advanced or accrued interest, withholds his hand from iniquity, executes true justice between contending parties, follows my statutes, and is careful to observe my ordinances, acting faithfully—such a one is righteous; he shall surely *live*, says the Lord God. (Ezek (18:5-9, emphasis added)

Ezekiel goes on to describe another son, in contrast, who "is violent, a shedder of blood, who does any of these things . . ., who eats upon the mountain, defiles his neighbor's wife, . . . He shall surely *die*." (Ezek 18:10-13, emphasis added)

These passages are wonderfully similar in form and intent to the saying of Jesus about sheep and goats in the gospel of Matthew that Senator John Kerry and Pastor John Hagee interpret so differently (see pages 21-23). The form is similar: Matthew and Ezekiel contrast those who do righteous things and those who don't using identical words for the contrast, one in a voice that is positive and the other, negative. The content is similar: both speak of feeding the hungry and clothing the naked. Finally, and importantly, both Ezekiel and Matthew are speaking of the prophetic choice between life and death: for Ezekiel, the choice is explicit ("he shall surely *live*"; "he shall surely *die*"); in Matthew, the choice is externalized as apocalyptic judgment: "And these will go away into eternal punishment, but the righteous into eternal life" (Matt 25:46).

Ezekiel prophesies that God will restore the righteous new generation to Judah using the people who choose life, and God will defeat and humiliate the enemy kingdoms who surround them. After the terror of Jerusalem's destruction and the hopelessness of exile, Israel will be sufficiently secure to live in peace, its people safe in their homes to enjoy the fruits of their fields:

> When I gather the house of Israel from the peoples among whom they are scattered, and manifest my holiness in them in the sight of the nations, then they shall settle on their own soil that I gave to my servant Jacob. They shall live in safety in it, and they shall build houses and plant vineyards. They shall live in safety, when I execute judgments upon all their neighbors who have treated them with contempt. And they shall know that I am the Lord their God. (Ezek 28:25-26)

God's chariot

After telling of his commissioning as a prophet, the book of Ezekiel opens with a chapter-long vision of the "likeness of the glory" of God. Jesus of Nazareth spent a lot of his time meditating on the glory of God, and this vision might have been what he imagined when he did. Therefore, I'll ask the reader's patience with a long extract:

> As I looked, a stormy wind came out of the north: a great cloud with brightness around it and fire flashing forth continually, and in the middle of the fire, something like gleaming amber. In the middle of it was something like four living creatures. . . . Their wings touched one another; each of them moved straight ahead, without turning as they moved. . . . In the middle of the living creatures there was something that looked like burning coals of fire, like torches moving to and fro . . . and lightning issued from the fire.
>
> As I looked at the living creatures, I saw a wheel on the earth beside the living creatures, one for each of the four of them. . . . Their appearance was like the gleaming of beryl; and the four had the same form, their construction being something like a wheel within a wheel. . . .
>
> Over the heads of the living creatures there was something like a dome, shining like crystal. . . . When they moved, I heard the sound of their wings like the sound of mighty waters . . . . And there came a voice from above the dome over their heads . . .
>
> And above the dome over their heads there was something like a throne, in appearance like sapphire; and seated above the likeness of a throne was something that seemed like a human form. Upward from what appeared like the loins I saw something like gleaming amber, something that looked like fire enclosed all around; and downward from what looked like the loins I saw something that looked like fire. . . . Like the bow in a cloud on a rainy day, such was the appearance of the splendor all around. (Ezek 1)

Taking airplanes and automobiles for granted as we do, we lack the awe of Ezekiel's listeners as they listened to this description of God's ride. But apart from our consideration of the spectacle, it's helpful to look closely at several aspects of Ezekiel's account of his vision.

First, Ezekiel doesn't see God; he sees "visions of God" (Ezek 1:1). He says he sees things that are "something [they] look like," so what Ezekiel describes is, in Petersen's words, "more surrealistic than realistic."[28] The authors of the books of Daniel and Revelation will use similar surrealism to describe the heavenly figures they see and hear.

Second, Ezekiel's visions of singing creatures recall the throne scene described by Isaiah in *his* commissioning as a prophet:

> I saw the Lord sitting on a throne, high and lofty; and the hem of his robe filled the temple. Seraphs were in a attendance above him: each had six wings: with two they covered their faces, and with two they covered their feet, and

---

[28] Petersen, *The Prophetic Literature*, 142.

with two they flew. And one called to another and said:
Holy, holy, holy is the Lord of hosts;
    the whole earth is full of his glory." (Isa 6:1-3)

This song of praise for God's glory and holiness will be sung by a heavenly choir in the visions in the book of Revelation, recalling both Isaiah and Ezekiel and their prophecies of hope (Rev 4:8). Their song also will be the form Jesus uses to address God in the prayer he taught his disciples: "hallowed [holy] be your name" (Matt 6:9). Indeed the song is the "Sanctus," sung today by Christians during the Catholic mass. The vision of the heavenly throne and the song of the living creatures that surround it are images of the lordship of God that bridge the Old and New Testaments and endure today.

Third, the wheels of the Lord's heavenly chariot touch the earth ("I saw a wheel on the earth"). The chariot's motion is not confined to heaven; it's connected to the earth, where the Lord's subjects reside. God has not removed himself from collaboration with people on earth, despite God's anger at their impurity and injustice.

Finally, the throne Ezekiel sees is *mobile*. God's presence is not confined to the temple, which has been destroyed, nor is God confined to the lands he promised to Abraham. God travels the earth and is the Lord of people wherever they may be. For Ezekiel and his colleagues in exile in Babylon, despite the temple's destruction and despite their involuntary sojourn in the belly of the beast, the Lord is with them and will not punish the next generation.

Three reassuring visions

Three reassuring visions close the book of Ezekiel.

In the first, the Valley of the Dry Bones, God assures Israel of its restoration. Because the prophet learns that "these bones are the whole of the house of Israel," this passage is not about the resurrection of the dead; it is about the promise that Israel will again be a vital nation in its promised lands:

> The hand of the Lord came upon me, and he brought me out by the spirit of the Lord and set me down in the middle of a valley; it was full of bones. . . . He said to me, "Mortal, can these bones live?" I answered, "O Lord God, you know." Then he said to me: "Prophesy to these bones, and say to them, O dry bones, hear the word of the Lord. Thus says the Lord God to these bones: I will cause breath to enter into you, and you shall live. . . . and you shall know that I am the Lord.
>
>   . . . Then he said to me, "Prophesy to the breath, prophesy, mortal, and say to the breath: Thus says the Lord God: Come from the four winds, O breath, and breathe upon these slain, that they may live." I prophesied as he commanded me, and the breath came into them, and they lived, and stood on their feet, a vast multitude.
>
> Then he said to me, "Mortal, these bones are the whole house of Israel. They say, 'Our bones are dried up, and our hope is lost; we are cut off completely." Therefore prophesy, and say to them, Thus says the Lord God: I am going to open your graves, and bring you up from your graves, O my

people; and I will bring you back to the land of Israel. And you shall know that I am the Lord. . . ." (Ezek 37:1-14)

In Ezekiel's second reassuring vision, Gog of Magog, Ezekiel describes a future cosmic battle that will assure Israel's security. The vision describes a battle between God and an alliance of armies from distant and exotic lands. God initiates the conflict, drawing out the beastly leader, Gog of Magog, with "hooks [put] into your jaws" (Ezek 38:4). God's defeat of Gog's huge armies is total; it will take Israel seven months to bury the dead, and seven years for fires to consume the armies' weaponry. Ezekiel is exaggerating, drawing on the symbolism of *seven* (the number of days God required to create the earth) to indicate *completeness*. The passage thus assures Israel that it will not face judgment again as it did from Babylon:

> I will display my glory among the nations . . . The house of Israel shall know that I am the Lord their God, from that day forward. And the nations shall know that the house of Israel went into captivity for their iniquity, because they dealt treacherously with me. So I hid my face from them and gave them into the hand of their adversaries, and they all fell by the sword...
>
> Now I will restore the fortunes of Jacob, and have mercy on the whole house of Israel; and I will be jealous for my holy name. . . . I will never again hide my face from them, when I pour out my spirit upon the house of Israel, says the Lord God. (Ezek 39:21-29)

We'll spend more time with the vision of Gog of Magog, an important source for end-times writers, in the next section.

The book of Ezekiel ends with a third reassuring vision, a detailed description of a perfect temple, to promise Israel that God will again make his home in Jerusalem. The design of the temple is neither of the one that was destroyed by Babylon nor of the new one that will be built after the exiles return. It has walls like a city's to defend God's sanctuary. It will enclose a garden like God's in Eden. A wide river will flow from the temple to the Dead Sea, freshening it and creating a fishery. The vegetation on the banks will bear fruit each month; "their fruit will be for food, and their leaves for healing" (Ezek 47:12). Ezekiel imagines an ideal holy city offering security and abundance to its people and a home for a peripatetic God.

The vision of the perfect temple joins the two passages that precede it— the Valley of the Dry Bones and Gog of Magog—as literary expressions of the same theme: during the exile in Babylon, a time and place where Israel lacks the familiar trappings of religion, it is still appropriate to hope for God's intercession.

Gog of Magog

Like many apocalyptic passages in the Bible, the Gog of Magog passage in Ezekiel reinterprets an earlier prophecy when events have overtaken it. Ezekiel himself asserts that the battle with Gog will fulfill earlier prophecies by having God ask Gog: "Are you he of whom I spoke in former days by my servants the prophets of Israel, who in those days prophesied for years that I would bring you against them?" (Ezek 38:17).

One of the earlier prophets to whom Ezekiel is referring is Jeremiah, who prophesied invasion from the north as a consequence for Israel's apostasy. Just as God sets hooks in Gog's jaws to draw him out, Jeremiah prophesied that God would provoke kings "from the north":

> The word of the Lord came to me . . . , saying, "What do you see?" And I said, "I see a boiling pot, tilted away from the north."
>
> Then the Lord said to me: Out of the north disaster shall break out on all the inhabitants of the land. . . . And I will utter my judgments against [the cities of Judah], for all their wickedness in forsaking me; they have made offerings to other gods, and worshiped the works of their own hands. (Jer 1:13-16)

The forces led by Gog of Magog are not just from the north, nor are they from the nations that actually threatened Israel during the prophet's times, which were Babylon and Tyre to the north and Egypt to the south:

> The word of the Lord came to me: Mortal, set your face toward Gog, of the land of Magog, the chief prince of *Meshech* and *Tubal*. . . . *Persia, Ethiopia,* and *Put* are with them, all of them with buckler and helmet; *Gomer* and all its troops; *Beth-togormah* from the remotest parts of the north with all its troops—many people are with you. (Ezek 38:1-7, emphasis added)

The names of most of these nations are listed in Genesis as the descendants of Noah, who repopulated the world after the Flood (10:1-5). Gomer, Magog, Tubal, and Meshech are among the seven sons of Noah's son Japheth; Togarmah is one of Japheth's grandsons; and Cush and Put are among the sons of Ham. In biblical history, they are the patriarchs and namesakes of the world's tribes, like Abraham's grandson Jacob who was renamed Israel. As the names of ancient peoples, they are also associated with geographical areas. Historian John Bright locates these places as follows:[29]

- *Cush* and *Put* refer, respectively, to present-day Ethiopia and Libya.
- *Persia* is Iran.
- *Meshech*, *Tubal*, and *Bethtogarmah* are areas in eastern Turkey, and *Gomer* is an area in southern Russia.

These places are in a geographical tier beyond Israel's traditional enemies (Egypt, Tyre, and Assyria), so they represent the ultimate enemy alliance, one much more dangerous and exotic than the ones Israel has historically confronted. In his annotation of the "Gog and Magog" story in the NRSV *Study Bible*, Petersen suggests that the identity of these various armies is "transhistorical"—their identities aren't limited by history.[30] Ezekiel's use of aboriginal names for the armies of Gog vividly reconstructs the family of man

---

[29] Bright, *A History of Israel*, Map CII.
[30] *NRSV Study Bible*, 1283, note for 38:1-39:29.

engaged in ancient rivalries that swirl around, then focus on the unresolved fate of Israel, characterizing not just the situation that Israel presently confronts but also her situation in the past and her hopeful future.

The geographical references in the Gog of Magog apocalypse have fascinated end-times writers for the past one hundred years, as I discussed in Part One. Considered within its context, however, the vision of Gog of Magog has a very different literary purpose from predicting the threat of Soviet Communism in the twentieth century or militant Islam in the twenty-first. Like the passages that precede and follow it—the Valley of Dry Bones and the perfect temple—the battle with Gog of Magog is a fantastic vision of hope for a people whose leaders are exiled in the capital of a conquering power and whose remnant in Jerusalem is suffering. Dry bones—exiles and the ruined remnant—will live again as Israel. The legendary destruction of exotic armies from beyond the horizon demonstrates that God will protect Israel as an exemplar of righteousness to all of the peoples of the world. And finally, a perfect temple encompassing all of Jerusalem will sanctify his faithful people.

Chapter 10
JOEL:
AN ARMY OF LOCUSTS

The brief book of Joel thrums with the noise of swarming locusts that threaten to destroy Israel's food supply. And God's in the lead! There's still time to repent; with repentance come productive fields and security from enemies.

Biographical or historical information that could date the book of Joel or identify the prophet is lacking; the first verse names his father, but he is otherwise unknown as well, so the book can't be accurately dated. The frequency with which the themes and even phrases of other classical prophets appear in Joel make it likely that the book comes after them, late in the period of classical prophecy; that was also a time when interest began to grow in the literature of apocalypse, which helps us understand some of Joel's more fantastic imagery.

Certain prophetic themes recur, especially the *day of the Lord*, but the borrowing isn't limited to imagery. For example, one description of the *day of the Lord* is lifted verbatim from Zephaniah:

> A day of darkness and gloom,
>> a day of clouds and thick darkness! (Joel 2:2; cf. Zeph 1:15)

In another example, Joel quotes Amos' opening prophecy:

> The Lord roars from Zion,
>> and utters his voice from Jerusalem. (Joel 3:16; cf. Amos 1:2)

Besides the piracy of other prophets' words, there are instances where Joel turns their prophecies upside down. In an ironic twist, Joel reverses the prophecies of Isaiah (and Micah) about peace, warning hostile nations to prepare their armies for the day of the Lord:

> Beat your plowshares into swords,
>> and your pruning hooks into spears. (Joel 3:10; cf. Isa 2:4, Mic 4:3)

Joel's borrowing of themes, words, and imagery is far more extensive than in all other classical prophets. At the same time, the book doesn't indicate, like other prophets, what offense has caused the plague of locusts to descend. Perhaps by his extensive borrowing, Joel is applying the prophecies of the great prophets to the present crisis, although God's instrument of judgment—a plague of locusts—is very different from those prophesied by the others, namely, military invasion and exile.

Locust swarms are not a trivial problem in Palestine and throughout the desert habitat of the southern shores of the Mediterranean, in the Middle East, and in the Near East. The swarms don't have the periodicity of the locusts we experience in the Americas; the Mediterranean swarms grow when climate factors cause rapid reproduction, swarms gather, then go airborne to seek food. A swarm may contain billions of locusts and be as large as 460 square miles; the swarm will travel as fast as the wind might carry it, cross astonishing distances, and consume 423 million pounds of food a day, stripping croplands and causing famine in areas dependent on subsistence farming.[31] To protect agriculture and prevent famine, swarms developing in northern Africa are now tracked by an international network of scientists and governments linked by technology and coordinated by the Food and Agriculture Organization of the United Nations, the very institution despised by end-times writer as the power base of the emerging antichrist.[32]

Reports on the last modern desert locust swarm, which emerged in the West African nation of Niger and invaded her neighbors in 2004, describe the catastrophe:

> Worry written on his face, a cell phone dangling from his neck, Oumar Sakho, 50, swept his arms across his fields.
> The enemy, he recalled, had descended by the thousands on the cabbage patch before him. They chomped on the fresh green crowns as though it were their very own smorgasbord, then blithely moved on. . . .
> In northern Mali, fields of millet have been overrun. In Mauritania, locusts have nibbled on vast swaths of pasture that normally feed herds of camels and goats. The chartreuse-winged pests have darkened the scrublands of Chad, threatening to move east to the patch of misery known as Darfur.[33]

Using the same metaphor as the modern reporter, the prophet Joel likens the plague of locusts to a military invasion, which by now has happened to Israel often enough. The approach of the locust swarm would resemble the sounds and sights of charging cavalry. Joel has taken this threat to Israel's food supply and made it a metaphor for the dynamic seen throughout biblical prophecy: Israel is punished by invasion, presumably for placing its trust not in God,

---

[31] "Locust," National Geographic. Online at: http://animals.nationalgeographic.com/animals/bugs/locust.html

[32] You can track the threat from north African locust swarms on a UN website here: http://www.fao.org/ag/locusts/en/info/info/index.html

[33] Somini Sengupta, "A Tiny Enemy Causes Broad Havoc on African Farms," NYT, October 10, 2004.

but in empty worship and in rulers indifferent to justice for the poor. With Israel's repentance, God remembers his love for his chosen people, defeats their enemies, and restores their prosperity.

The locust army is relentless and terrifying:

> They have the appearance of horses,
>   and like war-horses they charge.
> As with the rumbling of chariots,
>   they leap on the tops of the mountains,
>   like the crackling of a flame of fire
>   devouring the stubble,
> like a powerful army
>   drawn up for battle. (Joel 2:4-6)

The army of locusts brings life in Israel to a halt:

> The grain offering and the drink offering are cut off
>   from the house of the Lord. . . .
> The fields are devastated,
>   the ground mourns;
> for the grain is destroyed,
>   the wine dries up,
>   the oil fails. (Joel 1:9-10)

Abruptly, the narrative's tone changes to a message of repentance.

> Yet even now, says the Lord,
>   return to me with all your heart,
> with fasting, with weeping, and with mourning;
>   rend your hearts and not your clothing.
> Return to the Lord, your God,
>   for he is gracious and merciful,
> slow to anger, and abounding in steadfast love,
>   and relents from punishing. (Joel 2:12-14)

God responds immediately; in a prophecy that mixes past and future tense, God provides food for Israel and drives the swarm away.

> Then the Lord became jealous for his land,
>   and had pity on his people.
> In response to his people the Lord said:
> I am sending you
>   grain, wine, and oil,
>   and you will be satisfied; . . .
> I will remove the northern army far from you,
>   and drive it into a parched and desolate land . . . . (Joel 2:18-20)

At this point in the text, Joel takes on an increasingly apocalyptic cast. After God drives off the locusts, there's an outpouring of God's spirit:

> Then afterward
>   I will pour out my spirit on all flesh;

your sons and your daughters shall prophesy,
your old men shall dream dreams,
and your young men shall see visions. (Joel 2:28, emphasis added)

This outpouring of the spirit, after God has driven out the locusts and restored Israel's food supply, will be recalled on Pentecost after Jesus' death and resurrection, when Jesus' disciples receive the Holy Spirit and proclaim the kingdom of God using ecstatic forms of speech. In Joel, the outpouring of the spirit happens after the invasion is crushed ("then afterward"); in Acts, the passage is referenced but subtly changed to refer to the *present* and becomes a prophecy that the first Christian Pentecost fulfills:

In the last days it will be, God declares,
that I will pour out my Spirit upon all flesh,
and your sons and your daughters shall prophesy,
and your young men shall see visions,
and your old men shall dream dreams. (Acts 2:17, emphasis added)

Based on this passage of Joel and its reinterpretation by first-century Christians, occasions of ecstatic religious experience will be interpreted by many Christians thereafter as signs of the imminence of the messianic kingdom.

Like the classical prophets, Joel contains prophecies that judge foreign nations but here, too, the prophecies take on an apocalyptic cast. God summons their armies to the "valley of Jehoshaphat" (Joel 3:12), an otherwise unknown place; the name of an ancient king, the Hebrew word can be translated as "the Lord judges." Joel's prophecy of a gathering of armies in a valley will be recalled in the book of Revelation, but the valley will be called Harmageddon.

For his prophesy about the battle at Jehoshaphat, Joel borrows a metaphor from Isaiah:

Put in the sickle,
for the harvest is ripe.
Go in, tread,
for the wine press is full.
The vats overflow,
for their wickedness is great. (Joel 3:13)

The *wine press* metaphor is from Isaiah:

"I have trodden the wine press alone,
and from the peoples no one was with me;
I trod them in my anger
and trampled them in my wrath;
their juice spattered on my garments,
and stained all my robes." (Isa 63:3)

The *wine press* will also figure in Revelation, describing the battle at Harmageddon ("[Jesus Christ] will tread the winepress of the wrath of God" [Rev 19:15]), and it will enter the lexicon of American patriotic music in "The

Battle Hymn of the Republic":

> Mine eyes have seen the glory of the coming of the Lord:
> He is trampling out the vintage where the grapes of wrath are stored;
> He hath loosed the fateful lightning of His terrible swift sword:
> His truth is marching on.[34]

While the *day of the Lord* Joel describes is terrifying, it signals the beginning of an era of peace and prosperity. And as the book of Joel ends, the writer has transformed his vivid description of God's rescue of Israel from a plague of locusts into a prophecy of promise: if Israel makes the choice for life and repents, God will fulfill his promise to Israel that the nation will be a leader among the nations and secure forever in its land.

> Judah shall be inhabited forever,
>   and Jerusalem to all generations.
> I will avenge their blood, and I will not clear the guilty,
>   for the Lord dwells in Zion. (Joel 3:20-21)

✝

Joel appeals to end-times writers because it is a spare yet comprehensive template for their scenarios and appears to corroborate details they find in the book of Revelation, which was written four centuries later. In his commentary on Chapter One of Joel, Cyrus Scofield wrote:

> It is remarkable that Joel, coming at the very beginning of written prophecy (B.C. 836), gives the fullest view of the consummation of all written prophecy.
> The order of events is:
> • The invasion of Palestine from the north by Gentile world-powers headed up under the Beast and false prophet.
> • The Lord's army and destruction of the invaders.
> • The repentance of Judah in the land.
> • The answer of Jehovah.
> • The effusion of the Spirit in the (Jewish) "last days."
> • The return of the Lord in glory and the setting up of the kingdom by the regathering of the nation and judgment of the nations.
> • Full and permanent kingdom blessing.[35]

Scofield's précis of Joel has three significant problems: the unlikely dating of the book, the misinterpretation of its narrative as a sequence of *future* events,

---

[34] Cyberhymnal. Online at: www.cyberhymnal.org/htm/b/h/bhymnotr.htm.

[35] "Joel," "Introduction," *Scofield Reference Bible*, 1917. This excerpt is from "Search God's Word," an exceptionally useful online database of biblical passages in many translations as well as commentaries in the public domain, among them Scofield's. Online at: www.searchgodsword. org.

and the bald assertions in his first item. You will look through Joel in vain for "Gentile world-powers," the "Beast," or the "false prophet"; these major characters in the dispensationalist end-times scenarios don't appear in Joel.

Scofield's interpretation of the book of Joel as an end-times prediction obscures Joel's literary accomplishment in presenting God's word. The book's prophecies are prompted by a very real plague of locusts, then link the plague to historical prophecies about military invasion to call for the kind of repentance and dependence on the Lord's mercy that repelled conventional attacks.

Just as a swarm of locusts leaves fields empty of food, so the lack of heartfelt repentance makes Israel spiritually barren. By choosing to repent, Israel can renew its covenant with God, who intervenes to end the life-threatening plague and restore the faith of Israel. Unlike the punitive God of the end-times writers, Joel describes God as "gracious and merciful, slow to anger and abounding in steadfast love, and relents from punishing." Through repentance, Israel chooses life. The alternative, like famine caused by locusts, is death.

Chapter 11

ZECHARIAH:
THE RAPE OF JERUSALEM

Zechariah wanted the temple rebuilt, now that the Babylonian exile had ended and the exiles were returning to Jerusalem. Although the cornerstone had been laid, there had been little progress; he wanted priests, prophets, and secular leaders to cooperate, and he wanted to reassure them that the effort, which reflected God's favor, was worth it.

The Persian conqueror of Babylon, Cyrus, had permitted the exiles to return to Palestine in 539 BCE and expressly allowed them to rebuild the temple that had been destroyed by King Nebuchadnezzar's armies about fifty years earlier. The returnees found economic hardship and demoralization among the Jews who had remained behind after Jerusalem was destroyed. Contributing to low morale was the failure of many exiles to return; they chose to remain in Babylon where the living was easier. Still, laying a cornerstone for the new temple coincided with good harvests, and Zechariah spoke to the locals about this good sign:

> Thus says the Lord of hosts: Let your hands be strong—you that have recently been hearing these words from the mouths of the prophets who were present when the foundation was laid for the rebuilding of the temple, the house of the Lord of hosts. For before those days there were no wages for people or for animals, nor was there any safety from the foe for those who went out or came in, and I set them all against one another. But now I will not deal with the remnant of this people as in the former days, says the Lord of hosts. For there shall be a sowing of peace: the vine shall yield its fruit, the ground shall give its produce, and the skies shall give their dew; and I will cause the remnant of this people to possess all these things. . . . Do not be afraid, but let your hands be strong. (Zech 8:9-13)

Perhaps due to the encouraging prophecies of Zechariah and another prophet, Haggai, the new temple was completed and dedicated in 515 BCE, about seventy years after the first temple's destruction, thereby fulfilling

Jeremiah's prophecy. This *second* temple would stand almost six centuries and endure its defilement by Antiochus IV Epiphanes in 167 BCE, a defining moment that prompted the book of Daniel, and its expansion by King Herod the Great around the time of the birth of Jesus, framing the narrative of his life and ministry. It would ultimately be destroyed by Roman armies forty years after Jesus' death in 70 CE, when they brutally crushed a Jewish rebellion and burned Jerusalem to the ground.

The form and content of Zechariah's book are challenging. The first half consists of a series of obscure visions in prose form. The visions are interpreted to Zechariah by angels, which is typical of Jewish apocalyptic writing written centuries later but unusual among classical prophets (even in Ezekiel, it is God, not an angel, who interprets his visions). The appearance of angels as interpreters of visions reflects an evolution of prophecy under Israel's changed circumstances as a client state of large, powerful empires; it also represents the influence of Persian beliefs during the exile in Babylon. God seems to stand at a further remove from Israel's destiny; one commentator writes:

> Visions and a mediating angel who acts as interpreter—so great is the distance that now separates [the Lord] from man, and so indistinct has the divine voice become. [The Lord] has been enthroned high beyond the reach of man. He sits above the heavens, remotely transcendent. Not even prophets now have direct access to him.[36]

Halfway through the book, its form abruptly changes. There are no more visions; the passages resemble earlier classical prophecy but in prose form, and the oracles are increasingly apocalyptic, reflecting disenchantment with the optimism of the first eight chapters that a secure and prosperous nation would result from rebuilding the temple. The final chapter of Zechariah is thoroughly apocalyptic, describing the destruction of Jerusalem by military forces and culminating in an earthquake when God arrives and stands on the Mount of Olives. These are images used by end-times writers to predict phases of the battle between God and the antichrist that ends the tribulation and opens the millennium.

Almost certainly, the second half of Zechariah wasn't written by the author of the first. The historical Zechariah who described the visions and uttered the prophecies of the first half of the book had a foundational role in post-exile Judaism centered in the second temple; the author, or multiple authors, of the second half of the book seem to be on the fringes of a much later apocalyptic movement that likely spurned the temple cult but still foresaw God's continuing renewal of the faith of Jerusalem, which is firmly within the original Zechariah's prophetic scope.[37]

---

[36] D. Winton Thomas, "Zechariah, Introduction," *The Interpreter's Bible*, VI, 1055.

[37] Brueggemann, *An Introduction to the Old Testament*, 253 ff; Petersen, *The Prophetic Literature*, 207 ff.

Zechariah is a pivotal book in the Christian Bible, and not just because it has both prophetic and apocalyptic features that speak to God's transformation of the faith of Jerusalem. Several of its passages contribute traditions about Jesus and his ministry, and the book may have influenced Jesus in understanding his role in ushering in the kingdom of God. Visions and symbols in the first half of Zechariah foreshadow Jesus' ministry and trial: one vision describes the triumphant entrance into Jerusalem of a king in David's line, but on the back of a donkey (9:9); another describes a betrayal for thirty pieces of silver (11:12-13). The apocalyptic later chapters, especially the final chapter when a temple and a source of "living waters" spectacularly emerge, recall Ezekiel's perfect temple but also foreshadow Jesus' description of the good news in the gospel of John and visions of a New Jerusalem in the book of Revelation.[38] In Zechariah, apocalyptic hope for a cosmic victory by God is emerging from its larval stage as prophetic yearning for an earthly messianic kingdom recedes.

Zechariah's visions

The visions and oracles of the first eight chapters of Zechariah include an array of symbols that will be important as apocalyptic literature develops.

The opening visions reassure Israel that God's promises are still valid. A "young man" measures a new and greater Jerusalem that is home to both people and animals, living amicably together as in the Creation Epic and Isaiah's peaceable kingdom (Isa 11:6). They are protected not by walls but by God's power. An angel reports:

> "Run, say to that young man: Jerusalem shall be inhabited like villages without walls, because of the multitude of people and animals in it. For I will be a wall of fire all around it, says the Lord, and I will be the glory within it." (Zechariah 2:4-5)

Four horns, symbolic of kingship, are interpreted by an angel to represent the nations that oppressed Israel; the horns are destroyed by blacksmiths. (The horns will be a symbol used later by the author of the book of Daniel to describe the succession of foreign kings that resulted in the emergence of Antiochus IV Epiphanes, who violently repressed Judaism and defiled the second temple in the second century BCE.) Four chariots drawn by horses represent the "four winds of heaven" (6:5) and patrol neighboring lands to assure that Israel remains secure and at peace. A huge flying book crushes liars and thieves. The sins of the world, symbolized by a wicked woman in a basket, are carried away by female angels:

> Then the angel who talked with me came forward and said to me, "look up and see what this is that is coming out." I said, "What is it?" He said, "This is a basket coming out." And he said, "This is their iniquity in all the land." Then a leaden cover was lifted, and there was a woman sitting in the basket! And he

---

[38] Ezek 47:1-2; John 7:38; Rev 22:1-2.

said, "This is Wickedness." So he thrust her back into the basket, and pressed the leaden weight down on its mouth. Then I looked up and saw two women coming forward. The wind was in their wings; they had wings like the wings of a stork, and they lifted up the basket between earth and sky. Then I said to the angel who talked with me, "Where are they taking the basket?" He said to me, "To the land of Shinar, to build a house for it; and when this is prepared, they will set the basket down there on its base." (Zech 5:5-11)

"Land of Shinar" refers to Babylon, the traditional site of the tower of Babel from the book of Genesis and the center of the empire that destroyed Jerusalem and its first temple. Zechariah is saying that the construction of Jerusalem's new temple will send the sins of his nation packing to the archetypal kingdom of evil, the destroyers of the first temple, where they presumably belong.

This vision is extremely important to at least one modern end-times writer, Charles H. Dyer, Provost of the fundamentalist Moody Bible Institute. Dyer wrote his book, *The Rise of Babylon*, before Saddam Hussein's overthrow in 2003 by invading American armies, and viewed Saddam's investment in the reconstruction of the ancient city of Babylon as a harbinger of the tribulation:

> Yes. Zechariah's vision shows that the "house" of Babylon will rise again when it is ready. The time and place have not been right for thousands of years, but when God's prophetic plan is ready, Babylon will be rebuilt. Wickedness will again reign from the plain of Babylon. The city where humanity's rebellion against God began will be the site where that rebellion will take up residence.
>
> Every day that passes brings us closer to the end times, and every day the eyes of the world focus more closely on events in the Middle East and Mesopotamia. One key element in God's program of end-time activities will be the reestablishment of Babylon as a world power, when wickedness will again occupy the "city of man."[39]

Dyer's interpretation is preposterous (although it reflected the conservative theological underpinnings of American foreign policy at that time, which demonized Saddam Hussein's Iraq). Zechariah's vision of the wicked woman in the basket is among eight that build hope among the restored exiles that the new temple will provide security and prosperity—peace—for their renewed nation. Zechariah had no interest in wars, particularly wars over access to petroleum at the turn of the twentieth century, 2500 years later.

In oracles that punctuate the eight visions, Zechariah reassures Israel that its king and chief priest, as well as the new temple that the priest will use, are sanctified directly by the Lord. In one oracle, the chief priest stands before God and "Satan [stands] at his right hand to accuse him" (Zech 3:1). Historically, this is the first reference in the Bible to *Satan*, but it is a mistranslation: the Hebrew word *satan* means *the accuser*, the member of the divine counsel in God's heavenly court who makes an accusation, like a prosecutor, as part of a

---

[39] Dyer, *The Rise of Babylon*, 19-20.

hearing on the merits of a case, so it should have been translated as _the satan_. In any case, _the accuser_ is rebuked by God, who orders angels to throw away the chief priest's "filthy clothes" (Zech 3:4)—presumably, the chief priest's history of sin.

In another vision, a lamp between two olive branches is interpreted to represent the king and chief priest who, by rebuilding the temple, will provide a light to the world. Zechariah believed that the rebuilding of the temple by Joshua, the chief priest, and King Zerubbabel, Judah's governor and a descendant of David, celebrated God's continuing love for Israel, and he calls them _anointed ones_. However, Zechariah prophesied that God asked for just and righteous behavior and not simply religious fervor in return. A story about Zechariah is provided as an example of the collaboration God desires. As the seventieth year of exile approaches—the span of the exile predicted by Jeremiah—a delegation asks the prophet if they should continue their practice of fasting on the anniversary. Zechariah responds that God asks, in turn, "When you fasted and lamented . . . for these seventy years, was it for me that you fasted? And when you eat and when you drink, do you not eat and drink only for yourselves?" Consistent with classical prophecy, Zechariah poses the choice of life and its ethical consequences:

> "Render true judgments, show kindness and mercy to one another; do not oppress the widow, the orphan, the alien, or the poor; and do not devise evil in our hearts against one another." (Zech 7:9-10)

Zechariah also perceived a global mission for the rebuilt temple. He hoped that other nations would worship in the temple, recalling Isaiah's prophecy about the mountaintop banquet for the nations, to fulfill God's promise that Israel's righteousness would be an example to the world:

> Peoples shall yet come, the inhabitants of many cities; the inhabitants of one city shall to go to another, saying, "come let us go to entreat the favor of the Lord, and to seek the Lord of hosts; I myself am going." Many peoples and strong nations shall come to seek the Lord of hosts in Jerusalem, and to entreat the favor of the Lord. (Zech 8:20-22)

Zechariah's apocalypse

While the two halves of the book of Zechariah similarly shift abruptly from one exotic scene to another, their purposes are very different. The concern of the first half is to renew the sacrificial cult in a rebuilt temple, anoint civil and religious authority, and restore justice to Judah's society following the return of the Babylonian exiles to their ruined homeland. The concern of the second half, however, is to envision the future now that God's earlier promises to Israel—a Davidic king and victory over its enemies—have proven elusive. The second half of the book of Zechariah is a precursor of Jewish apocalyptic writing that will flourish in later centuries and continue after the destruction of the second temple, especially in the literature of the Christian church and particularly the book of Revelation.

An important apocalyptic theme in the second half of Zechariah is a cosmic battle instigated by God, who is called the *Divine Warrior*, on the *day of the Lord*. God approaches Palestine for the battle along the route used by Alexander the Great (Zech 9:1-8), serving as a way to date at least this passage in Zechariah: Alexander's march was in 332 BCE. After defeating nations that traditionally oppose Israel on his way, God installs a king who will usher in an era of peace—and not just in Jerusalem or all of Israel. Consistent with the close of the *first* half of Zechariah, the peace will be worldwide. In imagery immediately recognizable to anyone who's attended a Palm Sunday service, Zechariah prophesies this in the form of a hymn (signaled by the beginning word, "rejoice"):

> Rejoice greatly, O daughter Zion!
>   Shout aloud, O daughter Jerusalem!
> Lo, your king comes to you;
>   triumphant and victorious is he,
> humble and riding on a donkey,
>   on a colt, the foal of a donkey.
> He will cut off the chariot from Ephraim
>   and the war-horse from Jerusalem;
> and the battle bow shall be cut off,
>   and he shall command peace to the nations;
> his dominion shall be from sea to sea,
>   and from the River to the ends of the earth. (Zech 9:9-10)

Two other passages from the second half of Zechariah, both difficult to interpret otherwise, will later become traditions about Jesus. In one, Zechariah describes an irresponsible shepherd who, trusted by God with sheep that risked slaughter by unprincipled owners, abandons them. We can imagine Zechariah breaking his staff as he speaks to demonstrate the shepherd's betrayal:

> I took my staff Favor and broke it, annulling the covenant that I had made with all the peoples. So it was annulled on that day, and the sheep merchants, who were watching me, knew that it was the word of the Lord. I then said to them, "If it seems right to you, give me my wages; but if not, keep them." So they weighed out as my wages *thirty shekels of silver.* Then the Lord said to me, "Throw it into [the potter's field]—this lordly price at which I was valued by them. So I took the thirty shekels of silver and threw them into [the potter's field]. Then I broke my second staff Unity, annulling the family ties between Judah and Israel. (Zech 11:10-14, emphasis added)

A betrayal for thirty shekels of silver will also figure in a story in the gospel of Matthew about Jesus' betrayal by his disciple Judas, who may have been a revolutionary and saw Jesus' arrest as a way to prompt the *day of the Lord*. Thirty shekels was the amount the authorities paid Judas for his information about Jesus' whereabouts when they decided to arrest him. Later, racked with guilt, Judas will hang himself (Matt 27:3-10). It isn't simply the thirty shekels that recalls Zechariah's prophecy; like the corrupt shepherd in Zechariah's story, Judas betrayed an implicit promise of his discipleship. In the context of Zechariah's prophecy that this story recalls, Judas should have been dedicated to justice and compassion for the poor and oppressed, not involved in political maneuvers that seek apocalyptic outcomes.

In a second passage in Zechariah that is puzzling outside its later use in stories about Jesus' crucifixion, the descendants of King David and the inhabitants of Jerusalem raise their voices in a lament over "the one whom they have pierced" (Zech 12:10). The reference is unclear—there is no similarly wounded king, priest, or prophet in the Old Testament—so it most likely invokes Isaiah's songs of the suffering servant, which we saw earlier were metaphorical descriptions of Israel during its Babylonian exile.

Aside from Isaiah's song of the servant (which is about Israel) and perhaps Zechariah's allusion to a messiah who represents the suffering nation, there's nothing in the Old Testament about a Davidic king who will suffer. Russell writes that the idea of a "suffering Messiah" was actually anathema to Jews in Jesus' time.[40] Perhaps Jesus drew on the Isaiah tradition (as reinterpreted by Zechariah) to help his disciples understand the historical significance of his imminent arrest, torture, and death. Or, the gospels associated the hopeful messages of Isaiah and Zechariah with Jesus' death and resurrection, adding sacrifice and atonement to its significance.

The vision of the olive branches in the first half of Zechariah and prophecies about the servant in the second are variations on messianic themes. As Zechariah (or a later editor) wove his visions and prophecies together, he was developing new ideas about the messianic figure who will rule a world that enjoys safety and prosperity.

✝

Zechariah ends with a bang—catastrophe! The closing chapters of Zechariah are especially useful to end-times writers, because they contain a wealth of detail for their scenarios.

Like other prophecies of a final global battle, God takes the initiative but in this account, Israel's enemies are victorious at first:

> See, a day is coming for the Lord, when the plunder taken from you will be divided in your midst. For I will gather all the nations against Jerusalem to battle, and the city shall be taken and the houses looted and the women raped; half the city shall go into exile, but the rest of the people shall not be cut off from the city. (Zech 14:1-2)

Then God appears on the Mount of Olives, east of Jerusalem. The site will

---

[40] Russell, *The Method and Message of Jewish Apocalyptic*, 335. This characterization has been challenged by more recent research and scholarship.

be important in traditions about Jesus. It is from the Mount of Olives that he will enter Jerusalem on a donkey, invoking Zechariah's prophecy of the return of the Davidic kingship; in Luke's gospel it is the place where Jesus, having appeared to his disciples after his death, ascended to heaven.[41]

Upon God's arrival at the Mount of Olives in Zechariah's apocalypse, an earthquake splits the mountain in two, signifying the arrival of God on earth and creating a valley through which the inhabitants of Jerusalem may escape the rapacious armies plundering Jerusalem. The cleft in the Mount of Olives also has hydrological consequences: "living waters" now flow from a spring in Jerusalem, reaching as far as the Mediterranean to the west and the "ocean to the east" (14:8). No longer will visitors to the temple be forced to settle for ritual cleansing from a stagnant pool refreshed periodically from a nearby cistern. The waters flow fresh and abundant enough to reach two distant seas.

The armies pillaging Jerusalem are viciously destroyed: "This shall be the plague with which the Lord will strike all the peoples that wage war against Jerusalem: their flesh shall rot while they are still on their feet; their eyes shall rot in their sockets, and their tongues shall rot in their mouths" (Zech 14:12).

Foreign enemies who survive the plague, however, will be invited annually to attend Israel's fall festival of harvest and hospitality, the Festival of Booths, opening to them the opportunity of a faith relationship with Israel's God. Those who don't attend, however, will continue to be punished by plague and drought, reflecting the consequences of their prophetic choice of death. Here, Zechariah recalls Isaiah's prophecies of a time when the nations of the world will come in peace to Mount Zion.

The final part of the apocalypse is reminiscent of an earlier puzzling passage, where Zechariah condemns temple prophets who have evidently become trivial and irrelevant (10:2). As the book closes, the end of priestly responsibilities in the temple is prophesied:

> On that day, there shall be inscribed on the bells of the horses, "Holy to the Lord." And the cooking pots in the house of the Lord shall be as holy as the bowls in the front of the altar, and every cooking pot in Jerusalem and Judah shall be sacred to the Lord of hosts, so that all who sacrifice may come and use them to boil the flesh of sacrifice. And there shall no longer be traders in the house of the Lord of hosts on that day. (Zech 14:20-21)

Three remarkable themes emerge in this final passage. First, the celebration of the holiness of God is a sign of God's imminent victory over evil. The holiness of God will also be a crucial theme in Jesus' healing ministry; we'll review it in Part Five when we consider the meaning of the first petition in the Lord's Prayer, "Hallowed be your name."

A second theme is the sanctification of mundane things, making common

---

[41] Luke 24:50. The entry of Jesus into Jerusalem for the Festival of Booths is discussed at length beginning at page 369.

cooking pots as holy as the offering bowls on the altar in the temple. Here, the hope is that the ordinary life of Israel, not just the accoutrements of its temple, will become instruments for Israel's worship of God. This has consequences for an understanding of the importance to Jesus of table fellowship, which will also figure in Part Five.

Finally, the exclusion of traders from the temple and the inclusion of people from foreign nations in the Festival of Booths indicate that the temple will become a center of unbrokered worship for all the people of the earth. Priest and ritual become unnecessary. Jesus will seize on this passage to take prophetic symbolic action, like Zechariah's when he broke the shepherd's two staffs. Jesus' prophetic action, overturning the tables of the money-changers in the temple, will ultimately result in his death.

✝

The apocalyptic ideas in the second half of Zechariah were crucial to the development of traditions about Jesus. We've already touched on some of them: the humble entry of the Davidic king into Jerusalem on the back of a donkey; the suffering servant; the betrayal of a covenant for thirty pieces of silver; and the centrality of the Mount of Olives. Where Zechariah and gospel traditions intersect is in the Festival of Booths.

At the time of Jesus' ministry, the Festival of Booths, or *Sukkoth* in Hebrew, was an important annual festival in Israel. The booths were originally shelters built from branches by the Israelites during their wilderness experience in the Sinai, after the exodus from Egypt:

> The Lord spoke to Moses, saying: Speak to the people of Israel, saying: On the fifteenth day of this seventh month, and lasting seven days, there shall be the festival of booths to the Lord. . . .
>
> When you have gathered in the produce of the land, you shall keep the festival of the Lord, lasting seven days; a complete rest on the first day, and a complete rest on the eighth day. On the first day you shall take the fruit of majestic trees, branches of palm trees, boughs of leafy trees, and willows of the brook; and you shall rejoice before the Lord your God for seven days. . . . You shall live in booths for seven days; all that are citizens of Israel shall live in booths, so that your generations may know that I made the people of Israel live in booths when I brought them out of the land of Egypt: I am the Lord your God. (Lev 23:33-43)

In Jesus' time, tent-like booths were similarly built by Jews to recall their ancestors' vulnerability and utter dependence on God. The booths demonstrate that God, not shelter, protects his people. The Festival of Booths was also a fall harvest festival; Jews from all over the Mediterranean area visited Jerusalem to present animals and other fruits of harvest in the temple for sacrifice and local families opened their homes to visiting supplicants. Today, celebrating Jews invite Gentile neighbors and friends to visit their tents, linking hospitality with Zechariah's prophecies about the inclusion of all the nations in a feast. Fittingly, Zechariah's apocalypse is read during the festival.

In John's gospel account of Jesus' visit to the temple during the Festival of Booths (7:10-8:2), Jesus engaged in a theological dispute with the Pharisees who believed that scrupulous adherence to the Law was the path of righteousness. Jesus argued that righteousness is more a function of a person's spirit; a righteous spirit, not compliance with the procedures of ritual, sanctified the person, the relationship, and the event. Alluding to the "living waters" that will flow from the cleft in the Mount of Olives prophesied by Zechariah in his apocalypse, John reports:

> On the last day of the festival, the great day, while Jesus was standing there, he cried out, "Let anyone who is thirsty come to me, and let the one who believes in me drink. As the scripture has said, 'Out of the believer's heart shall flow rivers of living water.'" (John 7:37)

We'll talk more about the Festival of Booths in Chapter 15. For now, in this interplay of the themes of Zechariah and John, prophecy and gospel, we glimpse how Jesus and his followers may have viewed the meaning of his otherwise catastrophic death, and how the belief may have arisen among his followers that a transformed world like the one Zechariah prophesied became possible after his resurrection. Zechariah spoke of an Israel where people accepted their utter dependence on God's nurturance, where ordinary life could celebrate the closeness of God, and where Israel would be the time and place of the messianic banquet of reconciliation among the nations of the world. In the next three parts of my book, we will learn that Jesus reinterpreted Zechariah's themes to teach that people must become dependent like children on the nurturance and protection of God, like Israel in the desert; that the engine of transformation is forgiveness, flowing like living waters from the heart of the person who forgives; and that an ordinary table may be sanctified and become the messianic banquet of peace and reconciliation among the people who join it.

Part Three
APOCALYPSE

Now [the supporters of Epiphanes] erected a desolating sacrilege on the altar of burnt offering. . . . The books of law that they found they tore to pieces and burned with fire. Anyone found possessing the book of the covenant, or anyone who adhered to the law, was condemned to death by decree of the king. They kept using violence against Israel, against those who were found month after month in the towns. On the twenty-fifth day of the month they offered [their] sacrifice on the altar that was on top of [our] altar of burnt offering. According to the decree, they put to death the women who had their children circumcised, and their families and those who circumcised them; and they hung the infants from their mothers' necks.

But many in Israel stood firm and were resolved in their hearts not to eat unclean food. They chose to die rather than to be defiled by food or to profane the holy covenant; and they did die. Very great wrath came upon Israel.

—1 Maccabees 1:54-64, describing the repression of Judaism by Antiochus IV Epiphanes in 167 BCE.

.

Chapter 12
DANIEL:
THE TIME OF THE END

Classical Old Testament prophecy provides a doom-filled stage for end-times events, but the details for the scenarios of Tim LaHaye, John Hagee, and their peers are drawn mostly from the two apocalyptic books of the Bible: the book of Daniel in the Old Testament and the book of Revelation in the New. The next two chapters will use these two books as bookends, as it were, for a review of biblical literature in the two centuries before Jesus' ministry and the century following it to observe how apocalyptic thought influenced and reflected faith in Israel then, particularly the meaning and message of Jesus' ministry of teaching, healing, and forgiveness.

The Greek word *apokalypsis* is usually translated *revelation*, but it literally means *lifting of the veil*. To understand Jesus' first-century message, it is necessary to lift several veils, such as the yawning distance of two thousand years of history, the alien cultural inheritance most Americans bring to the Mediterranean experience of their writers, and the strange rhetoric of apocalyptic thought. There's one more veil that needs lifting, and it's the least transparent of all: the lurid misinterpretations by modern end-times writers that have dominated popular considerations of the Bible's apocalyptic writings.

A classical prophet was interested in history, and often said that certain events would occur if people didn't repent. When those events in fact occurred, particularly the destruction of Jerusalem and the exile in Babylon, it was apparent that God, acting through history, had vindicated the prophet. However, the point of prophecy was not to predict the future; it was to encourage repentance from the impurity, injustice, and other ways of betraying the trust God demanded. The classical prophets urged reform to avoid catastrophe, and with the ironic exception of Jonah (whom we'll review in Chapter 15), they were spectacular failures. Fortunately, the prophets were often on-target when a remnant was preserved to carry God's message of love and hopefulness to future generations.

When a prophet's prediction was confirmed by events, then the particular choice between faithlessness and righteousness that he commended to his listeners had been affirmed by God. As we have seen in our reviews of prophecy, the ethical dimensions of righteousness, the choice of *life* demanded by prophets on God's behalf, were clear: for individuals, humility and mercy; for leaders, justice for the poor. Sanctimonious religion absent justice in the land was never a substitute.

Apocalyptic writing also had its ethical side. Apocalypses announce that the victors with God in the coming battle are those who choose the often-difficult path of righteousness in a hostile, violent, and unjust society. The author of an apocalypse is more interested in how history, myth, faith, and future converge to reveal God's will. Apocalypse reinterprets prophesies of catastrophe that would ruin Israel; those prophecies are transformed into sequences of fantastic and cataclysmic events that end the troubles of the world as this era concludes. God's plan for Israel is no longer the restoration of a Davidic kingdom in Palestine; in apocalyptic writing, and in the Christian theology it influenced, God's purpose becomes the establishment of a perfect kingdom ruled by God that joins heaven and earth and returns the creation to God's original design, where God and people walk hand in hand.

In this part and the next, I will review the books of the Bible most influenced by apocalyptic thought and literature in the period surrounding the rise of Christianity. In the part that has now begun, I'll review the book of Daniel, written in the second century BCE; several letters of Paul and John written to early churches in the middle of the first century CE; and the gospel of Matthew, compiled in that century's concluding decades. The next part will be devoted to the book of Revelation, also written at the close of the first century CE, but it requires a part of its own.

As we proceed, we will observe how common themes in classical prophecy are developed into apocalyptic ones:

The struggle between Israel and its earthly enemies is transformed into a symbolic battle between God and an evil antagonist.

Israel's promised military triumph becomes God's assured cosmic victory.

A restored Jerusalem ruled by a king in accord with God's laws becomes a utopian community in a perfect time ruled by God.

The prophetic choice against death and for life becomes the punishment of the wicked and the acquittal of the good.

The new era when the people of Israel are safe and prosperous becomes a final time governed by God and enjoyed by the righteous reunited with martyrs resurrected from the dead.

A major issue for Jewish apocalyptic thought, discussed in Part Two, was the apparent withdrawal of God to a heavenly, cosmic plane where the battle with evil takes place. No longer is God speaking directly to prophets; angels have become intermediaries, and the life-and-death battle occurs on a cosmic plane, not on earth. The directness and intimacy of the relationship of God and person has been lost. Jewish religious thought will respond variously to the challenges of God's apparent remoteness, and Jesus of Nazareth will step into the fray.

✝

The excruciating boredom of my Sunday School classes was occasionally enlivened by the exciting stories and exotic names in the book of Daniel. Here we have the dreams of King Nebuchadnezzar, conqueror of Israel and enslaver of bright, heroic, young men; Belshazzar's feast and the spooky "writing on the wall"; Daniel himself, one of the young heroes, thrown into the lions' den by his enemies; his mellifluously named friends Shadrach, Meschach, and Abednego enduring the "fiery furnace."

According to the book, Daniel was a member of the aristocracy of Judah who was taken into exile in Babylon after Judah's defeat by Nebuchadnezzar at the opening of the sixth century BCE. The king drafts the most promising young men from the exiles to become courtiers. Because of their acumen, Nebuchadnezzar increasingly relies on them as advisers and administrators, although they continue to adhere to their Jewish faith.

Soon and repeatedly, Daniel and his colleagues are undermined by jealous Babylonian courtiers who cause first Nebuchadnezzar, then his son Belshazzar, then *his* successor to test their faith. Shadrach, Meschach, and Abednego survive an intensely hot furnace that kills the people who cast them into it. This raises their esteem in the eyes of the kings but enrages their rivals.

The tales have their most dramatic moment during a drunken royal feast enjoyed with wine vessels looted from the destroyed Jerusalem temple. With the party-goers in their cups, a disembodied hand writes the names of the units of money used in the kingdom on the wall. King Belshazzar is terrified. When the king's own advisors cannot interpret the words, he summons Daniel, who recognizes an allegorical pattern of puns on Aramaic verb-roots:[1]

> "This is the interpretation of the matter: MENE, God has numbered the days of your kingdom and brought it to an end [*mn, to number*]; TEKEL, you have been weighed on the scales and found wanting [*tkl, to weigh*]; PERES, your kingdom is divided and given to the Medes and the Persians [*prs, to divide*]." (Dan 5:26-28)

That night, Belshazzar is killed and is succeeded by "Darius the Mede." (Here the tale fulfills prophecies by Isaiah and Jeremiah[2] but departs history. Darius is not a contemporaneous historical character, and the Medes do not

---

[1] Pamela J. Milne, NRSV ^Study Bible^, 1315, note to 5:26-8.
[2] Isa 13:17-22 and Jer 50:9 among others.

conquer the Babylonians; the Persians do, under Cyrus the Great.) "Darius" continues to use Daniel as an administrator, but Daniel's rivals conspire to cause Darius to test Daniel's faith by throwing him into a caged den of lions. The lions don't attack, Daniel survives, and an impressed Darius issues this proclamation:

> "May you have abundant prosperity! I make a decree, that in all my royal dominion people should tremble and fear before the God of Daniel:
> For he is the living God,
>   enduring forever.
> His kingdom shall never be destroyed,
>   and his dominion has no end.
> He delivers and rescues,
>   he works signs and wonders in heaven and on earth;
> for he has saved Daniel
>   from the powers of the lions." (Dan 6:26-27)

Daniel continues to serve Darius and his successor, "Cyrus the Persian." Unlike Darius, Cyrus *is* historical: Cyrus the Great (580-529 BCE) conquered Babylon in 539 BCE. He immediately permitted conquered peoples including the Jews to return to their homelands and to resume their religious activities. Isaiah (actually a member of his school, for this would be long after the death of the original Isaiah) praised Cyrus as an *anointed one* (in Hebrew, *messiah*), the only non-Jew on whom the term is conferred in the Bible. This is a watershed for Israel; from now on, Israel's politics and religious life will be marked by dependence on (and the desire for independence from) empires for its safety and prosperity.

Daniel and his times

The book of Daniel is grouped in the Bible with the books of classical prophets who wrote during the centuries before, during, and immediately after the Babylonian exile. But aside from passages in the book of Daniel itself, there is no other evidence in the Bible or archaeology for a historical person in that period named *Daniel*. Also making it difficult historically to group the book of Daniel with other books of classical prophecy from that period is the absence of a typical passage introducing Daniel as someone's son or from a certain town who was active during a certain king's reign. Moreover, the book of Daniel is composed primarily of stories and visions, not the usual utterances introduced by, "This is the word of the Lord."

Instead of a classical prophetic form, the book of Daniel has the form of an apocalypse, a kind of Jewish literature common in the two centuries before Jesus' ministry and the century after. In addition to works handed down through the centuries, archaeologists have unearthed other examples of Jewish apocalypses from those times, particularly among the "Dead Sea Scrolls" found beginning in 1947 near the ruins of a Jewish monastery in the wilderness outside Jerusalem. Copies of the book of Daniel were found with them, as well. D. S. Russell identifies four characteristics of that literature, all of which apply to Daniel:

- "Esoteric in character": the content of the book had been secret, but it was revealed to the author through a dream or vision.
- "Literary in form": unlike the utterances of the prophets, which were primarily spoken and then written down and collected into book form at a later time, Jewish apocalypses originated as written documents.
- "Symbolic in language": animals and mythical beasts are used to symbolize oppressor nations, and numbers symbolically enhance the significance of events.
- "Pseudonymous in authorship": The person named as the author of the apocalypse is a historical or mythical figure whose authority and tradition lend additional meaning and importance to the revelation, but who isn't the actual author of the work.[3]

So who is Daniel? Elsewhere in the Bible, the name *Daniel* is mentioned twice by Ezekiel, another prophet of the exile period, but this *Daniel* is not a contemporary of Ezekiel's; he is a figure from the mists of history. In Ezekiel's first mention, *Daniel* appears with two legendary figures, Noah and Job, as paragons of wisdom:

The word of the Lord came to me: Mortal, when a land sins against me by acting faithlessly, and I stretch out my hand against it, and break its staff of bread and send famine upon it, and cut off from it human beings and animals, even if Noah, Daniel, and Job, these three, were in it, they would save only their own lives by their righteousness, says the Lord God. (Ezek 14:12-14)

In Ezekiel's second mention, *Daniel* appears in a sardonic aside about an enemy:

You are indeed wiser that Daniel;
    no secret is hidden from you. (Ezek 28:3)

There is, however, tantalizing archaeological evidence of a *Daniel* in the legends of the people of Canaan, who were the Israelites' neighbors in ancient Palestine. In his commentary on the book of Daniel, C. L. Seow writes that a legendary Canaanite named *Daniel* worshiped the god *El* who, like the Jewish God in the book of Daniel, revealed himself through dreams and visions.[4] Perhaps the author of the book of Daniel is tapping this legend by using the name as a pseudonym. The dreams that open the book certainly establish the biblical *Daniel* as an astute interpreter of dreams, like the *Daniel* in the

---

[3] Russell, *The Message and Method of Jewish Apocalyptic*, 104 ff. As soon as one defines the genre, one must make significant exceptions; for example, the book of Revelation, the only apocalypse that actually names itself an *apocalypse*, is *not* pseudonymous. John Collins describes several more recent attempts to define the genre in *The Apocalyptic Imagination*, 2-9, and provides a table illustrating the variety of apocalypses within it.

[4] Seow, *Daniel*, 3-4.

Canaanite legend, and as a source of great wisdom, like the *Daniel* in Ezekiel's prophecies. So the book may not have been spoken or written by a prophet named *Daniel*, but the author certainly meant to associate his book with the *Daniel* of these legends and give the book his cachet of *wisdom*.

Also arguing against the origins of the book of Daniel during the Babylonian exile, and for its creation centuries later, is the accuracy of the predicted history in the detailed visions that conclude it.[5] The focus of those visions is on the repression of Judaism by the Seleucid king Antiochus IV "Epiphanes" who ruled Judah four centuries after the exile, when the book of Daniel was purportedly written. According to historical accounts in 1 and 2 Maccabees, two books that are included in some traditions' Bibles but not others, the repression began with Epiphanes' instigation of the murder in 171 BCE of the legitimate chief priest and his appointment of a man outside the dynasty that traditionally filled the post.[6] The plot was part of strategy by Epiphanes, an advocate of the Hellenistic system of organizing urban life in the empire, to introduce Hellenistic law and institutions into Jerusalem and to make it a typical Greek city.

To give Jerusalem the cultural amenities of other Greek cities, Epiphanes authorized his handpicked chief priest, Jason, to build a *gymnasium* and an *ephebeum* where citizens could participate in athletics, military exercises, and scholarship. Traditionalist Jews feared that the exercises, which were performed without clothing, might cause families to abandon circumcision, an essential self-identification that set Jews apart;[7] other traditionalists were shocked by the appearance of the *ephebi*, the student participants who dressed in the short-pants attire of ancient Attic warriors.[8] The outrage was not entirely over immodesty but also about what participation in these sports required: Greek games were dedicated to pagan gods and entailed idolatrous worship.

Besides introducing Hellenistic institutions, Epiphanes looted the temple to support his army, stationed a foreign guard just outside the temple, and destroyed the walls that protected Jerusalem. The status of Jerusalem as Zion, much less as a Jewish enclave, was at risk.

When traditionalist Jews rebelled against his Hellenization of Jerusalem, Epiphanes reacted with appalling violence, as recounted in the epigraph that introduces this part of the book. Historian Woerner Foerster reports:

> The sabbath could now no longer be celebrated, and possession of the sacred books, together with the circumcision of newborn boys, was forbidden. A royal commission traveled up and down the country to supervise the carrying

---

[5] The inaccuracy of the prediction in Daniel 11:45 that the beast will meet his end encamped in Palestine ("between the sea and the beautiful holy mountain") leads scholars to date the origin of the book of Daniel just before Epiphanes' death in 164 BCE in Syria.

[6] Seow, *Daniel*, 125.

[7] Foerster, *From the Exile to Christ*, 34.

[8] Reicke, *The New Testament Era*, 53.

out of the decree. The temple in Jerusalem became a temple of the god of heaven under the Greek name of the Olympian Zeus; the Samaritan temple was likewise dedicated to Zeus; a smaller altar was set upon the great altar in Jerusalem and swine's flesh sacrificed upon it. . . . Temple prostitution now found its way even into Jerusalem. All over the country altars were erected and incense burned at the doors of the houses. The king's birthday-festival took place every month with a sacrificial banquet, in which the Jews had to participate; Dionysian festivals were celebrated. But the death-penalty was attached to the practice of the Jewish religion.[9]

At the zenith of the repression in 167 BCE, Epiphanes installed a statue of the Greek god Zeus in the Holy of Holies, the very center of the temple where the Jews believed God resided, and to it sacrificed a pig, usual for Greek gods but unsuitable for sacrifice under Jewish law. These outrages, occurring about three-and-a-half years after the repression began, sparked armed resistance by a movement organized by a family led by Judas Maccabee, and would end with the success of their revolution another three years later.

It was to make sense of the catastrophe of Epiphanes' repression and the armed revolt it provoked that Daniel was written. The author of the book of Daniel used the duration of the repression before the desecration of the temple, about three-and-a-half years or half a Sabbatical *week of years*, to prophesy that the repression would last a similar period following the desecration. The number *three-and-a-half* breaks the number *seven*, which in Jewish apocalyptic literature symbolized perfection, in half, and will come to symbolize, especially in the book of Revelation, a time when evil predominates. In modern times, the numerological symbols that communicated the evil nature of Epiphanes' historical repression will have morphed into the prediction by modern end-times writers that the antichrist and his false prophet, halfway through a seven-year tribulation, will desecrate a newly-built temple in Jerusalem.

The legendary *Daniel*, writing from the standpoint of the Babylonian exile four centuries before Epiphanes' repression, predicts the desecration in 167 BCE:

> Forces sent by him shall occupy and profane the temple and fortress. They shall abolish the regular burnt offering and set up the abomination that makes desolate. He shall seduce with intrigue *those who violate the covenant*; but *the people who are loyal to their God* shall stand firm and take action. *The wise among the people* shall give understanding to many; for some days, however, they shall fall by sword and flame, and suffer captivity and plunder. When they fall victim, they shall receive a little help, and many shall join them insincerely. Some of *the wise* shall fall, so that they may be refined, purified, and cleansed, until the time of the end, for there is still an interval until the time appointed. (Dan 11:31-35, emphasis added)

While the author is predicting that the repression will continue for a while, he is also making a prophetic statement about justice for the people

---

[9] Foerster, *From the Exile to Christ*, 35.

who are losing their lives resisting Epiphanes' repression, whom he calls "the wise among the people" and "people who are loyal to their God." Daniel's concern with justice for these martyrs underlies the stories about Daniel and his peers in Babylon that open the book; historian John Bright writes, "The stories of the blameless Daniel serve as examples of loyalty to the law, and of God's faithfulness to those who trust in him." The story of the fiery furnace was particularly poignant for martyrs who faced torture before their inevitable executions.[10]

"The wise among the people," called *Hasideans* in the Maccabean histories, first allied with the Maccabeans then abandoned their violent cause, suing for peace but with disastrous results:

> Then there united with [Mattathias and his friends] a company of the Hasideans, mighty warriors of Israel, all who offered themselves willingly for the law. (1 Macc 2:42)

> Then a group of scribes appeared in a body before [the high priest and governor] to ask for just terms. The Hasideans were first among the Israelites to seek peace from them. . . . The [high priest] spoke peaceable words to them and swore this oath to them, "We will not seek to injure you or your friends." So they trusted [the high priest]; but he seized sixty of them and killed them in one day. . . . Then the fear and dread of them fell on all the people, for they said, "There is no truth or justice in them, for they have violated the agreement and the oath that they swore." (1 Macc 7:12-18)

The Hasideans distinguished themselves not just by their loyalty to the law and its rituals, but also by the pursuit of a righteousness that reflected the wisdom behind them. Conceptualizing their movement as building a "fence around the law" and using a rubric of observant rituals that prevented disobedience, the Hasideans evolved over the next century into schools of thought that Josephus, a Romanized first-century Jewish historian, would call *parties: Pharisees*, who taught the law in synagogues and worked politically to expand their thinking's sway; *Essenes*, who withdrew to the wilderness and prepared themselves as the sanctified remnant of the world-changing catastrophe that would come soon; and, in reaction to them both, *Sadducees*, conservative but observant Jews who rejected fence-building rules and apocalyptic spiritualism.[11] A party of *Zealots*, who took up arms and eventually assassination as ways to hasten the inevitable catastrophe, developed later in the mix.

Apocalyptic thinking about a world separated physically and temporally from this one and dispensing justice for martyrs through their resurrection characterized the thinking of the Pharisees, Essenes, and Zealots. They focused their activities on the promise of a day of justification for Israel and the arrival

---

[10] 2 Maccabees 6:18 to 7:42, written not long after Epiphanes' repression, recounts horrific stories of torture.

[11] Josephus, *War* ii, in Barrett, ed., *The New Testament Background*, §135.

of God's kingdom. The persistence of these parties into New Testament times would assure that the book of Daniel, like the book of Zechariah, would be critical in the teaching and thought of Jesus and his apostles.

✝

We return to the times of Epiphanes' repression of Judaism in the second century BCE, when the book of Daniel was certainly written. Epiphanes' repression was extended to rural areas surrounding Jerusalem by the king's officers, who ordered Jews to make pagan sacrifices to demonstrate their loyalty to Epiphanes. The orders were made on the Jewish Sabbath, when armed resistance was prohibited by the Law and any Jewish resisters, rendered nonviolent by their Sabbatical beliefs, were easily put to death.

Unlike the nonviolent resisters the king's officers usually encountered on a Sabbath, a clan leader named Mattathias reacted violently, killing a Jew who collaborated with the officers and then the king's officers themselves: "Then Mattathias cried out in the town with a loud voice, saying: "'Let every one who is zealous for the law and supports the covenant come out with me!' Then he and his sons fled to the hills and left all that they had in the town" (1 Macc 2:27-29).

Mattathias' resistance sparked a general revolt, and it was successful. About three years after the temple's desecration, the temple was rededicated under the rule of the victorious Jewish rebels. It took another twenty years for Jewish forces to overcome imperial forces, but the temple's rededication in 164 BCE by Mattathias' son, Judas Maccabeus (d. 160 BCE), became a watershed event in Jewish history; it is still commemorated in the winter celebration, Hanukkah.

Notable for the movement begun almost two centuries later by Jesus, however, is evidence in the Mattathias story of *nonviolent* resistance to Epiphanes' oppression: except for Mattathias, Jews who refused to worship Greek gods stood passively before armed soldiers who threatened their lives. Nonviolent resisters had no popular hero like Mattathias, whose family's victory over the muddled and distracted forces of empire set a militant tone for the following two centuries and whose hegemony would be marked by intrigue, betrayal, and violence in Jesus' time.

The book of Daniel eminently qualifies as a literature of an emerging nonviolent reaction by the Hasidean movement. Daniel doesn't resist the Lion's Den, nor do his three friends resist the fiery furnace; they endure the tortures and are delivered. The *Hasidim*, the "pious, loyal ones," leave the armed rebellion and sue for peace and justice at the cost of their lives. Peasant Jews stand before armed soldiers and refuse their orders to worship pagan gods. The overarching message of the book of Daniel to those who resist Epiphanes' repression is to do so righteously and nonviolently, persevering because their justification (and resurrection) is promised when God is ultimately victorious.

Daniel's message of righteous nonviolent resistance to the fires of persecution will be recalled in the teaching of Jesus, Paul, and John the Revelator on how the faithful should react to insult, hatred, and threats, as we will see.

Apocalyptic visions

The martyrdom of the "wise ones" during Epiphanes' repression is the primary concern of the book of Daniel, and the book draws on ancient legends, numerology, and symbols to interpret the meaning of their sacrifices in God's as-yet-unfulfilled plan for Israel. By describing current events in fantastic terms from the viewpoint of a legendary Jew in sixth-century Babylon, the author of Daniel uses a perspective from the *past* to project *present-day* events into a *future* cosmic struggle, when God will ultimately be victorious and Israel will be vindicated. As in the book of Isaiah, in Daniel we encounter the blending of past, present, and future that characterizes prophetic and apocalyptic writing. The literature and theology of apocalypse transform our chronological sense of history and our dimensional sense of place to imagine a time and place where God is victorious over evil, a place and time that Jesus will enter and invite us along.

In the concluding chapters of the book, where Daniel recounts Epiphanes' rise to power and prophesies his ultimate defeat, we find many of the beasts and cryptic numbers that fascinate end-times writers. Four dreams that frighten Daniel are interpreted, as in Zechariah, by angels. In these passages, the legendary Daniel learns from interpreting angels that his dreams symbolically portray how the history of the Mediterranean world will unfold after the Babylonian exile ends. Finally, he's reassured by a vision where God defeats a particularly hideous beast.

In the first dream, Daniel recounts a nightmare about four strange creatures that rise out of a sea furrowed by winds.

> The first was like a lion and had eagles' wings. . . . Another beast appeared, a second one, that looked like a bear. It was raised up on one side, had three tusks in its mouth among its teeth. . . . Another appeared, like a leopard. The beast had four wings of a bird on its back and four heads; and dominion was given to it. . . . After this I saw in the visions by night a fourth beast, terrifying and dreadful and exceedingly strong. It had great iron teeth and was devouring, breaking in pieces, and stamping what was left with its feet. (Dan 7:4-7)

That the animals emerge from a windswept sea recalls the aboriginal chaos that God organized in the Creation Epic of Genesis. Seow notes that the disfigurements of the animals would have struck Jewish readers as "unclean"; the beasts would have struck Middle Eastern readers, in general, as ominous representations of evil.[12]

The first animal symbolizes the Babylonian Empire and Nebuchadnezzar,

---

[12] Seow, *Daniel*, 102.

whom *Daniel* served. The second, a grotesquely limping and devouring bear, represents the Median Empire that succeeded Babylon. The third, a caricature of the image of God described by Ezekiel, probably represents the Persian Empire, which succeeded the Medes.

Daniel's dreams of a succession of empires is typical of Jewish apocalypses: like dispensationalist theology, Jewish apocalypses often organized history into periods that move toward some purpose that is realized at its prophesied end. Biblical theologian John Collins writes:

> One effect of this periodization is the impression of an ordered universe where everything proceeds in a predetermined manner. . . . The schematization of history then shows that the greater number of periods has already elapsed and that the turning point is at hand. The use of an ancient pseudonym . . . permits a *vaticinium ex eventu* [foretelling after the event], a review of past history as if it were future, and so adds to the impression that all is determined in advance, and under divine control.[13]

The fourth beast, representing the present and climactic era of imperial history initiated by the conquest of Alexander the Great, is the beast that most interests the author of the book of Daniel. It grows ten horns, then another little one that springs up to replace three of the larger ones. In Israel, horns traditionally represented kingly power; because the number *ten* often symbolizes *totality* in apocalyptic writings,[14] that there were ten horns suggests the entire succession of kings who will succeed Alexander and culminate in the most recent, Epiphanes, the "little horn" that springs from the tenth:

> I was considering the horns, when another horn appeared, a little one coming up among them; to make room for it, three of the earlier horns were plucked up by the roots. There were eyes like human eyes in this horn, and a mouth speaking arrogantly. (Dan 7:8)

Other references in the Bible to Epiphanes are similarly derogatory. The Maccabean history, recounting his lineage, calls him a "sinful root" (1 Macc 1:10). Not only Jews held Epiphanes in low esteem; Seow writes that "some of his contemporaries reportedly referred to him as *Epimanes* ('Mad'), punning his self-designation as *Theos Epiphanes* ('God Manifest')."[15] Later in the book of Daniel, he's described in a prophecy that forms the basis of the characterization by end-times writers of the antichrist as a two-faced schemer, sort of like Batman's nemesis, the Penguin:

> At the end of their rule,
>   when the transgressions have reached their full measure,
> a king of bold countenance shall arise,
>   skilled in intrigue.

---

[13] Collins, *The Apocalyptic Imagination*, 64.

[14] Barr, *Tales of the End*, 8.

[15] Seow, *Daniel*, 176.

He shall grow strong in power,
    shall cause fearful destruction,
    and shall succeed in what he does.
He shall destroy the powerful
    and the people of the holy ones.
By his cunning
    he shall make deceit prosper under his hand,
    and in his own mind he shall be great. (Dan 8:23-25)

As *Daniel* fearfully observes the beasts in his nightmare, a fantastic chariot appears carrying an elderly man on a flaming wheeled throne, recalling Ezekiel's vision of God's fantastic chariot:

As I watched,
thrones were set in place,
    and an Ancient One took his throne,
his clothing was white as snow,
    and the hair of his head like pure wool;
his throne was fiery flames,
    and its wheels were burning fire. (Dan 7:9)

The white-robed *Ancient One* is served by a multitude of attendants and dispenses justice:

A thousand thousands served him,
    and ten thousand times ten thousand stood attending him.
The court sat in judgment,
    and the books were opened. (Dan 7:10)

The little horn is judged harshly: "As I watched, the beast was put to death, and its body destroyed and given over to be burned with fire" (7:11). In the legendary *Daniel's* dream, a "bystander" explains to *Daniel* the identities of the succession of beasts, although the beasts were caricatures obvious to many of his readers. The interpreter tells *Daniel* that the fourth beastly empire will spawn an evil king:

He shall speak words against the Most High,   .
    shall wear out the holy ones of the Most High,
    and shall attempt to change the sacred seasons and the law;
and they shall be given into his power
    for a time, two times, and half a time. . . . (Dan 7:25, emphasis added)

This passage seduces end-times writers because the last verse appears to provide a time frame for the antichrist's future reign. It corresponds to several other passages in the book of Daniel that have enigmatic time frames; they're all during the *week of years* that will be the span of Epiphanes' repression, but it's difficult to reconcile the numbers to historical events or even to one another. Here they are:

Another holy one said to the one that spoke, "For how long is this vision concerning the regular burnt offering, the transgression that makes desolate, and the giving over of the sanctuary and host to be trampled?" And he answered him, "For two thousand three hundred evenings and mornings; then the sanctuary shall be restored to its rightful state." (8:13-14)

He shall make a strong covenant with many for one week, and for half of the week he shall make sacrifice and offering cease; and in their place shall be an abomination that desolates, until the decreed end is poured out upon the desolator. (9:27)

From the time that the regular burnt offering is taken away and the abomination that desolates is set up, there shall be one thousand two hundred ninety days. Happy are those who persevere and attain the thousand three hundred thirty-five days. (12:11-12)

Because the historical account (1 Macc 1:54-4:52) indicates that sacrifice in the temple was suspended by Epiphanes for roughly three-and-a-half years, these passages together might be interpreted to mean that Daniel envisions Epiphanes' repression continuing *another* three-and-a-half years following the "abomination that desecrates," when Epiphanes installed a statue of Zeus in the temple and began pagan sacrifices.

But Seow notes that the time frames in the various passages coordinate poorly with the historical record; the usual translations of this passage may obscure the author's meaning. Seow translates the original Aramaic in verse 7:25 as "until a time, and times, and a portion of times," indicating to him that "the point is the temporal nature of oppressive rule, which may be for a period, any number of periods, or just part of a period. No matter, the rule will be only temporary."[16] Daniel's purpose is not to predict events; it is to reassure nonviolent resisters to Epiphanes' program of forced Hellenization that the time of their troubles is not long and that God's ultimate victory, in which they collaborate through their nonviolent resistance, is assured.

†

Daniel concludes his account of his vision of the beasts by introducing an angel-like figure termed in older versions of the Bible (such as the King James Version) "one like *the Son of Man*" (emphasis added). In more recent versions of the Bible such as the New Revised Standard Version, the figure in *Daniel's* vision is introduced like this:

I saw one like *a human being*
    coming with the clouds of heaven
And he came to the Ancient One
    and was presented before him.
To him was given dominion
    and glory and kingship,
that all peoples, nations, and languages

---

[16] Seow, *Daniel*, 112.

should serve him.
His dominion is an everlasting dominion
    that shall not pass away,
and his kingship is one
    that shall never be destroyed. (Dan 7:13-14, emphasis added)

The NRSV's translation of the first line reflects the ambiguity of *Daniel's* original meaning, which needs to be differentiated from its meanings in the gospels and in the book of Revelation that may color our views (or more pointedly, veil its meaning). In the gospels, Jesus commonly refers to himself as *son of man*, and the book of Revelation uses the term for a figure who ushers in the end of time. As a result, the so-called *son of man* passage in the book of Daniel is often interpreted as a prophecy about Jesus as a future Davidic king—the Messiah. Seow again points to contradictory evidence. In the original Aramaic, the indefinite article (*a* son of man) is used, not the definite article (*the* son of man). Furthermore, other Old Testament uses of the term indicate that it is better translated simply as *someone*.[17] Another interpreter of the book of Daniel, John Collins, compares the use of the term with preceding passages where beasts are described as "*one like a* . . . ." They represent "kings as well as kingdoms, but in addition they symbolize the chaotic power that these kingdoms embodied." Because the passages about the beasts use the same modifier, "one like a . . .," and the nature of the beasts is figurative, Collins concludes that *one like a son of man* is not some identifiable person but a symbol of the kingdom that God will install after the defeat of the empires that have oppressed Israel.[18]

The gospels' use of *son of man* says more about the apocalyptic times when Jesus lived (or later decades, when the gospels were written) than about the ability of the author of the book of Daniel to predict his coming. The uses of *son of man* in the gospels occur most frequently in apocalyptic passages, particularly a discourse by Jesus in Matthew 24-26 (on which I will spend considerable time later in this part). Some gospel passages that use *son of man* describe him in "clouds of heaven," and those are specific allusions to the son of man passage in Daniel 7:13 ("I saw one like a human being/ coming with the clouds of heaven"). One example is this, from Jesus' apocalyptic discourse:

> "[On the day of the Lord,] then the sign of the Son of Man will appear in heaven, and then all the tribes of the earth will mourn, and they will see 'the Son of Man coming on the clouds of heaven' with power and great glory." (Matt 24:30)

In a second example, Jesus responds enigmatically at his trial to the chief priest, who demands to know if Jesus claims to be the Messiah:

> "You have said so. But I tell you,

---

[17] Seow, *Daniel*, 108.
[18] Collins, *The Apocalyptic Imagination*, 103.

> From now on you will see the Son of Man
>> seated at the right hand of Power
>> and coming on the clouds of heaven." (Matt 26:64)

In the book of Revelation, the author has a vision of a Christ-like figure whom he describes using almost the identical phrase as Daniel 7:13, and he links the eternal life of the son of man he sees in his vision to the promise in *Daniel's* prophesy (7:14) that "his dominion is an everlasting dominion that shall not pass away":

> Then I turned to see whose voice it was that spoke to me, and on turning I saw seven golden lampstands, and in the midst of the lampstands I saw *one like the Son of Man*. . . .
>
> When I saw him, I fell at his feet as though dead. But he placed his right hand on me, saying, "Do not be afraid; I am the first and the last, and the living one. I was dead, and see, I am alive forever and ever; and I have the keys of Death and of Hades. (Rev 1:12-13, 17-18, emphasis added)

Here we see examples of New Testament texts recalling Daniel's *son of man* prophecy to interpret Jesus' ministry and his role in history. Written not long after a crisis similar to the one confronted by the author of Daniel (the destruction of Jerusalem and the second temple by Rome in 70 CE), the books of Matthew and Revelation link Jesus, who is a son of a man/human being, with the apocalyptic figure in the book of Daniel who is someone with God's favor and conquers evil and death. Jesus' frequent use of the term *son of man* to describe his role (as opposed to *messiah*, a description he usually denied), indicates that the apostles, if not Jesus himself, saw his role not so much in the messianic frame of the prophets but more in the apocalyptic frame of Daniel. Jesus was the representative of God in the ultimately victorious cosmic war with evil, yet he was *someone*, a human being on earth among us.

†

Subsequent dreams and visions recounted in the book of Daniel are variations on the first. The second recasts the symbolic imperial history using the figures of a ram and a goat; it repeats the symbolism of the "little horn" of the first, but this time the horn emerges from four horns on the goat's head: "Out of one of them came another horn, a little one, which grew exceedingly great toward the south, toward the east, and toward the beautiful land"(Dan 8:9). The ram-and-goat vision also provides symbols and numbers that readers and listeners of the second century BCE could link to current events, specifically Epiphanes' military movements as he approached Judah, "the beautiful land."

The next account of Epiphanes' rise to power over Israel is not in the form of a vision or dream but a lament, a confessional prayer that God answers. The legendary *Daniel*, who is supposedly writing during the Babylonian exile, is recalling the prophet Jeremiah's prediction that the exile would last seventy years; he "[turns] to the Lord God to seek an answer by prayer and supplication with fasting and sackcloth and ashes" (9:3) about when Israel's punishment would end:

> Open shame, O Lord, falls on us, our kings, our officials, and our ancestors, because we have sinned against you. . . .
>
> So the curse and oath written in the laws of Moses, the servant of God, have been poured out upon us, because we have sinned against you. He has confirmed his words, which he spoke against us and our rulers, by bringing upon us a calamity so great that what has been done against Jerusalem has never before been done under the whole heaven. . . .
>
> Now therefore, O our God, listen to the prayer of your servant and to his supplication, and for your own sake, Lord, let your face shine upon your desolated sanctuary. Incline your ear, O my God, and hear. Open your eyes and look at our desolation and the city that bears your name. We do not present our supplication before you on the ground of our righteousness, but on the ground of your great mercies. (Dan 9:8-18)

Here, the book of Daniel is invoking the ancient Sinai covenant recorded in the book of Leviticus that specifies rewards for obedience and imposes a sevenfold punishment for disobedience, the prophetic choice of death. Here are the rewards, in Leviticus, for obedience (the choice of life):

> If you follow my statutes and keep my commandments and observe them faithfully, I will give you your rains in their season, and the land shall yield its produce, and the trees of the field shall yield their fruit. Your threshing shall overtake the vintage, and the vintage shall overtake the sowing; you shall eat your bread to the full, and live securely in your land. (Lev 26:3-5)

On the other hand, the consequences for disobedience (the choice of death) are catastrophic and include the exile that the legendary *Daniel* is experiencing:

> And if in spite of [plague and military defeat] you will not obey me, I will continue to punish you *sevenfold* for your sins. . . .
>
> And you I will scatter among the nations, and I will unsheathe the sword against you; your land shall be a desolation, and your cities a waste. (Lev 26:18, 33, emphasis added)

The punishment, while harsh, fulfills the otherwise unobserved Sabbath Law because Israel's exile will be an opportunity for God to rest the lands from harvest: "Then the land shall enjoy its sabbath years as long as it lies desolate, while you are in the land of your enemies" (Lev 26:34).

God replies to *Daniel's* lament through an angel, Gabriel, who reinterprets Jeremiah's prophecy that Israel's punishment would last seventy years; the consequences will be *sevenfold* as prescribed by Leviticus 26 and will last not seventy years but seventy *weeks* of years, 490 years or about five centuries:

> "Seventy weeks are decreed for your people and your holy city: to finish the transgression, to put an end to sin, and to atone for iniquity, to bring in everlasting righteousness, to seal both vision and prophet, and to anoint

a most holy place. Know therefore and understand: from the time that the word went out to restore and rebuild Jerusalem until the time of an anointed prince, there shall be seven weeks; and for sixty-two weeks it shall be built again with streets and moats, but in a troubled time. After the sixty-two weeks, an anointed one shall be cut off and shall have nothing, and the troops of the prince who is to come shall destroy the city and the sanctuary." (Dan 9:24-26)

Using this scheme, the author of Daniel prophesies that Israel's punishment, beginning with its destruction in the seventh century BCE for failure to observe Sabbath years of rest, will extend to Epiphanes' repression of Judaism in the second century BCE. This is a radical reinterpretation of Jeremiah's prophecy, because other books[19] of the Bible say that Jeremiah's prophesy had been fulfilled by Cyrus' decree in 539 BCE that permitted the exiles to return to Jerusalem. However, the focus of the author of Daniel is not on the end of the exile in Babylon; he is concerned about the end of Epiphanes' repression, and he applies Jeremiah's prophetic imagination and the urgency of observing the Sabbath Law, an instrument of social justice, to Jerusalem's current predicament.

Modern end-times writers freely reinterpret the book of Daniel's reinterpretation of Jeremiah to predict when the tribulation will begin (69 *sevens* from some date in history) and how long it will last (seven years, with "an abomination that desolates" at its midpoint). But predicting a future occasion when God will return to reign over a perfect kingdom is not the purpose of the book of Daniel. It was written during a time of oppression to reassure the *holy ones* who face martyrdom that the time of trouble will be brief and God will ultimately dispatch their tormentors to the dustbin of history. Like *Daniel's* colleagues in the fiery furnace (and the recipients of Peter's letters to an early church about a *fiery ordeal* in their time), the persecuted and reviled are assured that God is ultimately victorious over evil and stands with those who have prophetically chosen the path of purity and justice--of *life*.

✝

The tenth and eleventh chapters of the book of Daniel provide still another version of recent imperial and military history, this time in a detailed symbolic account revealed to *Daniel* by an unnamed angel. The angel recounts the succession of the Babylonian, Persian, and Greek empires and Epiphanes' maneuvers; in particular, the account of the rise of the Greek empire closely tracks the historical account in 1 Maccabees. This time around, we can't fail to notice an unusual aspect of apocalyptic literature, and that's the repetition of its theme in varieties of narrative or poetic voices without much concern for the facts. Collins recalls Hermann Gunkel's insight that "'the apocalypses did

---

[19] Such as 2 Chr 36:22-23.

not aspire to conceptual consistency but could allow diverse formulations to complement each other,'"[20] and identifies the purposes of repetition:

> If a message has to be communicated in the face of distractions or "noise" [such as the fearsome chaos of a persecution], the communicator must use "redundance" by repeating the message several times in slightly different ways. In this way the basic structure of the message gets through. No one formulation exhausts the total message. This use of redundance is crucially important for our understanding of apocalyptic language. It implies that the apocalypses are not conveying a "literal" or univocal truth that can be expressed precisely in one exclusive way. Rather, they share the poetic nature of myth and allude symbolically to a fullness of meaning that can never be reduced to literalness.[21]

Later in Collins' book, in a study of 4 Ezra (a Jewish apocalypse not included in some traditions' Bibles), he identifies another purpose of repetition, the reassurance of martyrs:

> We can begin at this point to appreciate the purpose of the repetition. The angel is not engaged in rational argumentation but in the psychological process of calming fear and building trust.[22]

We see these aspects of inconsistent repetition in Daniel at a micro level in the passages about the three-and-a-half year period: the numbers are similar but not identical, yet signify the same events. At the macro level, Daniel characterizes Epiphanes' repression three different ways; while they differ radically in form and content, their structure is similar:

Event	Chapter 7 Four beasts	Chapter 8 A ram and a goat	Chapters 10-11 The great conflict
Imperial history	7:2-7;15-17, 19	3-8; 20-22	10:13, 11:3-20
Epiphanes' rise	7:8; 20-24	9-10; 23-24	11:21-30
Epiphanes' repression	7:25	11-12; 25	11:31-39
God's victory	7:9-1; 26-27	13-14; 25	11:40-45

The visions have a similar form and content but different symbols, and the visions escalate their apocalyptic imagery culminating in a victory by God and the resurrection of the dead. This spiraling course of mythological action reflects *Daniel's* primary concern, which is justice for the *wise ones* killed for refusing to worship pagan gods:

> But at that time your people shall be delivered, everyone who is found written in the book. Many of those who sleep in the dust of the earth shall awake,

---

[20] Collins, *The Apocalyptic Imagination*, 17.

[21] Ibid., 107-8.

[22] Ibid., 202-3.

some to everlasting life, and some to shame and everlasting contempt. Those who are wise shall shine like the brightness of the sky, and those who lead many to righteousness, like the stars forever and ever. (Dan 12:1-3)

✝

In *Daniel's* apocalyptic visions we have our first close encounter with the end-times themes of tribulation, judgment, and millennium. The archetypal opponent of God defiles the temple and persecutes the Jews for three and a half years. God returns, served by a retinue of tens of thousands. He holds court and opens the books. The Son of Man establishes a dynasty that rules all the nations. The righteous dead rise from the dead, and eternity begins.

But the visions of the latter half of the book of Daniel must be understood in the context established by the stories of the first half, where *Daniel* endures persecution during the Babylonian exile with integrity, wisdom, and courage and gains the restoration of the Jewish leadership to Jerusalem. This same *Daniel* is terrified by visions of evil empires that rival God's power and oppress the Jews, God's chosen people. God's angels assure him that while events on earth may not make it obvious, God is triumphant over evil. Moreover, God's reassurance is like a person's touch, recalling the humanity of the apocalyptic messiah, *the one like a son of man*:

> But then a hand touched me and roused me to my hands and knees. He said to me, "Daniel, greatly beloved, pay attention to the words that I am going to speak to you. . . . Do not fear, Daniel, for from the first day that you set your mind to gain understanding and to humble yourself before your God, your words have been heard. . . . [I] have come to help you understand what is to happen to your people at the end of days. . . ."
>
> Again one in human form touched me and strengthened me. He said, "Do not fear; greatly beloved, you are safe. Be strong and courageous!" (Dan 10:10-19)

Written for a second-century audience facing repression, the author has set contemporaneous events in wider historical (and mythical) contexts to interpret the significance of the present threat to those who endure it and are afraid. The book of Daniel is a timeless message to faithful people who fear that God's dominion is usurped by evil. The advice is: be strong; stay humble; persevere. God stands with you as a person would, on earth as well as in heaven, and victory over evil is assured.

Chapter 13
LETTERS TO THE THESSALONIANS:
THE DAY OF CHRIST

Thessalonica was one of many cities in the Roman Empire where the apostle Paul established a church in the decades following Jesus' death and resurrection. An important seaport, it was located along the Via Egnatia, the Roman military road between Appolonia, on the Ionian Sea facing Italy, and Byzantium, opposite present-day Istanbul on the Straits of the Bosporus. Thessalonica was the capital of the Roman province of Macedonia, which essentially comprises present-day Greece.

In Paul's time, midway through the first century after Christ's birth, the city was suffused with the cult of Caesar Augustus, the Roman Emperor who had been proclaimed "God" by the Roman Senate after his death in 14 CE, and with the cults of his descendants. Everywhere stood colonnades celebrating *Pax Romana*, the peace and security that had come with the victory of Roman legions over pagan tribes and rebellious factions of the Roman aristocracy. Local citizens' associations competed to honor Augustus and the current emperor with temples and statues; their likenesses were also on the local currency.

In Roman cities like Thessalonica, the religious practices of Jews were tolerated. Jews were allowed to assemble in synagogues and if they offered a prayer for Caesar, they weren't obliged to erect a statue for his worship. Christians enjoyed similar toleration to the extent that they were perceived by the authorities as a subdivision of the Jews, which originally they were. Early churches attracted traditionalist Jews who accepted Jesus as *messiah*, more modern Jews who desired a faith that was less strict in practice and accommodated some ways of the cultural life of the Greek city-state, but also Gentiles who were attracted by Christian moral teachings but couldn't comply with circumcision or other practical requirements of conversion to Judaism.

An upstart faith like Christianity that proclaimed a "son of God" other than Augustus' offspring and a way of achieving peace different from *Pax Romana* would not find official favor in a Roman city. If a Christian assembly was not perceived as a Jewish synagogue by the authorities, the church, like other outlawed associations, simply wasn't free to meet. Also, Christian churches that refused to pay the modest respect to the emperor that synagogues had agreed to provide, or consisted mostly of uncircumcised Gentiles, risked the attention of the authorities.

While there was an ever-present risk of the suppression of churches, there was no organized empire-wide persecution of Christians in the first century. The unstable Caesar Nero (37-68 CE) did undertake a local persecution against Roman Christians, whom he scapegoated for the fire that almost destroyed Rome in 64 CE; the persecution likely killed the Apostles Paul and Peter, but it was unlawful and criticized by members of the Roman Senate as another example of Nero's tyranny. Still, there were constant risks of denunciation everywhere to *individual* Christians, especially by traditionalist Jews who rejected how Christianity changed their ancient customs, and it was usually this risk that New Testament writers called *persecution* and fueled their negative characterizations of Jews.

It may have been a persecution like this that caused the Apostle Paul and his traveling companion, Timothy, to leave Thessalonica about 50 CE; they went to Athens.[23] Out of worry and curiosity (and perhaps guilt that other Christians suffered while he escaped[24]), Paul asks Timothy to return. After Timothy reports, Paul sends a letter of praise and encouragement. The letter, known as First Thessalonians, is the earliest Christian document in the Bible; it gives us a glimpse of Christianity about seventeen years after Jesus' execution and twenty years before the destruction of Jerusalem and its temple.

Paul's letter opens with praise for "God the Father and the Lord Jesus Christ," not Caesar and the Roman gods as would be the customary opening in usual correspondence in the Roman Empire. With his greetings he sends the central message of his gospel: "Grace to you and peace" (1 Thess 1:1).

Paul's purpose in writing is encouragement, but he also will send some cautionary words. The first three of the letter's five chapters are chatty, remembering the time that Timothy and he spent with the Thessalonians. Paul's concerns in the remainder of the letter will be positively framed, and they will be succinct. He will gently caution the church in Thessalonica about three things:

Sexual promiscuity. Roman morals were prudish, but Roman behavior was appallingly licentious; extramarital liaisons, heterosexual and homosexual, were common and marked by the power of the aggressor over the victim. Moreover, Thessalonica was the home of two mystery religions common throughout the empire and dedicated to the Greek gods of Dionysius and Orpheus, "both of them fertility cults, expressing themselves in phallic symbols and sexual

---

[23] Using the chronology of Acts; the foundation of the church in Thessalonica is referenced in Acts 17.

[24] Crossan and Reid, *In Search of Paul*, 168.

indulgences, in wild orgies and extravagant ecstasies."[25] Paul's caution is direct, based on his belief that the spirit of the new age inhabited Christian lives in the present:

> For this is the will of God, your sanctification: that you abstain from fornication; that each one of you know how to control your own body in holiness and honor, not with lustful passion, like the Gentiles who do not know God; that no one wrong or exploit a brother or sister in this matter . . . For God did not call us to impurity but to holiness. (1 Thess 4:3-7)

Sloth and dissension. In some of the earliest churches, members shared resources to fulfill in a practical way the lessons Jesus taught. This apparently created a disincentive to work among some members, and resentment by others who did: "Now concerning love of the brothers and sisters, you do not need to have anyone write to you, for you yourselves have been taught by God to *love* one another, and indeed you do *love* all the brothers and sisters throughout Macedonia" (1 Thess 4:9-12, emphasis added).

The "love of the brothers and sisters" is not simple affection: it is a word describing how Christians are expected to support one another in practical ways. John Dominic Crossan and Jonathan Reed interpret *love* as *share*:

> To love meant to *share*, a love assembly was a share-assembly, a love meal was a share-meal. . . . The sharing was from want to want rather than from plenty to plenty. And do not think of it as humanly extensive charity, a free giving of *our* stuff, but as divinely distributive justice, a necessary sharing of *God's* stuff. For Paul, a Christian assembly of sisters and brothers was one that had committed itself to sharing together just as in an ordinary family because it actually was a divine family, the family of God.[26]

The fate of church members who have died. Finally, Paul addresses a concern among the Thessalonian Christians about fellow church members who have died before seeing the return of Jesus Christ to fulfill the kingdom of God. They apparently believed that only those who are alive on the day of the Lord would join Jesus in the millennial kingdom. Here we encounter a belief of the earliest churches: Jesus would return to earth literally *within the lives of some in his generation.* This belief can be found also in the gospels, as in Matthew:

> [Jesus said,] "For the Son of Man is to come with his angels in the glory of his Father, and then he will repay everyone for what has been done. Truly I tell you, there are some standing here who will not taste death before they see the Son of Man coming in his kingdom." (Matt 16:27-28)

But there's been a delay in Jesus' return, now that almost two decades have passed since his death, and faithful Christians are reaching the ends of their lives without seeing the fulfillment of God's kingdom on earth. Some of them

---

[25] John W. Bailey, "Introduction, First and Second Epistles to the Thessalonians," *Interpreter's Bible*, XI, 245.

[26] Crossan and Reed, *In Search of Paul*, 175, emphasis original.

are dying horribly and unjustly as victims of persecution. Paul writes this to the Thessalonians:

> But we do not want you to be uninformed, brothers and sisters, about those who have died, so that you may not grieve as others do *who have no hope*. For since we believe that Jesus died and rose again, even so, through Jesus, God will bring with him those who have died. For this we declare to you by the word of the Lord, that we who are alive, who are left until the coming of the Lord, will by no means precede those who have died. For the Lord himself, with a cry of command, with the archangel's call and with the sound of God's trumpet, will descend from heaven, and the dead in Christ will rise first. Then we who are alive, who are left, will be caught up in the clouds together with them to meet the Lord in the air; and so we will be with the Lord forever. Therefore *encourage one another with these words*. (1 Thess 4:13-18, emphasis added.)

This is a key passage that end-times writers use to assert that a rapture will rescue the faithful before a future tribulation. But Paul's message here is not a prediction about events two thousand years in the future; he clearly states that his letter is pastoral encouragement to grieving people in *his* times "who have no hope" and who should "encourage one another with these words" with the expectation that the fulfillment of the kingdom of God could happen any day.

To encourage the Thessalonian Christians, Paul is using the Jewish apocalyptic belief of a general resurrection at the fulfillment of time, but he is writing to a congregation that is almost wholly Gentile: unlike most of his other letters, he doesn't address the usual conflicts between Jewish and Gentile Christians here. The Gentile Thessalonians find the notion of resurrection, commonplace among Jews, completely alien, so Paul is gently reminding the congregation of a key aspect of the good news that may still be obscure to them: the fulfillment of God's kingdom is an occasion when the dead will be joyfully reunited with the living.

Underlying the issue is the frustrated hope of a congregation which expected to see God's ultimate victory of good over evil in their lifetimes. Paul reminds the Thessalonians of Jesus' comments on when the kingdom of God would be fulfilled: "Now, concerning the times and the seasons, brothers and sisters, you do not need to have anything written to you. For you yourselves know very well that the day of the Lord will come like a thief in the night" (1 Thess 5:1-2). This recalls for his congregation the teaching of Jesus about vigilant observation of the faith:

> [Jesus said,] "Keep awake, therefore. For you do not know on what day your Lord is coming. But understand this: if the owner of the house had known in what part of the night the thief was coming, he would have stayed awake and would not have let his house be broken into. Therefore you also must be ready, for the Son of Man is coming at an unexpected hour." (Matt 24:42-3)

Paul seizes on the metaphor of darkness in Jesus' teaching about the "thief in the night." He contrasts those who sleep in the dark to the Thessalonian congregation, who are awake; they are the "children of the light" who are filled with the spirit of the new age and living the life of the kingdom *every* day because they expect, *any* day, the Lord's victorious return:

> But you, beloved, are not in darkness, for that day to surprise you like a thief; for you are all children of light and children of the day; we are not of the night or of darkness. So then let us not fall asleep as others do, but let us keep awake and be sober. . . . But since we belong to the day, let us be sober, and put on the breastplate of faith and love, and for a helmet the hope of salvation. . . . Therefore encourage one another and build up each other, as indeed you are doing. (1 Thess 5:4-11)

Here, apocalyptic faith is crucial for Paul's congregation. They are caught in the suspension of sacred time between Jesus' resurrection, which demonstrated that the kingdom of God had come, and the fulfillment of the kingdom, marked by the reunion of the dead with the living, which has yet to come but is soon. The Thessalonian Christians have chosen to live with patient endurance in the meantime in the spirit that Jesus' resurrection offers: a life of humility, morality, hard work, and mutual support reflecting Jesus' messages of selfless sharing. In terms of Paul's reinterpretation of the prophetic choice between life and death, the Thessalonians have accepted the assurance conveyed by Jesus' resurrection that God will ultimately defeat death, the last outpost of evil.

A tantalizing detail for dispensationalist end-times writers in the first letter to the Thessalonians is Paul's assertion that Christians who have died will rise first when God's kingdom is fulfilled, before the living rise into the heavens. Is there significance in Paul's ordering of the constituencies of the general resurrection? Crossan and Reed think so, noting that Paul calls the event *parousia*, a Greek word for the arrival of a dignitary to a city and suggesting that Paul may be "dancing fast and fancy on his theological feet."[27] In the Roman Empire, when a dignitary traveled by road to any important city, he would be greeted first by the mausoleums of the dead outside the city wall, then by the city's living residents once he entered the city's gate. Similarly, Paul teaches, Jesus Christ will enter the New Jerusalem to celebrate with them the grand reunion at the fulfillment of time. By using the word *parousia* and ordering the dead first in the general resurrection, Paul appropriates imperial custom to describe the transformation that will occur when the resurrected dead, then the living, welcome their Lord to a transformed world.

When Paul addressed the concern of the Thessalonians about the status of their deceased fellow members, he opened his advice with apocalyptic images of "meeting Jesus in the clouds," trumpets, and angels. Paul's words of encouragement to the Thessalonians provide the basis of rapture beliefs today,

---

[27] Crossan and Reed, *In Search of Paul*, 169-70.

but is Paul warning the members of the church in Thessalonica about being "left behind?" Is joining Jesus in the air the reward for faith? No. In their contexts, these words are Paul's assurances, using an apocalyptic frame, that no-one is excluded from the kingdom of God where the usual distinction between life and death becomes irrelevant because the ultimate enemy, death, has been conquered. The new era dawned with Jesus' resurrection; it will culminate with a general resurrection that reunites the living with their deceased brothers and sisters. Crucial in the meantime is living in the spirit of the new era, which early churches marked by hard work, respect for the sanctity of one's person, and mutual support among the faithful.

Early churches

The earliest primary sources of information about the first churches are the letters of Paul. The book of Acts records the history of the church in Jerusalem and Paul's missions, but it was written much later in the first century. Some information about churches also can be inferred from the book of Revelation, itself a letter to a group of churches, but Revelation was also written late in the first century and is certainly colored by the author's concerns about persecution and justice. We can burrow into the "synoptic" gospels of Matthew, Mark, and Luke, so-called because of their similarities in content; although they were written late in the first century, we can identify passages among them that are identical and therefore from an earlier source. The gospel of John is so unlike the synoptic gospels, and so polemical, that it is difficult to view it as a source of information; however, it opens a window on a tradition about Jesus that differs from the strands in the other three gospels and from Paul, so it expands our understanding of the diversity of early churches and their young traditions. Finally, there are two very recent additions to literature of early Christianity: the gospel of Thomas, a collection of sayings of Jesus discovered in nag Hammadi, Egypt, in 1947, and the *Didache*, a practical manual for Christians rediscovered in the nineteenth century.

Using these sources, James D. G. Dunn found wide diversity across common practices in the early churches, including Proclamation, Patterns of Worship, and Sacraments:

Proclamation

The message communicated by an apostle or gospel writer, in Greek *kerygma*, differs among New Testament writings but is characterized by Mark 1:15: "The time is fulfilled, and the kingdom of God has come near; repent, and believe in the good news." The proclamation of Acts and the gospel of John is the resurrection of Jesus; the synoptic gospels focus more on Jesus' mission to the poor and outcast, and Paul on how best to recreate those teachings in church assemblies. A tension is noticeable in New Testament writings between believers who expressed their beliefs through spirituality and those who expressed them more practically, but the writings finally included in the Bible have a common thread: salvation lay in the belief that Jesus' relationship with God was manifest during his ministry as well as in his resurrection so that Christian faith has both a spiritual and a humanitarian basis.[28]

Consistent with these findings, Christiaan Beker writes that Paul's proclamation is similar to the proclamation of the synoptic gospels; using theologian Oscar Cullman's terms, Paul's proclamation addressed the tension between the "already," the opening of the final age that began the transformation of life on earth with Jesus' resurrection, and the "not yet," the future fulfillment of the kingdom of God that will be announced by the general resurrection of the dead.[29] The following passage from Paul's first letter to the church in Corinth is an epitome:

> But in fact Christ has been raised from the dead, the first fruits of those who have died. For since death came through a human being, the resurrection of the dead has also come through a human being; for as all die in Adam, so all will be made alive in Christ. But each in his own order: Christ the first fruits, then at his coming those who belong in Christ. Then comes the end. . . . (1 Cor 15:20-24)

Patterns of worship

The book of Acts reports that after Jesus' death and resurrection, the apostles visited the Jerusalem temple daily, participated in the sacrificial cult, and conformed to Jewish practices such as repeating the traditional Jewish prayer, the *Shema*, twice daily (2:42-47). Christians met in one another's homes to share a meal and express their faith through songs and ecstatic speech ("prophecy" or "tongues"). From Acts 2:42, Joachim Jeremias concludes that the order of worship in home church assemblies was this:

> It began with (1) the teaching (*didache*) of the apostles; followed by (2) the fellowship (which we must probably understand as table-fellowship); after this came (3) the breaking of the bread, the Eucharist; and finally (4) the prayers. The instruction came at the beginning of the worship.[30]

Spontaneity, participation, and mutuality characterized the church Paul visited in Corinth: "When you come together, each one has a hymn, a lesson, a revelation, a tongue, or an interpretation. Let all things be done for building up" (1 Cor 14:26). However, a tension between spontaneity and spirituality on the one hand and ritual and tradition on the other is apparent throughout the gospels and letters, particularly after the martyrdom of the apostle Stephen, who argued that the sacrificial cult in the temple in Jerusalem was not essential to Christian belief and practice (Acts 7). Among Gentile church members outside Jerusalem, of course, the temple cult was meaningless. So, the clear tendency

---

[28] Dunn, *Unity and Diversity in the New Testament*, 11 ff.

[29] Beker, *Paul the Apostle*, 159.

[30] Jeremias, "The Sermon on the Mount," in *Jesus and the Message of the New Testament*, 28.

during the first century was in the organization of churches not around law or cult but around faith, as indicated in the gospel of Matthew: "For where two or three are gathered in my name, I am there among them" (Matt 18:20).[31]

Also revealing the nature of worship in the early churches are the fragments of hymns included in New Testament writings. Members of early churches would hear them when the book of Revelation and the opening chapters of the gospel of Luke were read (and perhaps, by cantors, sung); some, such as the *Magnificat* (Lk 1:46-9), are still sung in Christian worship services. Other Christian songs preserved in the New Testament are less traditional and more enthusiastic, especially the songs in the book of Revelation. Dunn writes,

> One can readily imagine gatherings for worship . . . where after a prophecy or psalm or prayer an exuberant worshipper cried out, 'Victory to our God who sits on the throne, and to the Lamb!' ([Rev] 7:10); or where an individual began a familiar doxology and all joined in, 'Amen! Praise and glory and wisdom, thanksgiving and honour, power and might, be to our God for ever and ever! Amen!' ([Rev] 7:12)[32]

Sacraments

Baptism, the earliest of Christian sacraments, was a rite of entry into the Christian church that entitled the convert to say the Lord's Prayer and participate in table fellowship. Baptism for the early churches recalled Jesus' baptism by John the Baptist in the waters of the River Jordan, where John prepared his followers for the final cosmic battle that closed the present age which he prophesied would be a baptism "with the Holy Spirit and fire" (Matt 3:11). But when John baptized Jesus, the "Spirit" of the new age descended, unexpectedly opening the era when the final battle would occur: "And when Jesus had been baptized, just as he came up from the water, suddenly the heavens were opened to him and he saw the Spirit of God descending like a dove and alighting on him" (Matt 3:16). So, it's reasonable to conclude that early churches saw baptism as a sign of the gift of the spirit of the new age to the person who was joining the church.[33]

Another very early sacrament was table fellowship. which rapidly evolved into a ritual we now call the *Lord's Supper,* a re-creation of the *Last Supper* Jesus had the night before his arrest and trial (Matt 26:26). Paul discusses the Lord's Supper only once in his correspondence (1 Cor 10 and 11), but it's clear from this passage that the supper was a common practice among the churches he advised. The ritual aspects of the meal (the identification of the bread and wine with Jesus' body) were embedded in a shared suppertime meal, emulating Mark's account of the Last Supper: "*While they were eating,* he took a loaf of bread . . ." (Mk 14:22, emphasis added). Acts reports that the apostles and their followers in Jerusalem

---

[31] Dunn, *Unity and Diversity in the New Testament, Third Edition,* 135 ff.

[32] Ibid., 145.

[33] Ibid., 166 ff.

had daily fellowship meals: "Day by day, as they spent much time together in the temple, they broke bread at home and ate their food with glad and generous hearts, praising God and having the goodwill of all the people" (Acts 2:46-7).

While baptism and the Lord's Supper were practiced differently among the early churches, the use of these sacraments to express their apocalyptic expectations was consistent. Excitement about the nearness of God and the virtual presence with them of the resurrected Jesus was the spirit that marked these celebrations. Ceremonies of baptism witnessed the descent on a new member of the fiery spirit that inspired Jesus, and rituals of table fellowship temporarily reunited the church with Jesus, who loved table fellowship during his life. Using the "already/not yet" tension of his proclamation, here is Paul writing about the Lord's Supper: "For as often as you eat this bread and drink the cup, you proclaim the Lord's death until he comes" (1 Cor 11:26).

Living apocalyptically

Members of early churches adhered to ethical programs that foreshadowed the fulfilled kingdom of God, and they practiced some or many of Jesus' radical teachings in their daily lives. These teachings often reversed the conventional wisdom in a violent and unjust empire, especially patronage relationships marked by power, submission, and debt.

Burton Mack lists the radical moral teachings of the earliest churches; the corresponding passages, from Luke, follow the aphorisms, which are Mack's:

- *Love your enemies*: "Love your enemies, do good to those who hate you, bless those who curse you, pray for those who abuse you" (Luke 6:27).
- *If struck on one cheek, turn the other*: "If anyone strikes you on the cheek, offer the other also; and from anyone who takes away your coat, do not withhold even your shirt" (6:29).
- *Give to everyone who begs*: "Give to everyone who begs from you. And if anyone takes away your goods, do not ask for them again" (6:30).
- *Judge not and you won't be judged*: "Be merciful as your Father is merciful. Do not judge, and you will not be judged; do not condemn, and you will not be condemned; Forgive, and you will be forgiven" (6:36-37).
- *First remove the stick from your own eye*: "Why do you see the speck in your neighbor's eye, but do not notice the log in your own eye? Or how can you say to your neighbor, 'Let me take out the speck in your eye,' when you yourself cannot see the log in your own eye? You hypocrite, first take the log out of your own eye, and then you will see clearly to take the speck out of your neighbor's eye" (6:41-42).
- *Make sure of God's rule over you*: "Strive for God's kingdom, and these [material] things will be given to you as well" (12:31).[34]

---

[34] Mack, *Who Wrote the New Testament*, 50. This list isn't complete; aphorisms I've omitted relate to the behavior Jesus expected from his disciples as missionaries who spread his teachings.

Many of these teachings were practical advice to people caught up in the grinding poverty caused by imperial and temple taxation, which resulted in chattel slavery, landlessness, and onerous debt unrelieved by the unobserved Sabbath and Jubilee Laws. Some early Christians responded to Jesus' ethical teachings by establishing networks of believers within which debts were forgiven, conflicts over power and wealth were abated, resources were shared, and people were encouraged to value practical work as opposed to deriving wealth from loaning money or accumulating slaves, land, and other material possessions. Other churches chose less radical forms, but a lapse into patronage would receive a stern caution, at least from Paul.

One sees how Jesus' teachings were translated into congregational life among the members of Paul's churches by reading the encouragement he gave them in his letters. To the church in Galatia:

> The fruit of the Spirit is love, joy, peace, patience, kindness, generosity, faithfulness, gentleness, and self-control. . . .
>
> My friends, if anyone is detected in a transgression, you who have received the Spirit should restore such a one in a spirit of gentleness. Take care that you yourselves are not tempted. Bear one another's burdens, for in this way you will fulfill the law of Christ. . . .
>
> So then, whenever we have an opportunity, let us work for the good of all, and especially for those of the family of faith. (Gal 5:16-6:10)

To the church in Ephesus:

> So then, putting away falsehood, let all of us speak the truth to our neighbors, for we are members of one another. Be angry but do not sin; do not let the sun go down on your anger, and do not make room for the devil. . . . Put away from you all bitterness and wrath and anger and wrangling and slander, together with all malice, and be kind to one another, tenderhearted, forgiving one another, as God in Christ has forgiven you. (Eph 4:25-32)

And in a final example, to the church in Thessalonica:

> Be at peace among yourselves. And we urge you, beloved, to admonish the idlers, encourage the fainthearted, help the weak, be patient with all of them. See that none of you repays evil for evil, but always seek to do good to one another and to all. Rejoice always, pray without ceasing, give thanks in all circumstances; for this is the will of God in Christ Jesus for you. (1 Thess 5:13-18)

These notions about how life should be lived are radically different from the social rules of cities in the Roman Empire. Life in them was marked by patronage, where power and wealth were only available by surrendering one's autonomy to someone with more power and wealth. Furthermore, Greco-Roman society was fiercely patriarchal; David Balch writes,

> Suspicions about foreign religions included the fear that conversion would reverse established hierarchical relationships and cause women to misbehave. Romans expected foreign religions [like Christianity] to cause immorality

(especially adultery), insubordination within the household, and sedition against the state. [35]

As a result of patronage and patriarchy, Greco-Roman society was splintered among factions led by powerful male patrons. Their clients were wedded together in jealous units that battled politically and sometimes criminally with competing factions for wealth and influence. Women and slaves, in turn, depended on and were at the mercy of men when power was exercised. Like *Pax Romana*, it was a system based on violence and brute power, and while it was intended to control the threat of lawlessness and civil war, in the view of Israel's prophetic choice it was a system based on death.

Christian churches rejected violence in relationships and condemned the patronage system. Paul's vision of congregational life was an assembly where no factions, no patrons, no separations existed. We see this particularly in this famous passage in his letter to the church in Galatia: "There is no longer Jew or Greek, there is no longer slave or free, there is no longer male and female; for all of you are one in Christ Jesus" (Gal 3:28). In another example, Paul encouraged a brotherly relationship between a Christian colleague and his slave, the Christian Onesimus, in his letter to Philemon: "no longer as a slave but more than a slave, a beloved brother" (Phil 16). He also encouraged reciprocal faith and trust between men and women in marriage:

> The husband should give to his wife her conjugal rights, and likewise the wife to her husband. For the wife does not have authority over her own body, but the husband does; likewise, the husband does not have authority over his own body, but the wife does. (1 Cor 7:3-4)

Beker writes:

> There can be no doubt that in the life of the early church racial, social, and sexual distinctions were abolished. . . . The transformation of the values of Hellenistic-Roman society within the church is revolutionary and has revolutionary implications for Christian life in society at large. Paul transforms the marriage ethic of his day by emphasizing the mutuality of the love relationship. The extension of the equality principle within the life of the church to the marriage relationship contains the seed for a transformation of the status of the woman in society.[36]

For Paul, the age of the spirit is marked by mutual support, not patronage; inclusion, not separation; peace from the heart, not from a sword; health from faith, not superstition. A life dependent on patronage, wealth, and power is the choice of death; conversely, a Christian chooses life in the spirit lived by Jesus, who defeated death to live among people again. The will to live this way, contrary to the overwhelming power of the empire to reward conformity and punish its lack, comes from an apocalyptic understanding of God's ultimate

---

[35] David L. Balch, "The First Letter of Peter," *NRSV Study Bible*, 2277.

[36] Beker, *Paul the Apostle*, 322.

victory: we live our ordinary lives in a spirit of daily expectation that death will be conquered for everyone soon.

The second letter

The second letter to the Thessalonians is a pessimistic revision of Paul's thoughts in the first, which are positive and optimistic. The most likely cause of the second letter's pessimism was the continuing delay of the fulfillment of God's kingdom.

The second letter claims to be by Paul, but scholars generally question his authorship.[37] That doesn't make it a forgery or a fraud; it wasn't unusual for literature of the time to be written in the name of someone else. We've already encountered this phenomenon in Isaiah, a book that is ascribed to an actual person in history but includes not just his prophecies but also those spoken much later by members of the prophet's school or tradition. We saw a different example in the book of Daniel, a document purporting to have been written four hundred years earlier and ascribed to a legendary figure associated with wisdom to bring that tradition to bear on the present. By writing in a predecessor's name, the later author can apply the original's insights to emerging situations, even hundreds of years later.

Indications that someone other than Paul wrote the second letter to the Thessalonians are obvious to even the casual reader who compares them. For example, we find a caution about a letter that might have given the wrong impression, maybe even a forgery—the first letter?

> As to the coming of our Lord Jesus Christ and our being gathered together to him, we beg you, brothers and sisters, not to be quickly shaken in mind or alarmed, either by spirit or by word or by letter, *as though from us*, to the effect that the day of the Lord is already here. (2 Thess 2:1-3, emphasis added)

And we observe the lengths to which the author goes to assure the reader of this letter's authenticity: "I, Paul, write this greeting with my own hand. This is the mark in every letter of mine; it is the way I write" (2 Thess 3:17). The author of the second letter is correct: Paul typically dictated his letters to a scribe but wrote a closing remark in his own hand, much as we might do in business correspondence in modern times to convey sincerity. But here, the author calls the reader's attention to an otherwise routine practice and mischaracterizes it as an authentication, and protests too much.

Another reason for suspecting a different author and a later date for the second letter is its correction of the first letter's teaching about living in an apocalyptic spirit, which expected God's victory over death soon. In the first letter, that day is expected imminently and the advice is to be vigilant because it will come like a thief in the night. In the second letter, on the other hand,

---

[37] Raymond E. Brown summarizes the controversy and concludes, "personally I can't decide with certitude." *An Introduction to the New Testament*, 596.

readers are cautioned that a series of end-times events must first occur: "Let no one deceive you in any way; for that day will not come unless the rebellion comes first and the lawless one is revealed, the one destined for destruction" (2 Thess 2:3-10). Crossan and Reed remark, "That is like saying that the night thief will not come unless there is first the sound of breaking windows and smashing doors."[38] The utter unpredictability of the day of the Lord in the first letter, which is consistent with sayings attributed to Jesus by the very earliest sources, is contradicted by this passage. Furthermore, the ideas of "rebellion" and "lawless one," commonplace in Jewish apocalyptic writing later in the first century,[39] are alien to the other New Testament letters that are more certainly Paul's.

The concerns of the second letter—about evil and the cosmic future— are *outside* the church, unlike those of the first letter, which are concerned with the daily rehearsal of sexual morality, hard work, and mutual support *within* it. Both letters frame their concerns using apocalyptic metaphors, but their stated purposes and tones are quite different. In contrast to the first letter's encouraging hopefulness, the second letter is harsh and speaks to the punishment of persecutors instead of the vindication of the faithful. The author of the second letter seems anxious about a recent victory of evil that God must avenge on a cosmic plane; the letter moves the focus away from the fulfillment of the kingdom toward a *day of the Lord* when a score will be settled, and it attempts to explain why justice has been postponed. We can suspect that the second letter was written after the destruction of Jerusalem's temple in 70 CE, which occurred twenty years after the first letter and forty years after Jesus' death.

The more Jesus' ministry in Galilee recedes into the past, the more the kingdom of God is separated from our daily lives; two thousand years later, end-times writers unfold it during a frightening and obscure scenario set in the future. The punishing chronology of time overwhelms Jesus' good news about the reign of God in our time.

---

[38] Crossan and Reed, *In Search of Paul*, 171.

[39] D. S. Russell, referring to a study by Bousset in *The Method and Message of Jewish Apocalyptic*, 191.

Chapter 14
WRITINGS OF JOHN:
NOW MANY ANTICHRISTS

A figure of consummate evil called *the antichrist* has the central role in dispensationalist end-times writings. In those scenarios, the antichrist is a charismatic leader emerging from the lands of the former Roman Empire who deceives and corrupts the world, seduces Israel but desecrates the temple, and leads the forces of evil at the battle of Armageddon. End-times writers derive the figure from the "lawless one" of the second letter to the Thessalonians, the boastful "little horn" in the book of Daniel, and various dragons and beasts in the book of Revelation, all of which we will encounter in the next part of this book.

However, neither Daniel nor Revelation, neither Second Thessalonians nor Matthew refers to the enemy of God as *antichrist*. That word never occurs in the Bible except in two brief pieces by someone named John, perhaps the author of the gospel of John but at least someone writing in his tradition.[40] The two pieces, an essay and a letter, were written late in the first century or early in the second, and we shouldn't be surprised that John's letter reflects the increasingly pessimistic view of Jesus' return as it was delayed long beyond the lives of Jesus' generation.

Given the absence of the word *antichrist* from the rest of the Bible, we must assume that John is referring to a figure in the mythology of his time when he writes, "Children, it is the last hour! As you have heard that antichrist is coming, so now many antichrists have come. From this we know that it is the last hour" (1 John 2:18).

In his study of the *antichrist* legend, historian Bernard McGinn concludes that Jewish apocalyptic thought during the two centuries preceding Jesus' ministry was increasingly convinced that "just as there was one malevolent angelic power who led the forces of evil throughout history, so too would

---

[40] Brown, *Introduction to the New Testament*, 383 ff.

human evil reach a culmination in the last days." McGinn suggests, just as Antiochus IV Epiphanes was the personification of evil for Jews in the second and first centuries BCE, the notion of an antichrist developed among some Christians in the first century CE as the evil opponent whom Jesus Christ must confront on his return.[41]

While John refers to an antichrist, he isn't predicting a tribulation, which for a Christian living apocalyptically is already present. The reference is almost offhand and introduces his primary concern, a doctrinal schism among members of his church: "They went out from us, but they did not belong to us; for if they had belonged to us, they would have remained with us" (1 John 2:19). The schismatics believed that Jesus of Nazareth had been a spirit, not a human being, a not uncommon belief in early Gentile churches. Several centuries later, these beliefs would be condemned as the heresy of Docetism. While accepting that the spirit of God was vital to faith—it prompted ecstatic forms of worship such as prophecy and speaking in tongues—John warns the church that the schismatics' belief is a deception: "Beloved, do not believe every spirit, but test the spirits to see whether they are from God; for many false prophets have gone out into the world" (1 John 4:1).

John tells the congregation that separating the spiritual aspect of faith in Jesus Christ from the humanitarian teachings of Jesus of Nazareth is antithetical to Christian teaching. By rejecting what Jesus taught about love, forgiveness, and healing among people and by rejecting the intimate relationship between the faithful and God that Jesus encouraged, the schismatics become the enemies of God. John writes that the schism was something his congregation should expect: the appearance of enemies of God who reject Jesus' ethical teachings is a crisis, a sign of the nearness of the kingdom of God. John appropriates the enemy-of-Christ legend to identify the former members who denied Jesus' humanity as *exactly* that enemy.

John's letter encourages his congregation to reject the schismatics' anti-Christ beliefs. Their love for one another and their knowledge of God's forgiveness, manifested in sharing and mutual support, sets them over against the antichrists. John employs the metaphor of light and darkness used by Paul in the first letter to the Thessalonians to describe the prophetic choice they must make:

> Whoever says, "I am in the light," while hating a brother or sister, is still in the darkness. Whoever loves a brother or sister lives in the light, and in such a person there is no cause for stumbling. But whoever hates another believer is in the darkness, walks in the darkness, and does not know the way to go, because the darkness has brought on blindness. (1 John 2:9-11)

Because the schism in John's church is a sign of the nearness of the kingdom of God, the congregation is urged to persevere in their righteousness and love:

---

[41] McGinn, *Antichrist*, 9, 33-56.

> I write these things to you concerning those who would deceive you. As for you, the anointing that you received from him abides in you, and so you do not need anyone to teach you. But as his anointing teaches you about all things, and is true and is not a lie, and just as it has taught you, abide in him. (1 John 2:26-27)

Antichrist is not a megalomaniacal United Nations bureaucrat with designs on the world's food supply and a desire to tattoo barcodes on people's foreheads. *Antichrist* is simply the antithesis of *agape*, a Greek word used by Christians in the first century for the selfless love encouraged by Jesus; for example, in this passage:

> [A Pharisee asked him,] "Teacher, which commandment in the law is the greatest?" [Jesus] said to him, "'You shall love the Lord your God with all our heart, and with all your soul, and with all your mind.' This is the greatest and first commandment. And a second is like it: 'You shall love your neighbor as yourself.' On these two commandments hang all the law and the prophets." (Matt 22:36-37)

For John, *agape* is central to the Christian's life:

> Beloved, let us love one another, because love is from God: everyone who loves is born of God and knows God. . . . God's love was revealed among us in this way: God sent his only Son into the world so that we might live through him. . . . Beloved, since God loved us so much, we also ought to love one another. No one has ever seen God; if we love one another, God lives in us, and his love is perfected in us. (1 John 4:7-12)

Thus, John clears away esoteric understandings of the Holy Spirit and leaves us with the spirit of the new age that dawned with Jesus' resurrection, which is love among children who are loved.

Chapter 15
GOSPEL OF MATTHEW: RUMORS OF WARS

On his last trip to Jerusalem, Jesus provoked the reaction by the authorities that would kill him.

By arriving on a lowly donkey but drawing similarly-sized crowds, he mocked the grand entrance at another gate of the city's Roman procurator, Pontius Pilate, who entered on a warhorse with a retinue of soldiers and musicians. He antagonized the temple priests by disrupting the cash market for sacrificial animals. He argued with learned teachers and called them "snakes." As his fate and its apocalyptic dimensions became obvious, his followers asked, "Tell us, when will this be, and what will be the sign of your coming and of the end of the age?" (Matt 24:3) Jesus' response provides a wealth of seeming detail for dispensationlist end-times scenarios.

First, Jesus describes a period of trouble:

> "You will hear of wars and rumors of wars; see that you are not alarmed; for this must take place, but the end is not yet. For nation will rise against nation, and kingdom against kingdom, and there will be famines and earthquakes in various places; all this is but the beginnings of the birth pangs." (Matt 24:6-8)

There is persecution:

> "Then they will hand you over to be tortured and will put you to death, and you will be hated by all nations because of my name. Then many will fall away, and they will betray one another and hate one another." (Matt 24:9-10)

And false prophets:

> "Beware that no one leads you astray. For many will come in my name, saying, 'I am the Messiah!' and they will lead many astray." (Matt 24:4-5)

The temple is desecrated:

"When you see the desolating sacrilege standing in the holy place, as was spoken of by the prophet Daniel . . . then those in Judea must flee to the mountains. . . . For at that time there will be great suffering, such as has not been from the beginning of the world until now, no, and never will be." (Matt 24:15-21)

There are signs in the heavens:

"The sun will be darkened,
　　and the moon will not give its light;
the stars will fall from heaven,
　　and the powers of heaven will be shaken." (Matt 24:29)

And the Son of Man, the apocalyptic figure in Daniel 7:13-14, appears with an army of angels to gather up the faithful remnant:

"Then, the sign of the Son of Man will appear in heaven, and then all the tribes of the earth will mourn, and they will see 'the Son of Man coming on the clouds of heaven' with power and great glory. And he will send out his angels with a loud trumpet call, and they will gather his elect from the four winds, from one end of heaven to the other." (Matt 24:30-31)

Good news to the poor

Matthew was written late in the first century CE, following the fall of Jerusalem to Roman armies in 70 CE, four decades after Jesus' death. Christians were increasingly pessimistic about Jesus' promised return within the lifetimes of his contemporaries; history was reshaping Jesus' original proclamations. However, the gospel of Matthew still includes some of the earliest records of Jesus' ministry, and its form and abundant Old Testament references reflect its ambition to inhabit the same prophetic frame of Isaiah, Ezekiel, Zechariah, and Daniel that inspired Jesus. Matthew is a window on the historical Jesus, and a critical review of Matthew will help lift the veil of history that stands between us and Jesus' ministry.

The gospel of Matthew opens the New Testament and, with the gospels of Mark, Luke, and John, is one of four narratives of Jesus' life that entered the biblical canon. Each gospel has a unique perspective using different organizing themes. They range in sophistication from Mark, the oldest, a straightforward chronological narrative, to John, the latest, which is organized around Jesus' theological controversies at the temple. When the gospels are compared, it's clear that each was collected from a variety of older oral or written traditions, and that each spoke to a different early community and tradition.

Matthew is concerned far more than the others with connecting Jesus' biography and teachings to the classical prophets of Israel. If Matthew has an organizing principle beyond sheer biography, it is that Jesus' birth, life, death, and resurrection fulfilled Old Testament prophecies about who the Messiah would be. The phrase "to fulfill what had been spoken by the Lord through the prophet" appears fourteen times, introducing numerology as another way that Matthew organizes his material: fourteen is the sum of the numerical equivalents of the Hebrew letters in the name of David, the archetypal messiah.

In another use of the number fourteen, Matthew counts three sets of fourteen generations that span Israel's history between Abraham and Jesus:

> So all the generations from Abraham to David are fourteen generations; and from David to the deportation to Babylon, fourteen generations; and from the deportation to Babylon to the Messiah, fourteen generations. (Matt 1:17)

Matthew's use of fourteen as a motif buttresses the messianic case: his basis for prophetic fulfillment is multidimensional, using not just prophecy but also genealogy and numerology.

The first of the fourteen passages where Matthew formulaically identifies an event in Jesus' life that fulfills a prophecy is Jesus' conception. Matthew suggests that Jesus' birth was miraculous because his mother, Mary, was a virgin when she conceived:

> All this took place to fulfill *what had been spoken by the Lord through the prophet*:
> "Look, the virgin shall conceive and bear a son,
> and they shall name him Emmanuel." (Matthew 1:22-23; emphasis added)

Matthew is recalling a prophecy of Isaiah: "Therefore the Lord himself will give you a sign. Look, the *young woman* is with child and shall bear a son, and shall name him Immanuel [God is with us]" (Isa 7:14, emphasis added). Matthew used a Greek translation of the Hebrew Bible that translated *young woman* as *virgin*, but either way the reference helps build Matthew's case that Jesus' birth fulfills a messianic prophecy. In particular, he is bringing Isaiah's overarching themes of God's sovereignty and God's steadfast love for Israel, manifested by the promise of an *anointed one, messiah,* to bear on the life of Jesus.

Other events in Matthew's account of Jesus' birth and youth recall Old Testament prophecies: his birth in Bethlehem fulfills a prophecy in Micah (Matt 2:3-6; Mic 5:2); his family's brief sojourn in Egypt recalls Hosea (Matt 2:13-15; Hos 11:1); his survival of King Herod's murder of young Jewish boys fulfills Jeremiah (Matt 2:16-18; Jer 31:15); his family's resettlement in Nazareth recalls the tradition of the Nazirites, the prophetic "branch" (Hebrew, *netzer*) of King David's line (Matt 2:19-23; Isa 11:1 *inter alia*). Rarely were the original prophecies *predictions*; a prophet spoke to the people of his time, not future generations. But in retrospect, the gospel summons the demands of these prophets for justice and purity, and their promises of prosperity and peace, for a faithful remnant when it narrates stories that fulfill their prophecies.

Details about Jesus' birth and early life in the two gospels that have them are difficult to verify because the only sources are the gospels themselves, and in some instances they are contradictory. What independent historical information may be available corroborates none of them. While their contents may not be historically accurate, Robert Funk identifies similarities between the forms of the gospels' birth narratives and Hellenistic biographies of Greek heroes of those times:

- A genealogy revealing illustrious ancestors

- An unusual, mysterious, or miraculous conception

- An annunciation by an angel or in a dream

- A birth accompanied by supernatural portents

- Praise or forecast of great things to come, or persecution by a potential competitor.[42]

Matthew and Luke likely filled this contemporaneous template of biography with traditions about Jesus' origins and sharpened them with prophetic allusions to persuade their audiences that Jesus, too, was a great man. But before we reject the birth narratives as created from whole cloth, we must differentiate our notions of *fact* from our notions of *truth*. Before the Enlightenment assigned a primary value to rational thought, myth was as important as fact, perhaps more so because myth conveyed *meaning*. Matthew provides details about Jesus' early life to recall prophecies about Israel and uses the contemporary literary form of the biography of a great man to emphasize Jesus' significance. The gospel writer brings history, prophecy, and literature to foreshadow the *meaning* of Jesus' ministry: the announcement on earth of an era of justice and peace.

✝

Gospel is the modern pronunciation of the Old English word *godspell*, a compound of the Old English words for *good* and *news*. In turn, *godspell* was the Old English translation of the Greek word *euangelion*, a Greek word used in the sense of *good news of victory (in battle)* that early Christians appropriated to announce the kingdom of God. In Matthew's account, the good news was marked by healings of people of their illnesses and incapacities:

> Jesus went throughout Galilee, teaching in their synagogues and proclaiming the good news of the kingdom and curing every disease and every sickness among the people. So his fame spread throughout all Syria, and they brought to him all the sick, those who were afflicted with various diseases and pains, demoniacs, epileptics, and paralytics, and he cured them. And great crowds followed him from Galilee, the Decapolis, Jerusalem, Judea, and from beyond the Jordan. (Matt 4:23-25)

---

[42] Funk, *Honest to Jesus*, 282. Funk credits Lane McGaughy for his outline of the Hellenistic birth narrative.

When Jesus commissioned his disciples to preach, he urged them to take the gospel to people who were dispossessed, disabled, mentally ill, or despised, and to the families of the dead:

> "Go to the lost sheep of the house of Israel. As you go, proclaim the good news, 'The kingdom of heaven has come near.' Cure the sick, raise the dead, cleanse the lepers, cast out demons." (Matt 10:6-8)

Not only would marginalized and grief-stricken people receive the good news, their healing *is* the good news. When Jesus receives a delegation from John the Baptist, who had been imprisoned, the group asks him on John's behalf whether Jesus is "the one who is to come [the Messiah], or are we to wait for another?" Using his usual indirection to questions about his theological identity, Jesus responds:

> "Go and tell John what you *hear* and *see*: the blind receive their sight, the lame walk, the lepers are cleansed, the deaf hear, the dead are raised, and the poor have good news brought to them." (Matt 11:4-5, emphasis added)

"What you *hear and see.*" The evidence that the kingdom of God is near but not yet here could be *seen* in Jesus' ministry of healing among the disposable people of Israel and *heard* when he spoke to the poor. Their disabilities and grief were no doubt a result of their grinding poverty or their separation (as unclean or sinners) from the rituals and customs that Jews used to celebrate their closeness to God. Jesus announced that God came close when marginal people were healed. God's victory over evil was then declared by the praise of people who had been too sick to fight.

Jesus' healing ministry among the poor of Galilee blended messianic themes from Israel's prophets and apocalyptic themes from Daniel and Zechariah into a radical makeover of the faith of his times. When we focus on Jesus' teachings, leaving aside the meaning of his execution and resurrection for now, we learn that he radically reinterpreted prophetic and apocalyptic ideas about the kingdom of God:

The kingdom of God is near, and it is present among people it gathers in its embrace.

The kingdom is characterized by love among people for God and for one another. They share. They forgive their enemies and their debtors. They deny divisions of race, class, and gender. They live morally. They pray daily that God's kingdom will come.

While the Law is essential, love is fundamental: people's love of God and their love of one another is the foundation of the Law.

The kingdom includes people who are sick, poor, oppressed, and despised. It includes people who help others make peace. Its inhabitants are children, or like children. These people of the kingdom are the remnant of God's historical judgments against Israel, and how we treat them is how God treats us.

People who join the kingdom may be separated from their families, but they will be loved; they may not be physically safe, but they will be at peace; they may not have a place to live, but they will have shelter and food every day.

Although the kingdom is here, it isn't complete. The faithful persevere in their love and forgiveness with patience, assured that God does triumph over evil despite the world's outward appearances.

The choice to join the kingdom is prophetic, and apocalyptic, a choice of life over death. The day the choice is made—and it must be made daily—is the day of the Lord.

The Sermon on the Mount

When the peasants of Galilee assembled to hear Jesus speak and see him heal the sick, they set down the plowshares and pruning hooks that provided their meager livings. The poverty of the peasantry can be estimated; Crossan quotes a study of German peasants in the Middle Ages, whose circumstances weren't much different from Jewish peasants at the dawn of the Christian Era, on a forty-acre farm:

> Its total annual *yield* was 10,200 pounds of grain crops. Of that, 3,400 pounds was immediately stored as *seed* for the next sowing and 2,800 as *feed* for the four horses. Of the remaining 4,000 pounds, 2,700 pounds went for *rent* to the landowner. In the end, therefore, only 1,300 pounds were left for the peasant family "yielding a per capita daily ration of 1600 calories." Since the physiological minimum is somewhere between 2000 and 3000 calories per day, that family would have to augment its daily caloric intake through other methods.[43]

"Other methods" included selling a family member into indentured servitude or going into debt; in either circumstance, the peasant was at the mercy of the owner or lender, and the dependence could last a lifetime. People on their own who lacked a supportive family member (such as widows and orphans or the disabled) were forced into prostitution or beggary that might or might not be relieved by the poor taxes raised by the temple. Compounding the predicament of the peasantry was the failure of Israel throughout its history to honor the Sabbatical Law (Deut 15), which required the remission of debts and the freeing of indentured servants every seventh year, and the Jubilee Law (Lev 25:9), which required every fifty years the restoration of family lands that had been sold to satisfy debts. Those failures had been denounced by the prophets of ancient Israel as "injustice" and "oppression," and things hadn't changed.

The one time the Old Testament says that the Sabbath Law may have been honored was under Nehemiah (445-? BCE), the governor of Judea who is credited with rebuilding Jerusalem following the return of the Babylonian exiles. Judea was impoverished; here's how petitioners presented their circumstances to Nehemiah at the time:

---

[43] Crossan, *The Historical Jesus*, 126, emphasis original.

"With our sons and daughters, we are many; we must get grain, so that we may eat and stay alive." There were also those who said, "We are having to pledge our fields, our vineyards, and our houses in order to get grain during the famine." And there were those who said, "We are having to borrow money on our fields and vineyards to pay the king's tax. Now our flesh is the same as that of our kindred; our children are the same as their children; and yet we are forcing our sons and daughters to be slaves, and some of our daughters have been ravished; we are powerless, and our fields and vineyards now belong to others." (Neh 5:2-5)

Galilean peasants in Jesus' time were no better off. Compounding their situation was double taxation: they paid tithes required by the Law to support the temple, its priests, and the poor, but they also paid taxes and customs imposed by Rome. Marcus Borg estimates that the various temple taxes came to about twenty percent of a farmer's production, the Roman taxes added about fifteen percent, and together they were an obscene burden. Borg writes:

> Many Jewish farmers could not [pay both taxes] without risking losing their land. Indeed, some small farmers could not pay even the Roman taxes and thus did lose their land, creating a growing number of landless day laborers, widespread emigration, and a social class of robbers and beggars. Many of the rest could save their land only by not paying the tithes commanded by the [Law]. The system of double taxation was generating a large class of "nonobservant" Jews, not because of the attractiveness of Roman and Hellenistic ways, but because of the economic pressure.[44]

Aggravating their circumstances was the way Roman taxes were collected. In lands ruled directly by Rome, like Judea in Jesus' time, a procurator was appointed to raise the tribute through a variety of taxes, tolls, and duties. However, collection was usually privatized: the procurator subcontracted it to a network of tax collectors, entrepreneurs who paid the expected taxes then aggressively dunned the powerless and pocketed the difference. Historian Bo Reicke writes, "We now find a well organized profession, not uncommonly rapacious and therefore detested."[45] Moreover, out of a healthy respect for incipient Jewish nationalism, the tax collectors in Jewish areas were predominantly Jews; therefore, "the people's hatred of the tax collectors rested on two grounds: first, their collaboration with the occupying forces; and second, the often unjust opportunities this class had to turn a profit."[46]

Centuries of unrelieved economic oppression punctuated by famine and warfare and now imperial taxes had created a large underclass of families and individuals who lived day to day, if that, and suffered the illnesses and disabilities to which a marginalized person is prone. To a crowd of people who are impoverished, hungry, sick, and above all powerless, Jesus, in Matthew,

---

[44] Borg, *Jesus*, 84-5.
[45] Reicke, *The New Testament Era*, 138.
[46] Ibid., 139.

addresses his first sermon thus:

> "Blessed are the poor in spirit, for theirs is the kingdom of heaven.
> "Blessed are those who mourn, for they will be comforted.
> "Blessed are the meek, for they will inherit the earth.
> "Blessed are those who hunger and thirst for righteousness, for they will be filled.
> "Blessed are the merciful, for they will receive mercy.
> "Blessed are the pure in heart, for they will see God.
> "Blessed are the peacemakers, for they will be called children of God.
> "Blessed are those who are persecuted for righteousness' sake, for theirs is the kingdom of heaven.
> "Blessed are you when people revile you and persecute you and utter all kinds of evil against you falsely on my account. Rejoice and be glad, for your reward is great in heaven, for in the same way they persecuted the prophets who were before you." (Matt 5:3-11)

These are *The Beatitudes* (from the Latin *beatus* meaning *blessed* or *happy*). Four of these sayings, the first three and the last, have parallels in Luke but not in Mark, indicating that they are part of the earliest narrative tradition about Jesus that we have. In Luke, a simpler and likely earlier version, the four original Beatitudes are:

> "Blessed are you who are poor,
> for yours is the kingdom of God.
> "Blessed are you who are hungry now,
> for you will be filled.
> "Blessed are you who weep now,
> for you will laugh.
> "Blessed are you when people hate you, and when they exclude you, revile you, and defame you on account of the Son of Man. Rejoice in that day and leap for joy, for surely your reward is great in heaven; for that is what their ancestors did to the prophets." (Luke 6:20-22)

The first, second, and fourth sayings are also in the gospel of Thomas; there, they read,

> Blessed are the poor for yours is the kingdom of heaven. (54)
> Blessed are they who are persecuted in their heart; these are the ones who have truly known the father. Blessed are those who are hungry, for the belly of the needy will be filled. (69)[47]

Later versions (like Matthew's) spiritualize the categories of the poor, the hungry, the sad, and the reviled who Jesus says will inherit the kingdom of God. Whom might Jesus have originally spoken of?

The poor: Certainly Jesus' audience included poor artisans and peasants like him, his disciples, and members of his family. But Crossan points out that *ptochos*, the Greek word for *poor* used in Luke and Matthew, is not a word used

---

[47] Dart and Riegert, *The Gospel of Thomas*.

in contemporary Greek literature to describe a peasant; it describes a beggar, "'someone who had lost many or all of his family and social ties. He often was a wanderer, therefore a foreigner for others, unable to tax for any length of time the resources of a group to which he could contribute very little or nothing at all."[48] Donald Goergen writes that *the poor* included people who were "socially ostracized and economically disadvantaged. . . . publicans, sinners, the uneducated and backward, the socially disreputable, the sick, those possessed by demons, children, women. They were living in economic poverty as well as without status in society."[49]

The hungry: While Jesus was certainly interested in enlisting people in his ministry who "hunger and thirst for righteousness," as Matthew puts it, again we must be cautious not to over-spiritualize Jesus' target: people who in fact were hungry for food *that day* and would likely go to bed hungry *that night*. If we accept the numbers Crossan provides above on the limited nutritional resources of a peasant family and add to them the burden of tithes and taxes, we can imagine their limited diets. The diet of beggars, who unlike peasants and artisans were excluded from the economic and social supports of neighbors and relatives, is unimaginable. At a minimum, Jesus was speaking to the basic needs of a significant (and scandalous) portion of the population of Galilee who had neither the nourishment nor the fellowship of the supper tables of their communities. At an apocalyptic remove, Jesus was including them in the banquet of the Messiah, an astonishing reversal of their present situation and an unprecedented administration of prophetic justice.

The sad: Jesus typically responded immediately to the mournful requests of people for healing.[50] The grief Jesus addresses in his ministry is a result of the overwhelming presence of death in the lives of the poor. Grief will also include sadness over illness, exclusion, or poverty, because these will inevitably result in death, but the target here is the bottomless sorrow of people who have been devastated emotionally and economically by the death of a provider, the enslavement of a child, the disability of a limb, the loss of sight or hearing, or the onset of an unclean disease. Jesus presented himself to people for whom death was not a choice but a default; these are the people who, in God's kingdom, will laugh with joy at their recovery of their abilities and their reunion with people they had lost.

The reviled: Again we are cautioned against the simplification of those who are persecuted on account of their discipleship to Jesus. Crossan rejects an interpretation limiting the persecuted to his followers because it would set them apart from others, which "is hardly thinkable for the Jesus of history,

---

[48] Crossan, quoting the doctoral dissertation of Gildas Hamel, in *The Historical Jesus*, 272.

[49] Goergen, *The Mission and Ministry of Jesus*, 222.

[50] There is one significant exception: he postponed going to his friend Lazarus when he was dying. I'll discuss the resurrection of Lazarus and its connection to the presence of the kingdom of God in Part Five.

whose appeal seems to have been precisely on the basis of a rejection and destruction of such language." Reviewing how *persecuted* occurs among the available sources with the words *reviled*, *hated*, *defamed*, and *excluded*, Crossan concludes that "what we seem to have . . . is a series of verbs meaning contemptuous abuse and social rejection slowly ceding place to the more lethal single verb of persecution," particularly as the early church, proclaiming the blessedness of the poor, found itself hated, then persecuted.[51] Besides people marginalized by their society, Jesus spoke to people who were *hated*.

✝

And what of the "kingdom of heaven" or the "kingdom of God," where the hungry have full bellies, the mourners laugh, and the excluded are amused? In prophetic and apocalyptic thought, it arrived in the future after a great military or cosmic struggle. Jesus, however, proclaims in the Sermon on the Mount that the kingdom is present precisely when the hungry are fed, the mourners laugh, and the persecuted are blessed. Crossan says that Jesus offered a "paradigm shift" in apocalyptic thinking away from anticipation of a future event toward a "collaborative eschatology" where the kingdom of God, which the prophets said was characterized by justice and mercy, is *present*.[52]

Matthew, who is not just recounting Jesus' life and ministry but also providing a catechism, a collection of teachings for his church, adds these instructive sayings to Luke's original four to describe how Christians might collaborate with God in the as-yet-unfulfilled kingdom:

> "Blessed are the merciful, for they will receive mercy.
> "Blessed are the pure in heart, for they will see God.
> "Blessed are the peacemakers, for they will be called children of God."
> (Matt 5:8-10)

When people share their resources with others in a spirit of fellowship, show others compassion and mercy, build up others and reduce controversy, they collaborate with God in establishing the kingdom *on earth*.

Goergen disagrees that "kingdom of God" adequately describes what Jesus is after in the Sermon on the Mount, but reaches conclusions similar to Crossan's. Goergen believes *kingdom*, whether of God or heaven, may connote to some a *future* time and *other* place that are not the time and place we currently inhabit. He prefers "reign of God," where *reign* characterizes *how* God rules, not where or when. Goergen writes: "Understanding Jesus' usage properly makes outmoded many of the discussions about whether the kingdom was present or future in the teaching of Jesus, for God is both here and coming. God cannot be confined within temporal categories." He concludes:

---

[51] Crossan, *The Historical Jesus*, 274.

[52] Author's notes, Crossan, Bellarmine University lectures, November 7, 2008.

We can picture the crowds composed of the poor, the hungry, the sad, the sick, the lame, the outcasts, the uneducated, the unclean. What could Jesus say to them that might have been a word of consolation? . . . He knew how his heavenly Father's love reached out to them. . . . And so he said all that he could say: God is yours. The message did not remove the poverty or hunger or pain. And yet it was a word of consolation. And it expressed one of the fundamental religious insights in the teaching of Jesus: GOD BELONGS TO THE PEOPLE. Nothing can separate them from God's love. They may fall outside the realm of the Law or social acceptability but they do not fall outside the realm of God. God belongs to *them*.[53]

Hope and conflict

Jesus attracted loyal followers and his teaching reached a wide and curious audience. His confrontation with the religious and political rulers of Jerusalem would result in his sudden execution, but the influence of his teaching would extend beyond his death. Within a dozen generations, even the Roman Emperor would embrace the beliefs of the stewards of his message.

To understand why Jesus' teaching was so successful, it's helpful to understand the historical and cultural circumstances of his times. His Mediterranean world was marked by the loss of tribal identity, the clash of cultures, and a growing separation between religious cults and political powers. For Jews, hope for a priest-king of David's stature was receding, calling into question God's past promises for secure borders and for Israel's leadership among the nations. Also, the integrity of the sacrificial cult of the temple, which had permitted Jews to live within the covenantal framework of ritual and law established by their ancestors, had been undermined by the corruption of recent kings and priests and more recently by the actual billeting of Roman troops in the temple compound.

The geo-political context of Jesus' ministry was the growing domination first of the Greek, then the Egyptian and Syrian, and finally the Roman empires. The response among Jews to imperial domination in the two centuries before Jesus' ministry had included the successful Maccabean revolt that later collapsed into rule by autocrats, most recently the Herods. It was a time of growing apocalyptic hope, if not for a military miracle, then a cosmic event that would restore Israel to its proper place among the nations, culminating its long and tumultuous history. But it was also a time of conflict over how that hope should be expressed and lived. Should the messianic kingdom be somehow hastened? Or did the kingdom's imminence justify more prayerful forms of expectation?

The schools of thought that evolved in reaction to the repression of Epiphanes in the second century BCE had hardened into religious "parties" by Jesus' time; they are identified and described by the contemporary Jewish

---

[53] Goergen, *The Mission and Ministry of Jesus*, 227, emphasis original.

historian Josephus, and several of them figure in the gospel narratives.

Sadducees included the priests of the temple and members of the aristocracy who identified with them. The main interests of the Sadducees were strict application of the Law and continuation of sacrifice at the temple under the supervision of the priestly class; they were, in our parlance, conservatives. At the time of Jesus, the Sadducees supported the Roman authorities and vigorously opposed any movements that resisted them. They did not accept the classical prophets or the growing body of oral tradition about the Law as authoritative, limiting their biblical canon to the five books of Moses. They also rejected spiritualism, belief in angels, and belief in resurrection, which had emerged as popular expressions of apocalyptic hope.

Pharisees were a party of lay teachers with a wide base of popular support. They believed that faithfulness entailed rigorous attention to requirements of the Law and how the great rabbis of history had applied it to everyday life. They hoped a popular movement that carefully followed the Law would emulate the covenantal community of Judaism that God had in mind in his revelations to Moses and the prophets. Reicke suggests that the modern equivalent of Pharisee might be "puritan."[54] Jesus would fall afoul of the Pharisees, for example, when he healed a person on the Sabbath. There is no end of controversy in the gospels, especially in the gospel of John, between Jesus and the Pharisees over the application of the Law to the lives of the poor, especially in situations where Jesus' acts of healing conflicted with the prohibitions of ritual piety.

Essenes believed the times required a faithful person to lead an ascetic life with a goal of purification while waiting for the day of the Lord. They resembled the Pharisees in their strict observance of law and tradition, but "they had their own peculiar interpretation of the law, their peculiar religious calendar, and they were pledged to a strict discipline which was rigorously enforced."[55] The "Dead Sea scrolls," discovered in caves in wilderness cliffs facing the Dead Sea in the twentieth century, is a collection of books preserved by an Essene community around the time of the destruction of the temple in 70 CE, and they have provided scholars with comprehensive information about Essene beliefs and practices. Their literature was apocalyptic, looking forward to an imminent day of the Lord, and they viewed themselves as the remnant that would be preserved following judgment. .

Zealots were religiously motivated militants who rejected the accommodation that Sadducees explicitly, and Pharisees implicitly, made with empire, which Zealots believed corrupted the temple's sacrifices. They believed that civil insurrection and resistance would hasten the day of the Lord. Although considered a party only after the beginning of the First Jewish War with Rome in 64 CE two decades after Jesus' death, zealotry in its forms of

---

[54] Reicke, *The New Testament Era*, 157.
[55] Bright, *A History of Israel*, p. 462.

armed resistance and banditry was well-established in Jesus' time.

In an example of how the early church was sometimes confused with the brigands and revolutionaries of their times, the book of Acts tells a story that mentions the movement of Judas the Galilean, who led a revolt in 6 CE, and a more contemporary rebel, Theudas. Soon after Jesus' execution (using the methods Romans reserved for revolutionaries and brigands), the Sadducees instigate the arrest of the leaders of the Jerusalem church, who had publicly accused Jerusalem's religious authorities of killing the Messiah. The Sadducees are furious, but a Pharisee member of the ruling council, Gamaliel, argues that the Christians should be spared:

> "Fellow Israelites, consider carefully what you propose to do to these men. For some time ago Theudas rose up, claiming to be somebody, and a number of men, about four hundred, joined him; but he was killed, and all who followed him were dispersed and disappeared; After him Judas the Galilean rose up at the time of the census and got people to follow him; he also perished, and all who followed him were scattered. So in the present case, I tell you, keep away from these men and let them alone; because if this plan or this undertaking is of human origin, it will fail; but if it is of God, you will not be able to overthrow them—in that case, you may even be found fighting against God!" (Acts 5:35-39)

This passage presents the historian with a difficulty; the contemporary historian Josephus says Theudas, a messianic figure who like John the Baptist organized his following at the Jordan River, was executed around 44 CE, which would be ten years after Gamaliel's speech.[56] Regardless, the passage in Acts places the movement begun by Jesus' resurrection among the movements roiling just below the surface of the Roman rule of Galilee and Judea that would soon break out into a series of wars, the first of which would result in the sack of Jerusalem and the destruction of the temple. Rome's brutal suppression of two later revolts would end significant Jewish settlement in Palestine until recent times.

The only use of *zealot* in the New Testament is the name of one of Jesus' disciples, "Simon the Zealot" (Lk 6:15; Acts 1:13), but the significance of his moniker isn't clear. However his movement may have been viewed, Jesus rejected a violent solution to the problem of Israel's nationhood. In Luke's narrative of Jesus' execution, Jesus differentiates himself from revolutionaries after he has been condemned to death and is led away through the streets of Jerusalem to the site of his execution:

> A great number of the people followed him, and among them were women who were beating their breasts and wailing for him. But Jesus turned to them and said, "Daughters of Jerusalem, do not weep for me, but weep for yourselves and for your children. For the days are surely coming when they

---

[56] *Antiquities* 20.97-98, as referenced in *NRSV Study Bible*, 2067.

will say, 'Blessed are the barren, and the wombs that never bore, and the breasts that never nursed.' They will begin to say to the mountains, 'Fall on us'; and to the hills, 'Cover us.' For if they do this when the wood is green, what will they do when it is dry?" (Luke 23:27-31)

Dry wood, gathered for fires because it burns briefly but hot, symbolizes zealotry. Jesus' nonviolent ministry of healing and reconciliation is more like green wood, which produces a low smoky fire that endures.[57] Forty years after Jesus' death and before Luke and the other gospels were written, a violent revolution instigated by Zealots will result in the siege of Jerusalem. Both the siege and the consummating sack, reported by Josephus in the epigraph to the next part of this book, will produce the fiery cataclysm that Jesus prophesied.

Jesus taught a message that crossed party lines and was consistent with a well-established apocalyptic tradition of nonviolent resistance, which we saw began with the Hasidean resistance to Epiphanes in the second century BCE. Another significant and successful nonviolent demonstration confronted a Roman attempt at Hellenization between 39 and 41 CE, less than a decade after Jesus' death when Emperor Gaius Caligula (31-41 CE) ordered a statue of Zeus (in Caligula's likeness) installed in the temple in Jerusalem, recalling the "desolating sacrilege" of Antiochus IV Epiphanes in the book of Daniel. Expecting resistance, Caligula authorized Petronius, his new legate to Syria, to take with him two legions (about 12,000 soldiers, a significant force because it was half the complement then guarding the eastern approaches to the empire[58]). After wintering with his troops in Ptolemais, on the Palestinian seacoast west of Galilee, Petronius met the Jewish authorities in Tiberias in Galilee. According to the Roman historian Philo, after learning what Petronius intended to do, the Jewish leaders "stood riveted to the ground, incapable of speech, and then while a flood of tears poured from their eyes as if from fountains they plucked the hair from their beards and heads."[59]

As if this spectacle wasn't enough, Petronius was soon confronted with a mass of unarmed Galilean peasants and their wives and children—tens of thousands, according to Josephus, who also wrote an account of the incident. More forthright than their leaders, they tell Petronius, "If we can't persuade you, we give up ourselves for destruction that we may not live to see a calamity worse than death."[60] Crossan estimates they camped for forty or fifty days until Petronius, aware of other instances of effective nonviolent resistance to Rome (Pontius Pilate had caved in to a similar protest several years earlier) and considering the potential economic impact of unplanted fields, decided to stall

---

[57] This interpretation relies on Robert Jewett, *Jesus Against the Rapture*, 105 ff.

[58] The estimate is from Crossan, *The Historical Jesus*, 131. My narrative follows his. He notes that the accounts of Philo and Josephus differ as to the location of the confrontation with Petronius; Philo has it occur in Ptolemais.

[59] Quoted in ibid., 131.

[60] Quoted in ibid., 131.

for time. He wrote Caligula and inaccurately reported that the wheat crop was ripe and that the Jews might destroy their crops if he suppressed the protest. This gave Caligula a military calculation to postpone a violent solution, and the protestors went home. With Caligula's assassination in 41 CE, the crisis passed.

From this incident we learn two things that bear on our evaluation of the apocalyptic literature of the New Testament:

First, there was more than one "desolating sacrilege" related to the erection of a statue of Zeus in the temple; the first occurred in 167 BCE at the instigation of Antiochus IV Epiphanes, but a second was attempted soon after Jesus' death and not long before all the documents in the New Testament were written. Installing an image of a "beast" in the temple, a staple of the dispensationalist end-times scenarios, is an artifact of at least these two historical events that had potentially catastrophic consequences because of their insult to Judaism. We should expect these events to figure significantly in the literature of apocalypse, which sets contemporary events in a wider historical and theological context to appreciate their significance.

The second thing we learn from these incidents is that there were significant examples of nonviolent Jewish resistance in these times of apocalyptic fervor. We encountered nonviolent resistance first during the repression of Judaism by Epiphanes when the Hasideans tragically sued for peace, and we encountered it again in the confrontation with Petronius at about the time Paul was beginning his mission to the Gentiles. Remarkably, in the later incident we discover nonviolent resistance among Galileans despite their reputation in Jerusalem for revolution and brigandry, as in Gamaliel's speech in the book of Acts.

Jesus stood within this tradition of nonviolent resistance, and it figures in the story of his arrest. When the temple police arrive, "one of those with Jesus" who is otherwise unidentified draws a sword and wounds one of the officers. Jesus orders his companion to stand down and says, "'Put your sword back into its place, for all who take the sword will perish by the sword'" (Matt 26:52). Confronting the forces of evil does not require violence. The bloody events in dispensationalist end-times scenarios obscure the insight that victory in the apocalyptic final battle requires nonviolent but assertive faith, and love and forgiveness by those who assert it.

Teaching and healing

Matthew's narrative of Jesus' ministry begins with his baptism by John the Baptist, who recognized Jesus' special spiritual gifts. But Jesus didn't follow John. After pondering his calling during a wilderness retreat and a dialogue with a tempting devil who suggests the alternative professions of magician, priest, and king, Jesus set out instead for the shores of the Sea of Galilee, near where he grew up. There he began an itinerant ministry.

Jesus used a variety of methods to communicate his new conception of the kingdom of God. Jesus' pithy sayings are attention-getting and memorable because they often contradict the conventional wisdom. For example, in the first Beatitude (in its version in Luke) Jesus says, "Blessed are you who are poor, for yours is the kingdom of God" (Lk 6:20). The notion then (and now) that wealth is a measure of happiness has been turned upside down.

Jesus also preached *sermons*, and here's an excerpt that has a parallel only in Luke and is therefore from the early source Q; notice the ordinary things Jesus uses as similes:

> "Do not worry about your life, what you will eat or what you will drink, or about your body, what you will wear. Is not life more than food, and the body more than clothing? Look at the birds of the air; they neither sow nor reap nor gather into barns, and yet your heavenly Father feeds them. Are you not of more value than they? . . . Consider the lilies of the field, how they grow; they neither toil nor spin, yet I tell you, even Solomon in all his glory was not clothed like one of these. But if God so clothes the grass of the field, which is alive today and tomorrow is thrown into the oven, will he not much more clothe you—you of little faith? Therefore do not worry, saying, 'What will we eat?' or 'What will we drink?' or 'What will we wear?' . . . But strive first for the kingdom of God and his righteousness, and all these things will be given to you as well." (Matt 6:25-33; cf. Luke 12:22-32)

Jesus also used *parables,* stories about ordinary affairs that end differently from what his listeners expect, to illuminate his thinking. A parable is a drama in two acts. Here are two parables, both from the early source, Q; note the ordinariness of the people and events in the dramas:

> "Someone gave a great dinner and invited many. At the time for the dinner he sent his slave to say to those who had been invited, 'Come; for everything is ready now.' But they all alike began to make excuses. The first said to him, 'I have bought a piece of land, and I must go out and see it; please accept my regrets.' Another said, 'I have bought five yoke of oxen, and I am going to try them out; please accept my regrets.' Another said, 'I have just been married, and therefore I cannot come.' So the slave returned and reported this to his master. Then the owner of the house became angry and said to his slave, 'Go out at once into the streets and lanes of the town and bring the poor, the crippled, the blind, and the lame.' And the slave said, 'Sir, what you have ordered has been done, and there is still room.' Then the master said to the slave, 'Go out into the roads and lanes, and compel people to come in, so that my house may be filled. For I tell you, none of those who were invited will taste my dinner.'" (Luke 14:16-24; cf. Matt 22:1-14)

> "Which one of you, having a hundred sheep and losing one of them, does not leave the ninety-nine in the wilderness and go after the one that is lost until he finds it? When he had found it, he lays it on his shoulders and rejoices. And when he comes home, he calls together his friends and neighbors, saying to them, 'Rejoice with me, for I have found my sheep that was lost.' (Luke 15:4-6; cf. Matt 18:12-14)

Jesus' teaching, through sayings, sermons, and parables, urged his listeners to reconsider their beliefs that the kingdom would arrive in the future via a messiah or an apocalyptic catastrophe. The kingdom of God, Jesus taught, is not Disneyland in the clouds; it's here among us if we choose to perceive it and act accordingly. The reunions we celebrate are with people who were lost, not with people who are safely with us. The kingdom is not a theological abstraction, but is best described in stories about birds, dinner parties, or shepherds. God's reign is not a future theocratic government, but a spiritual force that can shape everyday life today.

God's kingdom doesn't provide the kind of perfection we expect. People who lack hope are closest to God. Spurned people are the people God loves most. If God dresses flowers more colorfully than a person can possibly clothe himself, then the material things a person uses to define himself are unimportant. The rules of fairness, standing in line, and expecting more when you're first and less when you're last no longer apply when God loves all people, and especially the people who people love least.

✝

Jesus also challenged his audiences to *observe* the activities of his ministry in Galilee to learn more about God's reign. In chapters eight and nine of his gospel, Matthew assembles ten miracles, the number recalling the plagues that Moses conjured to frighten Pharaoh into letting the Jews leave Egypt.

Miracles, for those of us who live in times dominated by science, might persuade us that the gospels are describing powers that can't be rationally understood. To people of his time, miracles like the might acts performed by Jesus were either magic that tapped a perfectly ordinary well of spiritual power or they were God-given signs of the end-times.[61] But Jesus didn't heal to demonstrate unusual powers or to warn of approaching troubles; he healed to reveal the literal presence *with him and in his time* of the kingdom of God, his radical reinterpretation of the day of the Lord, the good news.

The subject of his first healing in Matthew is a leper, a person with a skin discoloration that may have been a symptom of the disease we now call leprosy but in those times included symptoms of other skin diseases. Compounding any physical suffering from the disorder was the leper's status in Jewish society: his skin condition was unclean and he was literally untouchable. The Law required a person with diseased skin to warn others that he or she was unclean and to live alone and outside settlements (Lev 13:45-6). The Law also provided, in Leviticus 14, a liturgical procedure priests could use to purify a leper so the person could participate in the temple sacrifice; it required the victim to

---

[61] Raymond Brown notes that the Greek word translated *miracle, dynameis,* is related to the English word *dynamite* and is more appropriately translated as *act of power. Introduction to the New Testament,* 133 n. 16.

sacrifice three lambs, a grain offering, and oil, not an easy investment for an outcast. Jesus took a more direct approach:

> When Jesus had come down from the mountain, great crowds followed him; and there was a leper who came to him and knelt before him, saying, "Lord, if you choose, you can make me clean." He stretched out his hand and *touched* him, saying. "I do choose. Be made clean!" Immediately his leprosy was cleansed. Then Jesus said to him, "See that you say nothing to anyone; but go, show yourself to the priest, and offer the gift that Moses commanded, as a testimony to them." (Matt 8:1-4)

Jesus touches the unclean man, violating the letter of the Law with his intimacy. Then Jesus cleanses the leprosy with his *touch*, ending the man's ostracism; he is no longer unclean, at least to Jesus, and ritual cleansing, which fails to heal, becomes irrelevant. The man's healing is primarily social; he is no longer an outcast. Jesus then recommends that the healed man express his thanks to God as others do. Observers would understand that Jesus is radically reinterpreting the prophetic message: God's Law requires healing for the sake of life, not purity for the sake of ritual.

In another healing, Jesus is approached by a woman who is unclean because of heavy menstrual bleeding. She *touches* him, making Jesus unclean, too. A more typical reaction then would be furious anger, but with Jesus it's mild surprise and compassion:

> Then suddenly a woman who had been suffering from hemorrhages for twelve years came up behind him and touched the fringe of his cloak, for she said to herself, "If I can only touch his cloak, I will be made well." Jesus turned, and seeing her he said, "Take heart, daughter, your faith has made you well." And instantly the woman was made well. (Matt 9:20-22)

Jesus' healing work among the people of Galilee was mostly among people who had been excluded from the Jewish sacrificial community. In the two examples I have used, the man with skin disease and the woman who hemorrhaged had been excluded because of their physical conditions. Others were excluded because they lacked the resources to purchase a sacrificial animal at the temple, or they were unmarried women and perhaps prostitutes, or they were the hated collectors of burdensome taxes. In Jesus' conception of the kingdom of God, society's pariahs were exactly the people who were most open to the good news that God loved people who loved God. The last becomes first, love is the basis of the Law, and healing trumps ritual purity.

Jesus, Zechariah, and the Festival of Booths

As Matthew continues his narrative of Jesus' ministry in Galilee, the numbers of his followers and their enthusiasm build. At the same time, there are rumblings of disapproval among the Jewish elite. They thought that Jesus' radical interpretation of Judaism was presumptuous at best and a threat to their perquisites at worst. Jesus certainly knew the risks. It was in the middle of his ministry in Galilee that Jesus received the news of the execution of John the

Baptist; Matthew reports, "now when Jesus heard this, he withdrew from there in a boat to a deserted place by himself" (Matt 14:13).

Whether Jesus knew he was fated to likewise be executed in Jerusalem and later revealed by his resurrection to be the Messiah, is arguable. Matthew says four times that he knew: "Jesus began to show his disciples that he *must* go to Jerusalem and undergo great suffering at the hands of the elders and chief priests and scribes, and be killed, and on the third day be raised" (Matt 16:21, emphasis added; cf. 17:22-3; 20:17-19; 26:1-2). These passages read like a creedal assertions developed after his death and inserted in the narrative; moreover, the use of the word *must* indicates the desire by the narrator to fit Jesus' journey into a larger apocalyptic plan. Still, the four gospels agree that Jesus went to Jerusalem and stirred up trouble, and his earlier, reflective reaction to John's execution shows he had considered the risks.

Details differ in accounts of his trip to Jerusalem in the gospels of Matthew, Mark, and Luke; the gospel of John recounts *five* different trips. If we compare all the accounts, however, we see broad agreement among them on the prophetic implications of his trip, if not the details, and thereby gain some helpful information about when and why he went (see table).

All four of the gospels agree that the Mount of Olives, a hill east of the temple, was an important destination in Jesus' travels to the Jerusalem area. Ezekiel prophesied that it was to the Mount of Olives that the Spirit of God had moved when Nebuchadnezzar's armies destroyed the first temple (11:23), and the Mount of Olives also figures in a prophecy of Zechariah as the place where God will stand on the day of the Lord (14:3-5). By using the Mount of Olives in his narrative of Jesus' arrival in Jerusalem, Matthew recalls these prophecies to associate Jesus' destination, as well as his mission, with their messages of God's steadfast love for Israel.

All four gospels describe Jesus' crowd-pleasing arrival in Jerusalem atop a donkey, a clear allusion to another prophecy of Zechariah (9:9). Arriving at the same time in Jerusalem would be the Roman procurator, Pontius Pilate, who typically made a ceremonial entrance with soldiers who reinforced the temple garrison during Jewish festivals to warn the hundreds of thousands of celebrants against revolutionary agitation. In contrast, Jesus' entrance on a donkey invokes Zechariah's prophecy about the Messiah who repudiates the use of military force in the pursuit of peace:

> He will cut off the chariot from Ephraim
> and the war-horse from Jerusalem;
> and the battle bow shall be cut off,
> and he shall command peace to the nations;
> his dominion shall be from sea to sea,
> and from the River to the ends of the earth. (Zech 9:10)

The four Gospels agree that the crowd greeted Jesus with cloaks or branches—cloaks on the donkey, cloaks on the road and on the donkey,

	Matthew 21:1-23:39	Mark 11:1-11	Luke 19:28-38	John 2:13-23	5:1 ff.	7:10-8:2	10:22	12:12-19
Occasion	Passover.	Passover.	Passover.	Passover.	Unnamed festival.	Festival of Booths.	Hanuk-kah.	Passover.
Arrival	Bethpage, near the Mount of Olives.	Bethpage and Bethany, near the Mount of Olives.	Bethpage and Bethany, near the Mount of Olives.	The temple.	Bethzatha Pools near the temple.		Portico of Solomon, in the temple.	Bethany, at the home of his friend Lazarus.
Entry into Jerusalem	On a donkey, with a colt tied to it, both draped with cloaks.	On a colt draped with cloaks.	On a colt draped with cloaks.			Secretly.		On a young donkey.
Popular greeting	Branches and cloaks spread on the road and Hosannas.	Branches and cloaks spread on the road and Hosannas.	Cloaks spread on the road and Hosannas.			Controversy: is he a good man or deceiving the crowds?		Branches of palm trees and Hosannas.
Jesus' temple activity	Drives out moneychangers; healing of the blind and lame.	Looks around.	Drives out people who sell things.	With a whip, drives out moneychangers.	None.	Teaches about his status as the Messiah.	Argues with opponents having been sent by "the Father."	
Result	Priests and scribes get angry.	Priests, scribes, and leaders begin scheming to kill him.	Many believed in him.		Pharisees send temple police to arrest him, but they don't.	His opponents threaten to stone and arrest him.		
Departure	To Bethany to spend the night.	To Bethany to spend the night. The next day, he drives moneychangers out of the temple (11:15-19).				To the Mount of Olives.	Across the Jordan to where John had been baptizing.	

branches of trees from fields or palm branches on the road, depending on how the author of the gospel interprets various passages in the Jewish Bible; spreading cloaks recalls how people greeted the ancient kings of Israel. Although five of the seven passages about Jesus' journey to Jerusalem time his arrival with the beginning of Passover, spreading branches is a ritual peculiar to the Festival of Booths, the seven-day harvest festival established by Mosaic tradition as a reminder of the Israelites' utter dependence on God in the Sinai wilderness. The frequent allusions to the prophecies of Zechariah in stories of Jesus' arrival in Jerusalem indicate that whatever the actual occasion, Jesus' entry to Jerusalem and the events leading up to his execution recalled the rich prophetic traditions of the Festival of Booths, even though the occasion may have been Passover.

Zechariah had prophesied that the Festival of Booths would be the occasion when the people of the world would unite after the day of the Lord to worship God; that ordinary meals would have the same sacrificial utility as the sacred fires of the temple cult; and that the coming of the day of the Lord would make unnecessary the temple's priests, its purity rituals, and its trade in sacrificial animals (14:16-20). Jesus' ministry, especially his enjoyment of table fellowship and his interest in healings as opposed to purity rituals, fulfilled Zechariah's prophecies in unexpected ways. The last verse of Zechariah's book is a stunning prophecy of the event that is the fulcrum of all the gospel execution story, Jesus' eviction of the money-changers from the temple: "And there shall no longer be traders in the house of the Lord of hosts on that day" (Zech 14:21).

Bruce Chilton imagines that Jesus' radical spirituality, the billeting of Roman soldiers at the temple, and Zechariah's prophesies about the perfection of worship all influenced Jesus' outburst at the temple after his arrival in Jerusalem.[62] Zechariah had described an ideal kingdom where purity no longer required ritual, sins were packed and sent to storage in crumbling Babylon, people excluded from sacrifice were included in worship, and the Gentile nations joined Israel at the messianic banquet table. Perhaps Jesus was acting impetuously on his disgust with the temple's marketplace, or he had been inspired by Zechariah to hasten the kingdom of God by picking a fight with Israel's religious authorities. Alternatively, Matthew and other witnesses to Jesus' life and death may have associated his activity with Zechariah's prophecies and believed they had been fulfilled, then shaped their narratives to support their views. Or it was a little of both, because in matters of the kingdom Jesus described, God chooses when we might glimpse a time and a place where love, justice, and mercy triumph over evil and peace breaks out absent military victory. But when the veil lifts, the kingdom is revealed, and we see.

---

[62] Chilton, *Rabbi Jesus*, 106, 116, 225, among others.

The sign of Jonah

All the gospels use his intensifying controversy with the Pharisees to plot Jesus' journey to the cross. In the gospels of Matthew, Mark, and Luke, the controversy begins when Jesus arrives in Jerusalem following his ministry in Galilee. In John, his controversies with the Pharisees are the organizing theme of the Gospel: the incident with the temple's money-changers actually opens the book.

Disputation was comon among thinking people in Jesus' time, and it took certain forms. We see remnants of those forms in the gospels, but their authors often make the rhetorical gambits of the Pharisees and Scribes, who were the research librarians of the temple, look like sneaky attempts to entrap Jesus in blasphemy. We have to look behind these accounts to imagine the actual dialogues. They must have been astonishing, for Jesus was from a family of rural artisans who lived in an area known for banditry and revolution, so his urban adversaries must not have expected much of a verbal fight. But he had the sympathy of many common people on whom the Pharisees depended for their strength as a party, so he couldn't be simply ignored; moreover, the gospels indicate that Jesus had the support of several influential Pharisees who hosted entertaining suppers for him in their homes and seemed to welcome the viewpoint he brought to the table.

Matthew devotes chapter 23 of his gospel to Jesus' denunciation of what he terms the "hypocrisy" of Pharisees, and the language escalates as the chapter proceeds. Several of the denunciations, a series of seven *woes* in the form of laments, are likely later editorial expansions of Jesus' teaching seen through the prism of his death. They culminate in a sorrowful condemnation in which modern dispensationalist end-times writers find references to the tribulation and the arrival of Jesus to slay the antichrist's armies:

> "Jerusalem, Jerusalem, the city that kills the prophets and stones those who are sent to it! How often have I desired to gather your children together as a hen gathers her brood under her wings, and you were not willing! See, your house is left to you, desolate. For I tell you, you will not see me again until you say, 'Blessed is the one who comes in the name of the Lord.'" (Matt 23:37-39)

But here, Jesus is *lamenting* how people have spurned God's nurturance, not promising God's wrath. Like the prophets, Jesus wants Jerusalem to choose life, not death. His prediction that they "will not see me again *until* . . ." is a portent of his resurrection. Still, the form of the passage, a prophetic lament that implies an answering reassurance from God, promises that those who rejected the gospel will embrace it once they see God's blessing of Jesus through his resurrection.

✝

Because many aspects of Jesus' teaching and his healing ministry to the poor were widely perceived as signs of the end-times, he was often asked if he was the Messiah. In the gospel of Mark, his responses are particularly elusive, prompting scholars to identify one theme of Mark's gospel as the "messianic secret" that Jesus and his disciples are careful to preserve. In Matthew, Jesus is not so much elusive as enigmatic:

> The Pharisees and Sadducees came, and to test Jesus they asked him to show them a sign from heaven. He answered them . . . "An evil and adulterous generation asks for a sign, but no sign will be given to it except the sign of Jonah." Then he left them and went away. (Matt 16:1-4)

Old Testament histories identify a prophet named Jonah who prophesied about the restoration of a border by King Jeroboam II of the Northern Kingdom (786-746 BCE) (2 Kings 14:23-27). That prophecy isn't preserved, nor is the historical situation anything like the one faced by the eponymous prophet in the brief and comical Old Testament book of Jonah.

In that brief book, God tells the legendary prophet to warn Nineveh that it must repent or be destroyed. The assignment is odious; Nineveh, east of the Northern Kingdom, is part of the empire of Assyria, Israel's enemy; it destroyed the Northern Kingdom of Israel in 722/1 BCE. Jonah believes that Nineveh deserves God's destructive wrath, not a warning, much less a warning from a Jewish prophet. Jonah disobeys God and flees in the opposite direction toward Tarshish, a city in what is now Spain but was emblematic then of the very edge of the world. To get there, he stows away on a ship.

The ship is engulfed by an epic storm. The crew, searching for what might have provoked the anger of a god, finds Jonah asleep below decks. He confesses: "I know it is because of me that this great storm has come upon you"; he suggests they throw him into the sea (Jonah 1:12). The crew charitably attempts to row him ashore, but they fail in the teeth of the storm. So they throw him overboard, and sure enough, the storm immediately ends.

Our reluctant prophet, drowning, is swallowed alive by a giant fish. In its belly, Jonah prays. The fish spits him out onto the seashore where God tells him, again, to warn Nineveh to repent.

Jonah reluctantly walks the streets of Nineveh for three days, repeating the briefest prophecy on record: "Forty days more, and Nineveh shall be overthrown!" (Jonah 3:4). Astonishing everyone, especially Jonah, the city repents. The king, his people, and in another humorous touch the city's work animals dress in sackcloth, sit on the ground, and fast. God is moved and spares Nineveh. Jonah is furious that God chose mercy instead of wrath:

> He prayed to the Lord and said, "O Lord! Is not this what I said while I was still in my own country? This is why I fled to Tarshish at the beginning; for I knew that you are a gracious God and merciful, slow to anger, and abounding in steadfast love, and ready to relent from punishing. And now, O Lord, please take my life from me, for it is better for me to die than to live."

(Jonah 4:1-3)

That night, God rubs it in:

> The Lord God appointed a bush, and made it come up over Jonah, to give shade over his head, to save him from his discomfort; so Jonah was very happy about the bush. But when dawn came up the next day, God appointed a worm that attacked the bush, so that it withered. When the sun rose, God prepared a sultry east wind, and the sun beat down on the head of Jonah so that he was faint and asked that he might die. (4:6-8)

God reopens the therapeutic conversation:

> "Is it right for you to be angry about the bush?" And [Jonah] said, "Yes, angry enough to die." Then the Lord said, "You are concerned about the bush, for which you did not labor and which you did not grow; it came into being in a night and perished in a night. And should I not be concerned about Nineveh, that great city, in which there are more than a hundred and twenty thousand persons who do not know their right hand from their left . . .?" (4:9-11)

Then God remembers the sackcloth . . . "and also many animals?" The book ends.

Jesus' reference to a "sign of Jonah" is puzzling. There are similar passages about signs of the end times in Mark and Luke, but those gospels don't refer to a "sign of Jonah." The passage about Jonah's sign occurs twice in Matthew, and in its earlier form, Jesus' resurrection is foreshadowed: "For just as Jonah was three days and three nights in the belly of the sea monster, so for three days and three nights the Son of Man will be in the heart of the earth" (12:40).

Crossan compares the various texts and concludes that Matthew's briefer reference to Jonah, without the reference to resurrection, is likely the more original.[63] (Interestingly, the book of Jonah does not say that Jonah stayed three days in the fish's belly, although three days was the duration of his reluctant perambulation of Nineveh after the fish spit him out.)

So what is the end-times sign of Jonah? God's primary concern is that the inhabitants of the city of Nineveh, a murderous Gentile city, not perish but repent. The prophetic choice between life and death was theirs, and when God's browbeaten prophet finally warned them, they chose life. Whether it is repentance or resurrection, the sign of Jonah is not seven years of troubles or the destruction of God's enemies on a blood-filled battlefield; it is a sign of God's steadfast love for his creation, including enemies—and their livestock![64]

Matthew's apocalypse

As Matthew's narrative of the controversies between Jesus and the

---

[63] *The Historical Jesus*, 251-253. Crossan in turn references the analysis of John Kloppenborg.

[64] This section benefitted from Jewett, *Jesus Against the Rapture*, 66ff.

Pharisees concludes, Jesus observes his disciples eyeballing the temple: "You see all these, do you not? Truly I tell you, not one stone will be left here upon another; all will be thrown down" (Matt 24:2).

This naturally sounds apocalyptic to his disciples, who ask him about the end times. Jesus had responded to a similar inquiry from a Pharisee with his brief and enigmatic remark about the "sign of Jonah." His response to the disciples is longer but no less indirect. The discourse anticipates events in the First Jewish Rebellion, after his death (and before Matthew was written): increasing Roman oppression, intensifying Jewish unrest, rebellion, the siege of Jerusalem, civil war and famine within the city's walls, Rome's destruction of Jerusalem and the temple, and the escape of Jerusalem's Christians. These catastrophes were within the memories of many in Matthew's immediate audience, and resentments, sorrows, and humiliations still simmered.

Jesus' apocalyptic discourse in Matthew is a series of seven sayings, each following a threefold form: a troubling sign, a comment on the sign's significance, and an apocalyptic conclusion (see table).

Saying	Trouble	Comment	Apocalyptic Conclusion	Reference
1	For many will come in my name, saying, "I am the Messiah!" and they will lead many astray. And you will hear of wars and rumors of wars.	See that you are not alarmed.	All this is but the beginning of the birth pangs.	24:4-8
2	Then they will hand you over to be tortured and will put you to death, and you will be hated by all the nations because of my name. Then many will fall away, and they will betray one another and hate another. And many false prophets will arise and lead many astray. And because of the increase of lawlessness, the love of many will grow cold.	But the one who endures to the end will be saved.	And then the end will come.	24:9-14
3	So when you see the desolating sacrilege in the holy place, as was spoken of by the prophet Daniel . . .	Those in Judea must flee to the mountains.	If those days of trouble had not been cut short, no one would be saved. But for the sake of the elect those days will be cut short.	24:15-22
4	For false messiahs and false prophets will appear.	Do not believe [them].	Then the sign of the Son of Man will appear in heaven.	24:23-31

Saying	Trouble	Comment	Apocalyptic Conclusion	Reference
5	From the fig tree learn its lesson: as soon as its branch becomes tender, you know that summer is near.	So also, when you see all these things, you know that he is near.	Heaven and earth will pass away, but my words will not pass away.	24: 32-35
6	But about that day and hour no one knows. . . only the Father.	You also must be ready.	The Son of Man is coming at an unexpected hour.	24:36-44
7	I was hungry and you gave me food, I was thirsty and you gave me something to drink, I was a stranger and you welcomed me, I was naked and you gave me clothing, I was sick and you took care of me, I was in prison and you visited me.	Truly I tell you, just as you did not do it to one of the least of these, you did not do it to me.	And [the goats] will go away into eternal punishment, but the righteous into eternal life.	25:31-46

In the first saying, Jesus warns about *trouble* from false messiahs and war: "'For many will come in my name, saying, "I am the Messiah!" and they will lead many astray.'" Here, Jesus could be speaking among many other contemporary self-styled messiahs like Theudas and Judas, the two men mentioned by the Pharisee Gamaliel in Acts' account of the persecution of the Apostles in Jerusalem (Acts 5:33-39). Jesus also warns, "'And you will hear of wars and rumors of wars.'" Jesus *comments*: "'See that you are not alarmed; for this must take place. For nation will rise against nation, and kingdom against kingdom, and there will be famines and earthquakes in various places: . . .'" Jesus concludes the first saying with an *apocalyptic conclusion*: "'All this is but the beginning of the birth pangs'" (Matt 24:4-8).

The second saying follows a similar form. Jesus warns of trouble from schism (like the one addressed by the first letter of John) and controversy caused by false prophets in the churches (a first-century problem we will encounter in the book of Revelation):

"Then they will hand you over to be tortured and will put you to death, and you will be hated by all the nations because of my name. Then many will fall away, and they will betray one another and hate one another. And many false prophets will arise and lead many astray. And because of the increase of lawlessness, the love of many will grow cold."

Jesus comments: "'But the one who endures to the end will be saved. And this good news of the kingdom will be proclaimed throughout the world, as a testimony to all the nations; . . .'" And Jesus concludes the second saying with an apocalyptic phrase: "'And then the end will come'" (Matt 24:9-14).

The rest of the sayings in the sermon are similarly arrayed; the discourse is a seven-by-three matrix (with an interrupting sermon) that contains some essential themes of Jesus' revolutionary conception of the imminence of the kingdom of God, set in an apocalyptic context and offering pastoral guidance on how first-century Christians should persevere.

When we perceive the form Matthew has used, we see how Jesus has taken popular signs of the end times and reinterpreted them within his conception of the kingdom of God, which is present but not yet fulfilled. For example, the first saying counsels against alarm at the appearance of self-proclaimed prophets, as if they were signs of a frighteningly imminent catastrophe; Jesus taught, on the contrary that the nearness of the kingdom of God is already manifested in the love, mercy, and forgiveness that we share presently with one another. The second saying advises patient endurance in the face of troubles because, in the kingdom of God, persecuted people of faith, not victorious warriors, are the conquerors.

A sermon and two parables separate the first six sayings from the seventh. We've visited the seventh, final saying before: it impelled Senator John Kerry to enter government service, but end-time writers use it as a prediction of the judgment that concludes the tribulation. The saying is Matthew's broadest account of how Jesus applied the prophetic choice between life and death to his first-century circumstances:

> "When the Son of Man comes in his glory, and all the angels with him, then he will sit on the throne of his glory. . . . Then the king will say, . . . 'Come, you that are blessed by my Father, inherit the kingdom prepared for you from the foundation of the world; for I was hungry and you gave me food, I was thirsty and you gave me something to drink, I was a stranger and you welcomed me, I was naked and you gave me clothing, I was sick and you took care of me, I was in prison and you visited me.'" (Matt 25:31-36)

The saying continues with a description of the "goats" who fail to feed the hungry and visit the prisoners. Then, Jesus provides his pastoral guidance: "'Truly I tell you, just as you did not do it to one of the least of these, you did not do it to me.'" The saying concludes in an apocalyptic frame: "And [the goats] will go away into eternal punishment, but the righteous into eternal life'" (Matt 25:37-46).

Recognizing their construction — trouble/ comment/ apocalyptic conclusion — helps us recognize that these sayings are spoken in the literary style of apocalypse. They speak of a veiled conflict in heaven, yet they are entirely consistent with Jesus' good news, that the kingdom is revealed when we forgive one another and extend our compassion to the despised, the sick, and the poor, today and here on earth. Christians must persevere despite frightening events that are interpreted by many as signs of the end of the world; the ultimate victory of God over evil is reserved for a time known only to God that we hopefully expect every day, but cannot predict.

The catastrophe of the cross

As the infuriated religious authorities of Jerusalem prepare to arrest him after he disrupted trade in sacrificial animals at the temple, Jesus convenes his disciples for a final meal together, the Last Supper. Together, they anticipate the catastrophe that will soon come. Instead of the somber and mutually supportive meal we might expect, injustice, betrayal, cowardice, and violence swirl around the group. Luke's account of the meal is an end-times scenario in miniature:

> When the hour came, he took his place at the table, and the apostles with him. He said to them, "I have eagerly desired to eat this Passover with you before I suffer. . . . But see, the one who betrays me is with me, and his hand is on the table. For the Son of Man is going as it has been determined, but woe to that one by whom he is betrayed!" Then they began to ask one another which one of them it could be who would do this.
>
> A dispute also arose among them as to which one of them was to be regarded as the greatest. But he said to them, . . . "The greatest among you must become like the youngest, and the leader like one who serves." . . .
>
> "Simon, Simon, listen! Satan has demanded to sift all of you like wheat, but I have prayed for you that your own faith may not fail; and you when once you have turned back, strengthen your brothers." And [Simon Peter] said to him, "Lord, I am ready to go with you to prison and to death!" Jesus said, "I tell you, Peter, the cock will not crow this day, until you have denied three times that you know me." (Luke 22:14-34)

Among his closest followers during their last of many meals together, Jesus must reconcile competitors and enemies. He warns Judas, perhaps a Zealot, that his betrayal will not set the apocalypse in motion; it will only result in his own doom. He ends an argument over status among them with his typical inversion, saying that the leader should be the servant of the others. He encourages Peter not to abandon the group, but anticipating that Peter's courage would fail him, he urges him to be a leader-servant afterward.

In the Last Supper, we see that the arrival of the kingdom is not a time for the exclusion of enemies like Judas or the vindication of leaders like Peter. The last become first, the weak become strong, and betrayers do not influence events but are by themselves destroyed. There is no wrath against the wicked, no rapturous escape for the righteous, no use for swords; what remains is the fellowship of a band of weak men who will be the leaders of his movement after Jesus' death. To the members of this peculiar table fellowship, Jesus gives the broken bread and poured wine as signs of his enduring presence with them despite his imminent death.[65]

†

---

[65] Robert Jewett speaks of the messianic banquet and the Last Supper as examples of the theme of the "Feast of enemies" in *Jesus Against the Rapture*, 134 ff.

The times following Jesus' death were tumultuous, no different from the times before it. Conflict continued, caused by Roman behavior and Jewish nationalism. Pontius Pilate was deposed and replaced in 36 CE after he sent soldiers to break up a crowd that a prophet had gathered, making things worse. As we've already seen, in 39 CE the Roman emperor Caligula ordered a statue of himself to be installed in the Jerusalem temple, sparking massive and successful nonviolent resistance by Galilean peasants and their families. In 44 CE, the emperor Claudius (41-54 CE) placed Judea under direct Roman authority. The Hellenizing initiatives of the emperor Nero (54-68 CE) fueled the alienation of traditionalist Jews in Palestine. Wildly different responses to Roman domination appeared in Palestine after Nero: Reicke and Crossan call them, variously, anarchists, robbers, fanatics, conjurers, magicians, prophets, bandits, messiahs, rebels, and revolutionaries.[66] Some Zealots in Jerusalem took to carrying daggers with which they killed collaborators; they were called *sicarii* in Greek, meaning *assassins*. The book of Acts refers to "the Egyptian . . . who recently stirred up a revolt and led the four thousand assassins out into the wilderness" (Acts 21:38); the contemporary Jewish historian Josephus says that "the Egyptian false prophet" led his followers "from the desert to the mount called the Mount of Olives," because "he wished to demonstrate from there that at his command Jerusalem's walls would fall down."[67] They didn't, and Felix, the procurator of Judea at the time, was obliged to attack the group with his guard, killing several hundred.

Crossan warns that contemporary historical accounts often failed to differentiate rural bandits and urban guerillas from pacific prophets imitating Moses who were attempting to jump-start the day of the Lord. Still, Reicke writes, "The Jewish nationalists gradually developed a burning hatred of foreign domination. Aristocratic patriots on the one hand and demagogic Zealots on the other set the mood and gradually succeeded in inciting the population to rebel."[68]

The simmering resentment exploded into organized armed revolt in 66 CE after a synagogue was desecrated and the local Roman garrison refused to intervene. The son of the chief priest led a small army that successfully attacked the Roman garrison at the temple. The collaborationist king fled to Galilee; the Roman legate in Syria attempted to restore order with a small force, but was decisively defeated by growing Jewish Zealot forces.

The emperor Nero then sent the general Vespasian with an invasion force of 60,000 seasoned Roman soldiers to Caesarea Maritima, Rome's seaport on the Palestine coast. Josephus recounts how Vespasian brutally suppressed the rebellion:

---

[66] Reicke, The New Testament Era, 207; Crossan, *The Historical Jesus*, 137-218.

[67] Josephus, quoted in Crossan, *The Historical Jesus*, 164-5.

[68] Reicke, *The New Testament Era*, 203.

At the first approach of spring, he marched the main body of his army from Caesarea to Antipatris [south and inland, toward Jerusalem]. After two days spent in restoring order in that town, on the third he advanced, laying waste and burning all the surrounding places . . . devastating with fire this and the neighbouring district and the outskirts of Idumaee . . . he put upwards of ten thousand of the inhabitants to death, made prisoners of over a thousand, expelled the remainder and stationed in the district a large division of his own troops, who overran and devastated the whole of the hill country over against Jerusalem. . . . The mass of the population, anticipating their arrival, had fled from Jericho to the hill country over against Jerusalem, but a considerable number remained behind and were put to death.[69]

Peasants fleeing Galilee's scorched earth joined the remaining resistance in Jerusalem, which the Roman army then besieged. The Romans surrounded the walls with crucifixes of resisters captured while foraging outside for food. Conflict among the different Jewish parties in the city radicalized the resistance and moderates fled; the hardships of the citizens who remained worsened. Christians, taking Jesus' advice to "flee to the mountains" when the day of the Lord arrives (Matt 24:16), left the city and became the nucleus of churches in Syria for which the book of Matthew was written.

Finally in 70 CE, Roman armies led by Vespasian's son Titus overcame Jerusalem's defenses, entered Jerusalem, and ransacked the city. The temple was looted, then destroyed by fire. Josephus estimated that 100,000 Jews died from famine during the siege; after the siege, another 100,000 were sold into slavery and deported.

Jewish resistance continued in isolated outposts, notably a heroic and ultimately suicidal defense of the mountaintop fortress Masada, but it all ended about three years after the sack of Jerusalem. The Romans minted coins commemorating Israel's humiliating defeat as a warning to other subject peoples throughout its empire. Titus, the victorious general, refused a wreath of victory, saying that there is "no merit in vanquishing people forsaken by their own God."

This, the dry wood consumed, is the catastrophe Jesus foresaw.

---

[69] Josephus, quoted in Crossan, *The Historical Jesus*, 195.

Part Four
REVELATION

Pouring into the alleys, sword in hand, [the Romans] massacred indiscriminately all whom they met, and burnt the houses with all who had taken refuge within. Often in the course of their raids, on entering the houses for loot, they would find whole families dead and the rooms filled with the victims of the famine, and then, shuddering at the sight, retire empty-handed. Yet, while they pitied those who had thus perished, they had no similar feelings for the living, but, running everyone through who fell in their way, they choked the alleys with corpses and deluged the whole city with blood, insomuch that many of the fires were extinguished by the gory stream.

—Josephus on the sack of Jerusalem in 70 CE.[1]

---

[1] *War*, in Barrett, *The New Testament Background*, 167.

Chapter 16

INTRODUCING REVELATION

The Christian Bible closes with an exquisite symphony of imagination to encourage the compassionate people of God to patiently endure despite a violent and unjust world that spurns them. The book of Revelation still fuels the hopes of oppressed people of faith, as signified by this call-and-response song originally sung in the twentieth century by the African-American bluesman "Blind Willie" Johnson:

> Well who's that writin'?
>   John the Revelator
> Who's that writin'?
>   John the Revelator
> Who's that writin'?
>   John the Revelator
> A book of the seven seals
> Well ooh ooh why me, thousands cried holy
>   Bound for some, Son of our God
> Daughter of Zion, Judah the Lion
>   He redeemeth, and bought us with his blood
>   (refrain)[2]

Although a recording of another of Johnson's blues songs, "Dark Was the Night," is among the recordings the spacecraft Voyager I is taking across the universe to announce earth's humanity to any alien civilization that may encounter it,[3] very little is known about Johnson's life, reflecting the anonymity accorded to Africa-Americans in the Jim Crow South. A birth certificate reveals

---

[2] "John the Revelator (song)," Wikipedia. Online at: http://en.wikipedia.org/wiki/John_the_Revelator_%28song%29

[3] "Music from Earth," NASA Jet Propulsion Laboratory. Online at: http://voyager.jpl.nasa.gov/spacecraft/music.html

its span (1897-1945), but Michael Corcoran, writing in the Austin *Statesman*, says:

> The document doesn't tell you how he lived from 1930, when his recording career ended, until his death. It doesn't tell you how many times he was married and how many kids he fathered. It doesn't tell you how he learned to play such a wicked bottleneck guitar or which Pentecostal preachers he modeled his singing voice after. It doesn't verify the widespread legend that Willie was blinded when a stepmother threw lye in his face at age seven to avenge a beating from his father. The certificate reports the cause of death as malarial fever, with syphilis as a contributing factor. But when it also lists . blindness as a contributor, the coroner's thoroughness becomes suspect.[4]

"John the Revelator" was sung to a responsive group of listeners who knew oppression. Similarly, Revelation is a book that was written to be read aloud, from beginning to end, to evoke a response in its listeners. The book itself makes this clear at the outset: "Blessed is the one who *reads aloud* the words of the prophecy, and blessed are those who *hear* and who keep what is written in it; for the time is near" (1:3, emphasis added).

So, to best appreciate the book of Revelation, imagine a meeting of a first-century Christian assembly. It's in someone's home because many churches couldn't afford a meeting place or they were forbidden to have one. We're in the interior courtyard of the large home of one of the wealthier members, next to a fountain and outside the room where afterward we'll share supper (it's likely pot-luck!).[5]

Our assembly includes slaves as well as free people, women as well as men, Jews as well as Gentiles. With that diversity, our church already contrasts the kingdom of God with the empire of Rome, where these distinctions were firmly drawn in social settings. Even among citizen men at meetings of Roman associations, the men were arrayed by status: the host would take his meal at the room's head, and others would position themselves according to their relationship with him, those most distant closest to the door. In contrast, God's kingdom is victorious and near when the diverse members of our church gather and sit where they want to listen to this thrilling book.

Typical of first-century Christians, our church values meditative and ecstatic forms of religious expression, so John's visions and songs aren't peculiar. Dreams, prophecy, and speaking in tongues were commonplace ways to experience and express God's grace in the early church. Paul writes about spiritual gifts that early church members shared: "When you come together, each one has a hymn, a lesson, a revelation, a tongue, or an interpretation" (1 Cor 14:26). In some early churches the differing abilities of members to enter

---

[4] "The Soul of Blind Willie Johnson," Austin Statesman, no date. Online at: www.austin360. com/music/content/music/blindwilliejohnson_092803.html.

[5] These imaginings are drawn on a reading of Chapter 6 of *In Search of Paul* by Crossan and Reed.

ecstatic states caused divisions; some members were perceived (or perceived themselves) as more faithful or righteous than others based on their ability to summon visions or to prophesy. The outpouring of prophecy and praise sometimes obscured the central purpose of the church; Paul cautioned them:

> Now you are the body of Christ and individually members of it. And God has appointed in the church first apostles, second prophets, third teachers; then deeds of power, then gifts of healing, forms of assistance, forms of leadership, various kinds of tongues. Are all apostles? Are all prophets? Are all teachers? Do all work miracles? Do all possess gifts of healing? Do all speak in tongues? Do all interpret? But I strive for the greater gifts. And I will show you a still more excellent way.
>
> If I speak in the tongues of mortals and of angels, but do not have love, I am a noisy gong or a clanging cymbal. And if I have prophetic powers, and understand all mysteries and all knowledge, and if I have all faith, so as to remove mountains, but do not have love, I am nothing. If I give away all my possessions, and if I hand over my body so that I may boast, but do not have love, I gain nothing. (1 Cor 12:27-13:3)

In our first-century church, the spontaneous songs, prophecies, and prayers that open our meetings have concluded and it's time for a reading before we share our supper. The reader opens a book and begins. The book is from John, an evangelist who visits our church. He composed it on an island off the coast "in the Spirit" on the Lord's Day, the day of the week we celebrate as the day Jesus left his tomb. The reader begins; John turns toward a voice he hears, and sees

> seven golden lampstands, and in the midst of the lampstands I saw one like the Son of Man, clothed with a long robe and with a golden sash across his chest. His head and his hair were white as white wool, white as snow; his eyes were like a flame of fire, his feet were like burnished bronze, refined as in a furnace, and his voice was like the sound of many waters. In his right hand he held seven stars, and from his mouth came a sharp, two-edged sword, and his face was like the sun shining with full force. (1:12-16)

When we hear this, we recall Daniel's vision of *the Ancient One*, a white-haired king on a throne who we might assume is God, as well his vision of a messianic figure he called *one like a son of man* (Dan 7:9-10, 13-14). But we're taken aback: in John's revelation, *one like a son of man* has the white hair of the *Ancient One*. This is difficult for us, because *son of man* is a term Jesus uses for himself in the gospels and we may think of the phrase as code for *messiah*. John sees that the *one like a son of man* has the appearance of the *Ancient One*, so John has joined Daniel's two figures into a single heavenly figure who has an aspect of humanity as well as an aspect of divinity. John's focus on the human aspect of this figure is not unimportant; it was the cause of the schism in the church to which another John wrote, where the deniers of Jesus' humanity were the "antichrists."

John's vision of the white-haired figure who has both divine and human aspects, whom I will call *the Lord*, radically reinterprets Daniel's messianic vision to suggest the solidarity of God in heaven with the people of the earth. After all, the Creation Epic reports that God looks like us: "Then God said, 'Let us make humankind in our image, according to our likeness'" (Gen 1:26). As Revelation proceeds, we will witness the rising and insistent chorus of the angels in heaven, people on earth, and creatures of land and sea who finally celebrate the joyous reunion of heaven and earth at its close. John roots the white-haired figure in both the divine and human experiences. John will develop his surprising reinterpretation of Daniel as the reading continues.

These opening verses are full of Old Testament allusions. John's auditory vision of the Lord's voice as "the sound of many waters" is reminiscent of Ezekiel's vision of God's chariot, moving through the heavens supported by winged creatures: "When they moved, I heard the sound of their wings, like the sound of mighty waters" (Ezek 1:24). The seven golden lampstands recall descriptions of the temple used by the Israelites in the wilderness of Sinai, an elaborate tent:

> The Lord spoke to Moses, saying: Command the people of Israel to bring you pure oil of beaten olives for the lamp, that a light may be kept burning regularly. Aaron shall set it up in the tent of meeting, outside the curtain of the covenant, to burn from evening to morning before the Lord regularly; it shall be a statute forever throughout your generations. He shall set up the lamps on the lampstand of pure gold before the Lord regularly. (Lev 24:1-4)

That the Lord might have a deadly weapon in his mouth—"from his mouth came a sharp, two-edged sword"—recalls Isaiah's announcement in his servant songs of God's appointment of Israel to be a priest for the nations of the world:

> He made my mouth like a sharp sword,
> in the shadow of his hand he hid me;
> he made me a polished arrow,
> in his quiver he hid me away. . . .
> "I will give you as a light to the nations,
> that my salvation may reach to the end of the earth." (Isa 49:2, 6)

John will use the sword-in-mouth image later in his book, in the culminating battle with evil: a sword in the mouth of the leader of the Lord's army will defeat the armies of the beasts and the nations assembled at Armageddon (Rev 19:15). A sword-wielding mouth is a jarring metaphor; an instrument of war is in the mouth, the source of breath (which to ancients represented spirit) and of words (referring to the word of God). There was no little irony when early Christians used a Greek term for military public relations, *euangelion*, "good news of victory (in battle)," for Jesus' *good news*, the nonviolent victory of love and forgiveness over evil and death.

The many references to Old Testament images in this early passage of Revelation tell us a lot about the book. Recalled are images in the Law (the menorahs), the Prophets (the Word as sword and the appearance and sounds of God), and in the Wisdom tradition (Daniel's messianic figure, *one like a son of man*). We might conclude that John was thoroughly familiar with Jewish traditions and he was likely a Jew by heritage. We might also conclude that many of the listeners in our early church are Jewish Christians who appreciate the rich associations with Old Testament prophecy in his visionary imagery, or are Gentiles who have undertaken the study of the Old Testament to better understand the good news.

John recalls images in the Old Testament not just to prove a point. While the fulfillment of prophecy is as important to John as it was to the gospel writers, more important still are the messages these images bring when they are recalled. When John recalls the menorahs in the tent in the desert where the Israelites worshiped God, he is framing his visions in the wilderness tradition of Israel, where God reveals himself to a nation that is utterly dependent on God's grace; moreover, he is reminding us of a time when worship was in a tent and not in a temple, which by John's time had been destroyed. When John uses images from Isaiah, he is recalling the prophet's teachings about the sovereignty of God, Israel's hopes for redemption, and Israel's servant role in hosting Gentile nations at the messianic banquet of peace and prosperity. When he uses images from Ezekiel, he is recalling Ezekiel's prophecies during the exile that the breath of faith will inhabit Israel again, God will defeat her Gog-like enemies, and the perfect temple will be built. All these important images swirl around our early church's meeting room as we listen to John's opening chapter, which has set the stage for the visions to come.

✝

The book of Revelation is a circular letter to seven first-century churches. After messages to each of the individual churches (to which I'll soon turn), the book records John's vision of the fulfillment of time, a time that is "near" and coming "soon" (Rev 1:1,3). In the vision, the inhabitants of heaven announce and celebrate God's destruction of evil in a narrative dominated by symbols and myths. Seven scenes of worship punctuate the vision, like the refrain in a ballad that introduces the song, repeats after each verse of the ballad, and concludes it. The scenes of worship become more inclusive of the faithful in heaven and on earth and more magnificent in their glorification and praise of God as the book proceeds and the heavenly stage widens to include the heavens and the earth—the entire creation. At the same time, the book provides scenes of conflict and catastrophe that are increasingly detailed, lurid, and violent as the vision proceeds. While the seven scenes of worship expand cyclically in participation and scope, the visions of conflict have a plot whose episodes follow a familiar prophetic pattern: emerging troubles, a warning by God, the designation of a remnant, a persistent choice by the wicked of the way of death, and finally widespread death and destruction of the unrepentant. (A one-page outline of the book's organization is in Appendix 2.)

The structure of the book of Revelation is important to an understanding of its meaning and it helps determine the interpretation a reader will make. If one believes that Revelation is a prediction of how the end-times will unspool in the future, as do dispensationalists,[6] then the catastrophes on earth are the main event and the angels and the saints are in the bleachers, making appropriate noises as the plagues and meteor showers and battles swirl before them, then cheering as Jesus Christ swoops in to save the day. However, this interpretation requires a studied ignorance of the book's opening and closing chapters, which (literally!) describe the book as a letter to seven churches about issues they presently face. The best modern interpretations account for the *entire* book, rejecting dispensationalist and other *a priori* notions about how it should be read.

The book of Revelation is what it says it is, a revelation about Jesus Christ to first-century churches, not a prediction of twenty-first century calamities. The book is an *apocalypse*, the Greek word that is translated in English as *revelation* and whose Greek roots mean *a lifting of the veil*.[7] An apocalypse reveals a truth that is otherwise hidden; it is not a view of the future through a magic knothole. The Lord in heaven tells John to "write what you have seen, what is, and what is to take place after this" (1:19), but the three tenses of past, present, and future he uses in that passage mirror the preceding sentence, which concerns the timelessness of the Lord's existence: "I am the first and the last, and the living one. I was dead, and see, I am alive forever and ever" (1:17-18). John has visions that transcend time and space, and their sharing is intended to shape a Christian's experience of the kingdom of God and inform his or her moral decisions.

Any attempt to comment on Revelation struggles with the organization of the book. In my view, the book is a series of envelopes containing others that contain the truth the book intends to reveal. The three nested envelopes tell the listener the *context* of the message they contain. That there are three envelopes reflects the depth to which the revealed truths are hidden.

The envelopes that provide the context for the message they contain are these:

---

[6] For example, Tim LaHaye introduces his popular commentary on the book of Revelation: "With the exception of chapters 12 and 17, most of Revelation unfolds chronologically. It is easier to understand this book if one expects it to fall into chronological sequence except for these two chapters." *Revelation Unveiled*, 17.

[7] Although the genre of apocalyptic writings is broad, the book of Revelation is the only one that is titled "Apocalypse."

Envelope	Reference
1 Greetings-- Alpha and Omega	1:1-8
2 One like the Son of Man	1:9-20
3 Messages to the Seven Churches	chapters 2-3
The scroll	chapters 4-20
3 The New Creation	21:1-8
2 The New Jerusalem	21:9-22:7
1 Benediction--Alpha and Omega	22:8-21

The outer envelope conveys the greetings and benedictions at the beginning and end of the book, typical of Christian letters in the first century. They assert the timelessness of God and his love of life on earth, using the metaphor of *Alpha and Omega*, the first and last letters of the Greek alphabet. The opening asserts, "'I am the Alpha and the Omega,' says the Lord God, who is and was and who is to come, the Almighty" (1:8); the closing concludes, "'I am the Alpha and the Omega, the first and the last, the beginning and the end'" (22:13).

The next interior envelope describes the world-changing agents that God uses to transform life on earth to conform it to the ways of heaven. The agent as the book opens is *one like the Son of Man*, a reference to the messianic figure in the book of Daniel; as the book closes, the agent is the *new Jerusalem*, the millennial city representing the earth transformed as heaven descends to earth.

The most interior envelope encloses God's message, a scrolled decree. The envelope opens with letters to the "conquerors" in the seven churches who are encouraged to resist the idolatry of empire despite the sacrifices resistance entails. The envelope closes with the assurance that in the new creation, "mourning and crying and pain will be no more" (21:4).

These nested envelopes persuade the listener that the scroll they contain describes God's present transformation of the world, a process that until now has been hidden. When the scroll is unsealed and scenes of victory and praise surround them, members of our first-century church will learn that they are a catalyst for the new creation. The visions affirm that Jesus' sacrifice and God's imminent gift of the New Jerusalem are renewing the partnership between divine and human begun at the creation. Our first-century church joins the angels in heaven, the faithful who have died, and the faithful alive today to celebrate God's timelessness and the certainty of God's repudiation of evil. We must persevere: evil will not prevail.

Chapter 17
THE SEVEN CHURCHES

The book of Revelation was written to encourage first-century Christians to "patiently endure" in their loving fellowship despite the coercive allure of the economic, social, and cultural ways of the Roman Empire.[8] Several generations had passed since Jesus' death; understandings among the earliest Christians that he would return within their lifetimes to lead a worldwide kingdom of God had proven inaccurate, and individual Christians continued having practical difficulties keeping a faith that asked them to reject important parts of the empire's way of life. Moreover, confronted by Roman authorities with their religious nonconformity, some Christians were forced to choose between death and the shame of falling away from sacred vows taken before their friends and families.

As the book begins, God tells John that the seven lampstands illuminating the throne in heaven are the seven churches to whom he writes (1:20). That the seven churches illuminate the heavenly throne startles our first-century church; Craig Koester, in his commentary on the book of Revelation, writes,

> Its message is that the churches are not alone, but have Christ in their midst, both as savior and judge. This disclosure of the presence of Christ may be reassuring or unsettling depending upon the position of the reader. For those that are insecure, the disclosure of Christ's presence is assuring. For those who would prefer to keep their distance from Christ, this intrusion can be unsettling.[9]

The seven churches were in Roman cities in what today is western Turkey,

---

[8] The term "patient endurance" or "endurance" occurs in the book's opening at 1:9; in announcements to three of the seven churches at 2:2, 2:19, and 3:10; and in two exceptional comments by John at 13:10 and 14:12, pivotal passages we'll look at more closely as this part proceeds.

[9] Koester, *Revelation and the End of All Things*, 54.

inland from the Aegean Sea. They may have been a circuit that John visited as an itinerant apostle, like Paul, but no known road connected them. *Seven* is an organizing principle for many scenes in Revelation (its catastrophes are organized by seven seals, seven trumpets, and seven bowls), and *seven* was symbolic in prophetic and apocalyptic literature of *completeness,* echoing the seven days of the Creation Epic.[10] From the churches' number, then, it is possible to interpret the churches as representative of the range of problems faced by early churches.

The locations of the churches may also have been symbolic: all were in cities that were centers of Roman administration, culture, or trade. The chief priests of the temples honoring the late Caesar Augustus in six of the cities met annually in a provincial assembly.[11] One of the cities, Pergamum, was the site of the Great Altar of Zeus built in the third century BCE, and John may be referring to it when he speaks of a monument in the city that he calls "Satan's Throne" (2:13).[12] The churches literally live within the belly of the beast that the book will later describe.

Koester lists the challenges facing the seven churches as *assimilation, persecution,* and *complacency,* and we'll look at the churches using those categories.[13]

Assimilation

The churches in Ephesus, Pergamum, and Thyatira had been divided by false apostles or teachers who encouraged members of the church to "eat food sacrificed to idols and practice *fornication*" (2:14, 20, emphasis added). Two groups of false teachers are named and condemned: the Nicolaitans (2:6, 15), who are otherwise unknown to history, and "those who hold to the teaching of Balaam" (2:14), the name of an infamous charlatan in the Old Testament (Num 22:2-24:5). Also condemned at Thyatira is Jezebel, the name of a pagan queen of Israel who employed hundreds of false prophets to seduce the nation into the worship of alien gods (1 Kings 18:19). Except perhaps for the Nicolaitans, John is using pseudonyms for the false prophets in the three churches; in the cases of Jezebel and Balaam, he is likely using the names to associate what he condemns in the churches with behavior that was condemned by the prophets.

Nor is John's use of the word *fornication* necessarily literal; in prophecy, *fornication* was often condemned but usually referred to the worship of pagan idols. I provided several examples in the second part where the prophets

---

[10] Ibid., 48. Barr, in *Tales of the End*, 8, interprets seven as "perfection," 6. See table. The number *seven* occurs over fifty times in the book of Revelation.

[11] Reicke, *The New Testament Era*, 231.

[12] The throne will become a monument in the twentieth century to the persistence of evil: Adolf Hitler's architect modeled the ceremonial reviewing stand at the Nuremburg parade grounds after the temple to Zeus in Pergamum. Learn more online at: http://en.wikipedia.org/wiki/Albert_Speer.

[13] Koester, *Revelation and the End of All Things*, 57-69.

denounced Jerusalem as a prostitute for her abandonment of the purity of the Law. So, when John uses "practice of fornication" to describe a danger to one of the churches, it may refer to the extramarital liaisons with women and boys that pagan men in Greco-Roman cities might exploit, which were common enough, but the more likely meaning is worship of a pagan god, in particular consuming food sacrificed at pagan altars. The accusation is serious: idolatry had all the moral ramifications of fornication but was committed spiritually, making it even more pernicious.

Paul didn't oppose eating food sacrificed (made sacred) to a pagan god, arguing that pagan gods didn't exist so the food couldn't be sacred (1 Cor 8-10). However, John condemned it. Behind the issue of eating food sacrificed to pagan gods, there was a more general question: may Christians participate in the social and political activities of empire that celebrate its culture of domination and violence? The answer to that question is more elusive, but John's parodies of Greco-Roman politics and religion in the rest of the book suggest that Christians must avoid the ways that the empire's culture separated people from the love of one another, and of God.

Assimilation into city life in Greco-Roman society was difficult to resist. The empire was based on power, patronage, and conformity in all relationships, whether in business, politics, religion, or sex. The empire's power was celebrated in elaborate temples financed by sycophantic associations, constructed by slaves, and erected in cities created for discharged soldiers, so the physical environment itself was a monument to *Pax Romana*. The very atmosphere must have smelled of power generated from violence—figuratively and literally, for the smell of roasted meat sacrificed to various gods often wafted down city streets. Access to power was the empire's seduction. The church in Ephesus is commended for resisting it, but is warned that they have done so at the cost of "abandoning the love you had at first" (2:4), the earliest churches' practices of sharing resources and meals.

Persecution

John's messages for the churches in the cities of Smyrna and Philadelphia indicate that they were suffering from persecution by the Roman authorities.

Except for the brutal pogrom in 64 CE against Christians in Rome by the Emperor Nero, persecution of Christians in the Roman Empire ensnared individuals rather than targeted groups. Imperial authorities tolerated the refusal of Jews and Jewish Christians to participate in Greco-Roman sacrificial practices, and since the reign of Julius Caesar (48-44 BCE), Judaism had enjoyed a right of social association forbidden to others. But as time passed, Christians and Jews differentiated themselves from one another and as a result, Christians no longer enjoyed the tolerance given to the more ancient faith (like the church in Thessalonica, discussed in Part Three). An accusation would be leveled, the Christian would be confronted, and, if the Christian refused to worship the Roman gods, a judicial decision would be made. Exile, a judgment that may have put John on the island of Patmos, was an unusual punishment reserved for aristocrats with connections; more usual was torture and execution. Koester quotes a letter from a Roman official of the time who says that after Christians were denounced to him, he

> asked them in person if they are Christians, and if they admit it, I repeat the question a second and a third time, with a warning of the punishment awaiting them. If they persist, I order them to be led away for execution; for whatever the nature of their admission, I am convinced that their stubbornness and unshakable obstinacy ought not to go unpunished.[14]

To churches enduring persecution, John's message is reassurance. Although the persecution will continue, death will not result in the exclusion of martyrs from the kingdom of God; they will be welcomed, paradoxically, as *conquerors* (2:7, 11;2:17, 26, 28; 3:5,12, 21). For the persecutors, justice comes in the fulfillment of time, which is soon. The horrible visions of the book of Revelation that follow the messages to the seven churches will illustrate the gravity of their tormentors' fate.

Complacency

The churches in Sardis and Laodicea evidently didn't have the problems of assimilation and persecution facing the other churches. They are not warned about idolatry, nor are they urged to persevere against the risk of death. However, they are told that they are unprepared for membership in the kingdom of God.

To the church in Sardis, the message is: "'I know your works; you have a name of being alive, but you are dead. Wake up, and strengthen what remains and is on the point of death, for I have not found your works perfect in the sight of my God'" (3:1-2). To the church in Laodicea, the message is:

> I know your works; you are neither cold nor hot. I wish that you were either cold or hot. So, because you are lukewarm, and neither cold nor hot, I am about to spit you out of my mouth. For you say, 'I am rich, I have prospered, and I need nothing.' You do not realize that you are wretched, pitiable, poor, blind, and naked. (3:15-17)

Both churches are urged to be conquerors, but with the term's counterintuitive, peculiarly Christian meaning. In contrast to Roman conquerors, who brought peace to their subjects through overwhelming and ruthless military might, Christians become conquerors and bring God's peace through acts of love and mercy. In victory they celebrate their fellowship meal with Jesus Christ: "Listen! I am standing at the door, knocking; if you hear my voice and open the door, I will come in to you and eat with you, and you with me" (3:19-20).

---

[14] Ibid., 65. quoting Pliny, *Letters*, 10.96:3-4.

Chapter 18
THE FIRST SCENE OF WORSHIP

Following the messages to the seven churches, the book's vision of the destruction of evil begins, but with a scene of worship. Considering the focus by end-times writers on Revelation's descriptions of catastrophe and judgment, it's not insignificant that the first scene of John's vision of evil's destruction is the worshipful glorification of the Lord using songs that were likely familiar to the members of our first-century church.

The worship opens in the heavens. A door opens in the sky to admit John, and there he encounters

> a throne, with one seated on the throne! And the one seated there looks like jasper and carnelian, and around the throne is a rainbow that looks like an emerald. . . . Coming from the throne are flashes of lightning, and rumblings and peals of thunder." (4:2-3)

The gemlike appearance of God's throne reminds listeners of Ezekiel's description of God in his chariot. The thunder and lightning remind listeners of God's appearance to Moses in the book of Exodus, when the Israelites approach Mount Sinai: "On the morning of the third day there was thunder and lightning, as well as a thick cloud on the mountain, and a blast of a trumpet so loud that all the people who were in the camp trembled" (Ex 19:16).

Prowling the area around the Lord's throne are four winged animals, the cherubim who support the wheeled throne in Ezekiel's vision. The creatures chant:

> "Holy, holy, holy,
> the Lord God the Almighty,
>   who was and is and is to come." (Rev 4:8)

This song is familiar to the members of our first-century church who are listening. We can imagine them singing along as the reader, becoming cantor, sings the chant of the cherubim. The source of the chant is ancient, Isaiah's vision of singing seraphim:

> I saw the Lord sitting on a throne, high and lofty; and the hem of his robe filled the temple. Seraphs were in attendance above him. . . . And one called to another and said:
> "Holy, holy, holy is the Lord of hosts;
> the whole earth is full of his glory." (Isa 6:1-3)

During the worship in heaven, twenty-four elders dressed in white prostrate themselves before the throne, throwing their crowns at its foot. There's no explanation of their number, but from the book's interest elsewhere in Israel's tribes, we can infer that it's the sum of their number (12) and the number of Jesus' disciples. The elders complete the hymn of praise begun by the creatures:

> "You are worthy, our Lord and God,
> to receive glory and honor and power,
> for you created all things,
> and by your will they existed and were created." (Rev 4:11)

Together and abbreviated, these songs will also be familiar to modern Christians. Recalling the hymn sung to God by the seraphim in Isaiah, Roman Catholics hear them in the "Sanctus":

> Holy, holy, holy,
> Lord God of Hosts;
> Heaven and earth are full of your glory.
> Hosanna in the highest.

Protestants also know the song from a nineteenth-century hymn by the Anglican bishop Reginald Heber, usually set to the music *Nicaea* by John B. Dykes:

> Holy, holy, holy! All the saints adore Thee,
> Casting down their golden crowns around the glassy sea;
> Cherubim and seraphim falling down before Thee,
> Who was, and is, and evermore shall be.[15]

Koester contrasts this scene of worship with another that will be familiar to the members of our first-century church: the adulation and worship of emperors, kings, and their representatives who visited the cities of the Empire. Koester writes:

> Public appearances of the emperor often featured him sitting on a throne and accompanied by a crowd of friends, advisors, and attendants. When the emperor traveled, communities would send representatives, sometimes dressed in white, to greet him and present him with golden crowns to show their recognition of his sovereignty.[16]

---

[15] Presbyterian Church of the United States et al, *The Hymbook*, 22-23, v 2.

[16] Koester, *Revelation and the End of All Things*, 75.

From these songs and their setting in heaven we learn these things about Revelation. First, the book uses the trappings and mythology of the Roman Empire to compare the kingdom of God in heaven with its corrupt imitation on earth. Second, the book of Revelation has been a resource for Christian worship throughout the ages and even now. Aside from its inappropriate uses in dispensationalist end-times scenarios, we see the book's most enduring influence in worship, a theme to which I will return.

Chapter 19
THE LAMB

As the songs of praise quiet and echo throughout the heavens, a scroll appears in the right hand of the Lord. The scroll is sealed with seven wax seals, a practice of those times that assured a document's authenticity. The number of seals—seven—symbolizes the comprehensiveness of the scroll's decree.

An angel asks if anyone in heaven or on earth is "worthy" to break the seals on the scroll. No one rises to the occasion until John *hears* an elder announce "the Lion from the Tribe of Judah, the Root of David"—the messiah-king of Jewish hopes—who "has conquered, so that he can open the scroll and its seven seals" (5:5). But what John *sees* when he turns is not a lion, but a lamb, "standing as if it has been slaughtered" (5:6).

Here is the first example in Revelation that contrasts what John *hears* with what he *sees*: he sees a peasant executed on a cross, not the powerful king victorious in battle that the elder's announcement would cause him to expect. The Messiah is not the figure we anticipated; it's a person slaughtered, not a military victor standing proudly among the bleeding bodies of his enemies.

The slaughtered Lamb is an allusion to the customary Passover sacrifice. The Lamb is not just a symbol of Jesus Christ, but a visionary image of Jesus in his sacrificial aspect, a *person* who was sacrificed at Passover, when a lamb is sacrificed to commemorate God's release of Israel from its bondage. Similarly, the Lord on the throne who greets John at the beginning of the book is not just a symbol of God but a visionary image of a divine being who is *like a human being*, merging Daniel's visions of the *Ancient One* and the *one like a son of man*. The images of the Lamb and the Lord are two sides of the same coin: both have divine and human aspects. Koester notes that it would have been easy enough for John to identify the Lamb as Jesus Christ (and, I interpolate, the white-haired *one like a son of man* as God), but John doesn't; in fact, he won't name Jesus as *the Christ* until very late in the book when he sees the general resurrection and the millennial kingdom (20:4).[17]

Appreciating that the Lamb and the Lord represent the human as well as heavenly aspects of their divinity is essential for understanding Revelation's purpose: to establish that Christians presently live and hope for the reign of God *here on earth* among earth's creatures, as Isaiah prophesied and Jesus taught in Galilee. For first-century Christians and Jews, this is a radically new way of thinking about apocalyptic prophecy but it is not inconsistent with either Jesus' announcement of the arrival of the kingdom in Galilee or the "already but not yet" announcement of Paul. The kingdom of God is not some other-worldly place in some future time separated from us by seven years of trouble; it is already among us now, and it will be fulfilled soon.

Upon the appearance of the Lamb, the numbers surrounding the throne expand until all the creatures of the earth respond to the song of praise raised by uncountable numbers of angels:

> "Worthy is the Lamb that was slaughtered
> to receive power and wealth and wisdom and might
> and honor and glory and blessing!"

> Then I heard every creature in heaven and earth and under the earth and in
> the sea, and all that is in them, singing,

> "To the one seated on the throne and to the Lamb
> be blessing and honor and glory and might
> forever and ever!" (Rev 5:12-13)

The Lamb begins to break the seven seals so the scroll may be unrolled and God's decree announced. However, breaking the seals will release horrible images of a profane, unjust, and violent world in the process of its own destruction.

---

[17] Ibid., 78.

Chapter 20
"HOW LONG?"

As the Lamb opens the seven seals of the scroll before an audience of the inhabitants of all heaven and earth, John sees catastrophes.

The release of the first four seals unleashes four visions of horses with riders who "were given power to destroy a fourth of the earth by war, famine, disease, and wild beasts" (6:1-8):

A white horse ridden by a hero wearing a crown signifies the bogus peace brought by Roman legions, such as those who conquered Jerusalem in 70 CE, twenty or thirty years previously.

A red horse whose rider "was permitted to take peace from the earth, so that people would slaughter one another," signifies the ever-present danger of civil strife, such as the civil unrest, assassination, and banditry that preceded the first Jewish revolt in the decade preceding Jerusalem's destruction.

A black horse whose rider carried scales to measure wheat or barley signifies economic catastrophe and famine like those that befell Jerusalem when it was besieged by Roman legions.

A pale-green horse whose "rider's name was Death, and Hades followed with him," rounds out the foursome and through the horse's ghastly color signifies death's horrible intimacy.

Members of our first-century church do not limit the symbolism of the horsemen to a future catastrophe. War, civil war, and famine recently destroyed Jerusalem and continue to ebb and flow within the empire, leaving death the apparent conqueror. That this is true serves the symbolism of these first four wax seals on God's decree, for the seals are signs of the scroll's authenticity.

The opening of the fifth seal reveals "the souls of those who had been slaughtered for the word of God and for the testimony that they had given" (6:9). This seal represents unprosecuted justice for martyrs and murdered prophets, and the souls ask, "Sovereign Lord, holy and true: *how long* will it be before you judge and avenge our blood on the inhabitants of the earth?"

(6:10, emphasis added). The fifth seal is another indisputable truth: justice for martyrs has been postponed.

How long? Let's leave our first century church and jump to 1965 and the steps of the State Capitol in Montgomery, Alabama. The catastrophic heritage of slavery continues to unfold in American history. The Reverend Martin Luther King, Jr., is speaking to an assembly a couple of weeks after "Bloody Sunday," a turning point in the Civil Rights movement when peaceful marchers were attacked by state and local police at the Pettus Bridge outside Selma, a nearby city. Dr. King must speak not just to the present injustice of the brutality his followers have most recently experienced, but also to a dismal three-hundred-year history of bondage, exploitation, rape, poverty, lynching, shootings, bombings, and myriad other injustices that the white oppressors of black people in southeastern America had used to perpetuate their hateful prejudices and economic control. He asks his followers to persevere and to remain committed to the nonviolent teachings of Jesus Christ, for certainly they would be conquerors:

> And so I plead with you this afternoon as we go ahead: remain committed to nonviolence. Our aim must never be to defeat or humiliate the white man, but to win his friendship and understanding. We must come to see that the end we seek is a society at peace with itself, a society that can live with its conscience. And that will be a day not of the white man, not of the black man. That will be the day of man as man. (*The audience responds, Yes*)
>
> I know you are asking today, "How long will it take?" (*Speak, sir*) . . . Somebody's asking, "When will wounded justice, lying prostrate on the streets of Selma and Birmingham and communities all over the South, be lifted from this dust of shame to reign supreme among the children of men?" . . . (*Yes, sir*)
>
> I come to say to you this afternoon, however difficult the moment, (*Yes, sir*) however frustrating the hour, it will not be long, (*No, sir*) because "truth crushed to earth will rise again." (*Yes, sir*) . . .
>
> How long? Not long, because the arc of the moral universe is long, but it bends toward justice. (*Yes, sir*)
>
> How long? Not long, (*Not long*) because:
>> Mine eyes have seen the glory of the coming of the Lord; (*Yes, sir*)
>> He is trampling out the vintage where the grapes of wrath are stored; (*Yes*)
>> He has loosed the fateful lightning of his terrible swift sword; (*Yes, sir*)
>> His truth is marching on. (*Yes, sir*)[18]

When we hear the souls of martyrs crying "How long?" we learn this about the book of Revelation: for those who choose nonviolence and forgiveness to overcome injustice and oppression, the book has been a source of encouragement and hope for almost twenty centuries.

---

[18] From "Our God Is Marching On," Online at:
www.stanford.edu/group/King/publications/speeches/Our_God_is_marching_on.html

✝

Visions of natural catastrophes swirl before John's eyes when the sixth seal is removed:

> There came a great earthquake; the sun became black as sackcloth, the full moon became like blood, and the stars of the sky fell to the earth as the fig tree drops its winter fruit when shaken by a gale. The sky vanished like a scroll rolling itself up, and every mountain and island was removed from its place. (Rev 6:12-14)

The vision recalls many prophets' descriptions of the *day of the Lord*, but it also recalls Matthew's description of natural events during Jesus' death on the cross: "From noon on, darkness came over the whole land . . . . The earth shook, and the rocks were split" (Matt 27:45,51). The authenticity of the scroll signified by this seal is attested by Jesus' death on the cross, a difficult but defining truth for Christians: the leader of their movement, a man many welcomed as the Messiah, was executed in the most painful and humiliating way the Roman Empire could devise.

Unlike the appearance of the four horsemen and the cries of the martyrs, which had no effect, the failure of the foundations of heaven and earth resulting from the opening of the sixth seal strikes fear into the powerful, "the kings of the earth and the magnates and the generals and the rich and the powerful" (6:15). With everyone else, they hide in caves from "the face of the one seated on the throne and the wrath of the Lamb" (6:16).

Death is at large, martyrs wail, and the heavens and the world are collapsing, but the opening of the seventh seal is postponed. John now sees four angels at the four corners of the world subdue the winds and everything becomes still. Another angel stands where the sun rises and thunders, "Do not damage the earth or the sea or the trees, until we have marked the servants of our God with a seal on their foreheads" (7:3), an allusion to baptism. [19]

John then witnesses an assembly of these servants of God. He *hears* 12,000 people from each of the twelve tribes of Israel for a total of 144,000 people who receive seals to protect them against the trouble to come. (These become the "Jewish evangelists" in the dispensationalist end-times scenario.) To appreciate the meaning of the number 144,000, an understanding of apocolyptic numerology is essential. David Barr provides these equivalences based on his analysis of the book of Revelation:

---

[19] Barr, *Tales of the End*, 87.

Number	Symbolizes
Three	The spiritual order
Four	The created order
Seven	Perfection (contrast six)
Ten	Totality
Twelve	Israel (God's People)
Three-and-one-half	The number of evil
Multiples and repetitions	Intensification

Using these symbolic equivalencies, the number *twelve* symbolizes *the people of God*; the number *ten*, *totality*; the number *three*, the spiritual order. *Twelve* multiplied against itself then multiplied by *ten* multiplied *thrice* symbolizes *all* people who accept God's grace through baptism and reject the worship of evil throughout history, past, present, and future.[20] To protect this remnant, the crisis that will be caused by the opening of the seventh seal has been forestalled.[21]

A third scene of worship then begins, restarting the cycle of visions that alternate worship and catastrophe as the book forges forward to its resolution. John sees

> a great multitude that no one could count, from every nation, from all tribes and peoples and languages, standing before the throne and before the Lamb, robed in white, with palm branches in their hands. They cried out in a loud voice, saying,
> "Salvation belongs to our God who is seated on the throne, and to the Lamb!" (7:9-10)

John *hears* the group of 144,000 who receive seals, and he *sees* "a great multitude"—another group, or the same? In this passage we observe the indeterminate nature of John's visions. Sometimes his visual and auditory perceptions of a vision differ, indicating that his powers of perception are insufficient to embrace the full scope of what the visions reveal.

In response to the crowd's song, the angels, elders, and animals around the heavenly throne fall on their faces, singing:

> Amen! Blessing and glory and wisdom
> and thanksgiving and honor
> and power and might
> be to our God forever and ever! Amen. (7:12)

---

[20] Barr, Tale of the End, 8.

[21] As it happens, the number of sealed saints is in the same order of magnitude of the number of Christians Bo Reicke estimates in Asia Minor at about the time that the book of Revelation was written: 80,000. Reicke, *The New Testament Era*, 304.

An elder explains to John that the survivors of "the great ordeal" who have "washed their robes and made them white in the blood of the Lamb," an unexpected outcome of that peculiar laundry, are the *conquerors*, the faithful who rejected idolatry, rejected assimilation, and aren't complacent in their faith. The elder tells John:

"They will hunger no more, and thirst no more;
    the sun will not strike them,
    nor any scorching heat;
for the Lamb at the center of the throne will be their shepherd,
    and he will guide them to springs of the water of life,
and God will wipe away every tear from their eyes." (7:14-17)

Chapter 21
THE SEVENTH SEAL

We return to the Lamb's announcement of God's decree. The first six seals have been removed from the scroll in quick succession, but the removal of the seventh has been postponed by visions of catastrophe and worship. The Lamb's removal of the final, seventh seal will permit the scroll to unroll so God's decree may be read. The anticipation of the listeners in our first-century church has been aroused by the refrain of worship that has just concluded. John now reports, "there was silence in heaven for about a half an hour" (8:1).

In our first-century church, perhaps our reader pauses here, too, for a few minutes of silence. After a round of coughing and shuffling of feet, the assembly quiets and meditates on the timeless presence of God that the silence in John's vision is intended to represent.

Silence in the Old Testament often invokes the presence of God. Moses commanded silence when he convened the Israelites to announce the Law:

> Then Moses and the levitical priests spoke to all Israel, saying: Keep silence and hear, O Israel! This very day you have become the people of the Lord your God. (Deut 27:9)

The Psalmist sings of silence in the face of persecution:

> For God alone my soul waits in silence;
>   from him comes my salvation. (Ps 62:1)

Zephaniah begins his prophecy against Judah:

> "Be silent before the Lord God!
> For the day of the Lord is at hand." (Zephaniah 1:7)

When the silence ends, an angel carrying a gold censer ignites its incense and hurls it to earth, resulting in "peals of thunder, rumblings, flashes of lightning, and an earthquake" (8:5). Perhaps we turn our heads to observe the incense censer on the altar in our church with a new appreciation, for here in the book of Revelation we have our first indication that the spiraling glorification of God in heaven prompted by the Lamb's unsealing and opening of the scroll has begun to impinge on the earth. When the silence ends, the heavenly censer ignites and perfumes the sky and the land below.

The breaking of the seventh seal is announced by seven angels who take turns blowing trumpets that accompany a series of catastrophes on earth. A fiery hail scorches a third of the earth; a blazing mountain turns the seas to blood, killing a third of its creatures; a huge star wipes out a third of rivers and springs; the brightness of the moon, stars, and suns are reduced by a third. The breakings by *thirds* symbolize a disruption of the spiritual order; the portents are reminiscent of the plagues visited by God on Egypt to persuade Pharaoh to release the Jews from slavery.

The next two trumpets call out hideous visions of doom. A swarm of venomous locusts the size of war horses appears after the fifth trumpet blast, recalling the day of the Lord in Joel. The sixth blast releases four evil angels "who are bound at the great River Euphrates" (9:14), which separated the Roman Empire from the feared Parthian tribes; here it is a symbol, like *Babylon* or *armies of the north*, for threatening enemies. With the four evil angels comes a hideous and huge cavalry; John says he "*heard* their number and . . . *saw* the horses in my vision" (9:16-17), repeating the form of expression where his auditory visions complement (or contradict) the spectacle that he sees. The noses of the cavalry's horses breathe fire and brimstone, recalling the account of the destruction of Sodom and Gomorrah in Genesis 19:24, and they destroy a third of humanity. Amazingly, the survivors are oblivious of the imminent threat:

> The rest of humankind, who were not killed by these plagues, did not repent of the works of their hands or give up worshiping demons and idols of gold and silver and bronze and stone and wood, which cannot see or hear or walk. And they did not repent of their murders or their sorceries or their fornication or their thefts. (9:20-21)

Once again, however, the fulfillment of a set of seven catastrophes is postponed. Before the seventh trumpet blast, another angel wrapped in a cloud and a rainbow descends from heaven and stands with one foot on the earth and the other on the seas. He is announced by seven thunderclaps whose message John is forbidden to record—it must be God again. The angel holds a scroll and announces, "There will be no more delay, but in the days when the seventh angel is to blow his trumpet, the mystery of God will be fulfilled, as he announced to his servants the prophets" (10:6-7). This is puzzling. If there will be no more delay, then why postpone the fulfillment of the mysterious message of the thunderclaps to the indeterminate future? What are we waiting for? *How long?* Here John's visions escape our ordinary notions of time. The time necessary to break the seventh seal has already been stretched by the trumpet blasts; the scroll, we begin to understand, has significance that transcends time and makes meaningless our usual understanding of its measured pace.

As the suspense of the seventh and fulfilling trumpet blast continues, John is instructed to measure a temple that has been revealed to him, a task that reminds listeners of the measure of a perfect temple in Ezekiel (40:3 ff) and a restored Jerusalem in Zechariah (2:1 ff). However, he's told not to measure the forecourt of the temple because it will be used by the Gentile nations for "forty-two months" (11:2)—three and a half years, the time frame used by the author of Daniel for the period of beast-trouble in *his* apocalypse. Here, John is saying that the troubles his listeners endure will persist, but as in David, temporarily.

Two witnesses appear dressed in sackcloth, the way the prophet Elijah dressed in the Old Testament and John the Baptist in the New, signifying a time of repentance. John sees the two witnesses as "two olive trees and two lampstands that stand before the Lord of the earth" (11:4). These visions recall Zechariah's vision where two lampstands were symbols of the "anointed ones," the king and priest whom Zechariah credits with rebuilding the temple following the Babylonian exile (Zech 4). That there are two witnesses also recalls Moses and Elijah, who oral tradition said would return as a sign of the nearness of the day of the Lord.[22]

The two witnesses will have supernatural powers and prophesy for "1260 days" (11:3), again recalling the time frame of trouble in the book of Daniel. When that period ends, "the beast that comes up from the bottomless pit will make war on them and conquer them and kill them, and their dead bodies will lie in the street of the great city" (11:7-8). But the two dead prophets will be resurrected and lifted to heaven. At the same time, an earthquake will destroy a tenth of the city and kill seven thousand people; the rest "were terrified and gave glory to the God in heaven" (11:13).

That only a tenth of the city is destroyed and seven thousand killed precisely reverses the results of two Old Testament prophecies by Isaiah and Amos.[23] Furthermore, just as earlier visions of judgment in the book were marked by obstinate apostasy among the unrepentant, this judgment vision is characterized by widespread repentance. Koester believes the book is making these points: "The witness, death, and vindication of the community of faith accomplish what the prospect of judgment alone does not do. It brings people of many tribes, languages, and nations to fear God and to give him glory."[24]

While modern end-times writers puzzle over future practical considerations related to these visions, like how the temple might be rebuilt or who the two witnesses may be, our first-century church audience wouldn't have trouble fathoming the meaning of these symbols. The witnesses are the persecuted churches who have inherited the ancient traditions of Elijah and Moses and

---

[22] Barr, Tales of the End, 91-92.

[23] Isa 6:13; Amos 5:3; cf. 1 Kings 19:18.

[24] Koester, *Revelation and the End of All Things*, 111.

are announcing Jesus' faith to the world; the lampstands illuminating the Lord are the testimony of the churches that allows the rest of the world to see the faith that has been revealed; the temple where the illumination occurs has no specific site within the kingdom of God, because, like Ezekiel's chariot, the kingdom is everywhere. The responsibility of the churches is to call the world to choose life marked by justice, compassion, and reconciliation over against the choice of death, which is participation in the violence and injustice of military empires. Like Jesus, the churches may be persecuted, but those who patiently endure following Jesus' teachings are the conquerors.

Chapter 22
THE SEVENTH TRUMPET

The seventh trumpet finally sounds, announcing at last the unsealing of the scroll. Its unsealing is the apocalypse, the unveiling of what is hidden, God's decree, "the mystery of God . . . fulfilled" (10:7). What is unveiled, however, is not a future tribulation full of famine, disease, and civil wars culminating in a gory battle, but another scene of worship around God's throne.

The assembled voices of heaven sing:

"The kingdom of the world has become the kingdom of our Lord
    and of his Messiah
and he will reign forever and ever."

The twenty-four elders respond:

"We give you thanks, Lord God Almighty,
    who are and who were,
for you have taken your great power
    and begun to reign." (Rev 11:15-18)

Our first-century listeners know these songs and sing along. Then, John observes that "God's temple in heaven was opened, and the ark of his covenant was seen within his temple; and there were flashes of lightning, rumblings, peals of thunder, an earthquake, and heavy hail" (11:19). The most interior and sacred part of the first temple, built by Solomon, contained the ark, or conveyance, of the stone tablets given by God to Moses to memorialize God's covenant with Israel on Mount Sinai. It was a gilded box lost when the first temple was destroyed by Nebuchadnezzar's armies. In both the first and second temples, the most interior part, the Holy of Holies, was visited just once a year, and by only one man, the chief priest. When the most sacred part of heaven's temple is revealed to John and, through his book, to *all* members of God's kingdom, not only is heaven impinging on the earth but the holiest place on earth where God resides is opening to all of the earth's inhabitants.

The Lamb has announced the scroll's decree. It institutes the kingdom of God, in heaven *and* on earth. The kingdom's heart, its virtual Holy of Holies, is now accessible to everyone. God's name is praised throughout heaven and earth in a hymn that everyone can join. The prayer Christians say daily is fulfilled: .

> Our father in heaven,
>> hallowed be your name.
>> Your kingdom come,
> Your will be done,
>> on earth as it is in heaven. (Matt 6:9-10)

Now, a series of visions punctuated by two scenes of worship and another set of seven plagues describes how evil is destroyed. The visions of the destruction of evil are drawn from Hebrew, Greco-Roman, and Persian stories, and their exotic imagery tantalizes end-times writers. But John's purpose in recounting them is not to mysteriously predict the future. The visions challenge his listeners to rethink the power of evil and encourage them to patiently endure. Their love and compassion, in partnership with God's love for them, conquer the brutal and seemingly invincible forces of evil that confront them.

The woman, the child, and the dragon

The first vision of the destruction of evil tells a story about "a woman clothed with the sun, with the moon under her feet, and on her head a crown with twelve stars" who is giving birth to a male child "who is to rule all nations with a rod of iron" (12:1-6). By adorning the woman with heavenly bodies, the setting here is heaven and the expected child is the Messiah; the reference to childbirth reminds us of apocalyptic characterizations of the coming of the kingdom of God as "birth pangs" (Matt 24:8). The child is threatened by "a great red dragon, with seven heads and ten horns, and seven diadems on his heads," recalling the archetypal beast of the seventh chapter of the book of Daniel. The child is "snatched away and taken to God and his throne," indicating Jesus' ascension to heaven following his resurrection. The woman "fled into the wilderness, where she has a place prepared by God, so that she can be nourished for one thousand two hundred sixty days," indicating the escape of the church from the destruction of Jerusalem and using the time frame symbolic of a period of evil from the book of Daniel as a symbol for the troubles the church must endure.

Then, the archangel Michael and his angels, figures drawn from the book of Daniel and other apocalyptic writings,[25] defeat the dragon: "the great dragon was thrown down, that ancient serpent, who is called the Devil and Satan, the

---

[25] In his study notes on the book of Revelation in the NRSV Study Bible, David Aune identifies these passages as potential sources for Michael, Gabriel, and the seven archangels: Dan 10:13 and 12:1; Jude 9; Tob 12:15; 1 Enoch 20:1-17; Lk 1:19;and Rev 1:4. Aune, "Revelation," *NRSV Study Bible*, 2310 and 2324.

deceiver of the whole world—he was thrown down to the earth, and his angels were thrown down with him" (12:9). The dragon's defeat occasions a song that explains the story's meaning: Satan is no longer a force in heaven thanks to the sacrifice of Jesus and the martyrs of the church, but Satan's expulsion to earth is the cause of the current persecution, which won't last long:

> Rejoice then, you heavens,
>   and those who dwell in them!
> But woe to the earth and the sea,
>   for the devil has come down to you
> with great wrath,
>   because he knows that his time is short! (Rev 12:12)

On earth, the dragon again pursues the woman who this time flees on the wings of an eagle, but again to the wilderness, "to her place where she is nourished for a time, and times, and half a time" (12:14), again invoking the evil time frame from the book of Daniel. That she is rescued on the wings of an eagle reminds us of Revelation's continuing relevance to Christian worship; the metaphor in Revelation is from Isaiah 40:31, a source of the refrain in the popular modern religious song, "On Eagle's Wings."[26]

Besides the symbolism of three-and-a-half, the variations on a theme in these stories remind us of the variations on the history of the rise of the beast in Daniel's times, Antiochus IV Epiphanes. The two variations of the story of the woman, her son, and the dragon are typical of apocalyptic writing, as we saw in the discussion of the book of Daniel; the repeated theme helps the listener understand an abstract thought that otherwise might be elusive and reassures the listener with its repetition. Here, the times are parallel: the dragon's defeat in heaven has occurred, but its defeat on earth will come in the fulfillment of time.

Koester identifies the source of the vision of the woman, her child, and the dragon as a Roman myth that was popular when the book of Revelation was written.[27] The myth was about the Roman god Apollo, a favorite of the emperor Nero, notorious for his persecution of Roman Christians in 64 CE. Nero liked to think that he was the "son" (Apollo) in the pagan version of the story who pursues the dragon and kills it, ushering in a period of peace and prosperity.

Most of our first-century church listeners would have known the Apollo story and enjoyed the irony in John's adaptation. It takes a myth about Rome's power and transforms it into an apocalyptic story of victory for the people who reject it. But our congregation would also recognize through the story that while God had defeated evil through Jesus' resurrection, evil in one of its many manifestations was still at large in the Roman world, and still dangerous.

---

[26] The song itself adapts Psalm 91. The "eagle's wings" metaphor is also found in Ex 19:4.
[27] Koester, *Revelation and the End of All Things*, 118.

The beast from the sea

The dragon pauses and two beasts emerge. The first beast—called *Leviathan* in a contemporary Jewish apocalypse, 2 Esdras[28]—rises from the sea,

> having ten horns and seven heads; and on its horns were ten diadems [crowns], and on its heads were blasphemous names. And the beast that I saw was like a leopard, its feet were like a bear's, and its mouth was like a lion's mouth. . . . One of its heads seemed to have received a death-blow, but its mortal wound had been healed. (Rev 13:1-3)

The beast's ten horns make it resemble the dragon, and both now recall the beast of the seventh chapter of the book of Daniel. The origin of the beast, the sea, would remind listeners in our first-century church of other sea-dwelling monsters in Jewish traditions. For example, a beast from the sea appears in Isaiah's apocalypse, where the battle between God and the sea monster is set in the future: "On that day the Lord with his cruel and great and strong sword will punish Leviathan the fleeing serpent, Leviathan the twisting serpent, and he will kill the dragon that is in the sea" (Isa 27:1).

Some details in John's vision of the beast from the sea contribute to the end-times writers' profile of the antichrist: he is "haughty" and "blasphemous," and he is given authority "over every tribe and people and language and nation, and all the inhabitants of the earth will worship it" except the saints of the church (Rev 13:5-8). The listeners in our first-century church realize that the beast may represent the Roman emperor but also know that *a beast from the sea* signifies a primordial and persistent evil whose source is chaos and who has bedeviled God's people throughout history. This evil existed at the creation of the world and is still dangerous. The beast is more than a myth: in its guise as Babylon, it destroyed the first temple and sent the elites of Judah into exile; personified in Antiochus IV Epiphanes, it murdered Jews who persisted in their faith; as Nero and his henchmen, it tortured and murdered Christians in Rome; and in its form as the Roman legions, it recently destroyed Jerusalem and the second temple. This is the beast who threatens the churches of Asia Minor whom John writes to warn about assimilation, persecution, and complacency.

At the end of his description of the hideously corrupt beast from the sea, John speaks directly to his listeners, almost like an actor in a movie who momentarily leaves his role to speak for himself to the audience. This sudden departure from apocalyptic style gets our attention:

> Let anyone who has an ear listen:
>> If you are to be taken captive,
>>> into captivity you go;
>>> if you kill with the sword,
>> with the sword you must be killed.
>> Here is a call for the endurance and faith of the saints. (13:9-10)

---

[28] 6:49-52.

John is pointedly recalling Jesus' warning to his disciples about armed resistance to his arrest (Matt 26:52); he is making a startling call to his listeners for nonviolent endurance under persecution.

In the dragon and the beast from the sea, we have formidable symbols of the evil that has been, is being, and will soon be conquered by God and the Lamb. Now, meet the beast from the earth.

The beast from the earth

As the dragon watches, the second beast, called *Behemoth* in 2 Esdras, rises from the earth to be the priest of the beast.

> It had two horns like a lamb and it spoke like a dragon. It exercises all the authority of the first beast on its behalf, and it makes the earth and its inhabitants worship the first beast, whose mortal wound had been healed. It performs great signs, even making fire come down from heaven to earth in the sight of all; and by the signs that it is allowed to perform on behalf of the beast, it deceives the inhabitants of earth, telling them to make an image for the beast that had been wounded by the sword and yet lived; and it was allowed to give breath to the image of the beast so that the image of the beast could even speak and cause those who would not worship the image of the beast to be killed. (Rev 13:11-15)

End-times writers find many useful details in this description of the second beast and its priestly activity for the first. For them, the vision describes a false prophet who will be the antichrist's second-in-command. But to our early church listeners, the beast and his priest are lampoons of contemporaneous monsters they encounter when the representatives of empire visit their cities.

They notice a contrast between this pair of figures, who are the center of violence on earth, and the two figures who are the center of worship in heaven. On one hand, there are the Lord and the Lamb presiding over the inhabitants of heaven and the saints on earth; on the other hand there are two beasts, the first scary and blasphemous, the second with the appearance of a lamb but acting like a dragon. On one hand is the Lamb, the messenger of love and forgiveness who healed the sick; on the other, the second beast fooling people with magic tricks. On one hand is the Lamb, slaughtered yet alive and presiding over the unsealing of God's decree establishing the kingdom of God; on the other, two beasts that received mortal wounds yet survive like vampires, usurping the earth with their lies.

The priest-beast requires everyone to wear the "mark of the beast" on their forehead or right hand; "no one can buy or sell who does not have the mark, that is, the name of the beast or the number of its name" (Rev 13:17). Because another seal was placed on the foreheads of the saints to protect them from the wrath of God when the kingdom of God is fulfilled, we see the contrast between the beasts' protection racket, whose outcome is death, and the Lamb's system of grace, whose object is life.

Describing the first beast's heads, John had said that one "seemed to have received a death-blow, but its mortal wound had been healed" (13:3). The second beast makes an image of the beast that "had been wounded by the sword and yet lived" (13:14). The riddle of their identity concludes with another: "Let anyone with understanding calculate the number of the beast, for it is the number of a person. Its number is six hundred sixty-six" (13:18).

Jewish and Christian apocalyptic literature as well as other ancient cultures of the time were fascinated by numerology, and in one common enterprise people summed the numbers associated with the letters in people's names to calculate a numerical symbol. The number 666 is the sum of the Hebrew letters for "Caesar Nero." With the other clues, it dawns on many listeners in our first-century church that these two beasts may be incarnations of a beastly figure on earth, the emperor Nero, persecutor of the Christians of Rome. The beast's scarred and misshapen head is an allusion to Nero's suicide: he slit his own throat. That the wound had healed refers to a common belief in those times that Nero survived his death to continue his persecutions as an undead stalker. The gloomy Sibylline Oracles, a collection of ancient mystical writings, some of which may be contemporary to Revelation, include this allusion among others to the dead but still-feared Nero, a lover of chariot-driving:

And one whose mark is fifty shall be lord,
A dreadful serpent breathing grievous war,
Who sometime stretching forth his hands shall make
An end of his own race and stir all things,
Acting the athlete, driving chariots,
Putting to death and daring countless things;
And he shall cleave the mountain of two seas
And sprinkle it with gore; but out of sight
Shall also vanish the destructive man;
Then, making himself equal unto God,
Shall he return; but God will prove him naught.[29]

Nero's posthumous reputation reflected his murderous pleasures, including his persecution of Christians following the fire that almost destroyed the city of Rome in 64 CE. The fire resulted in widespread homelessness, and Nero set up barracks to house refugees on a park he owned next to the Tiber River. Senators conspiring against Nero agitated the refugees with the rumor that Nero had purposely set the fire; to distract his critics and amuse the refugees, Nero blamed the Christians for the fire and held public circuses of their torture and death.

A somewhat contemporary account of the horrors endured by Christian victims of Nero's persecution is provided by the Roman historian Tacitus (ca. 56-ca. 117 CE):

---

[29] Internet Sacred Text Archive, Sibylline Oracles 5:39-49. Online at http://www.sacred-texts.com/cla/sib/sib07.htm

Nero fastened the guilt and inflicted the most exquisite tortures on a class hated for their abominations, called Christians by the populace.... Accordingly, an arrest was first made of all who pleaded guilty; then, upon their information, an immense multitude was convicted, not so much of the crime of firing the city, as of hatred of mankind. Mockery of every sort was added to their deaths. Covered with the skins of beasts, they were torn by dogs and perished, or were nailed to crosses, or were doomed to the flames and burnt, to serve as a nightly illumination when daylight had expired. Nero offered his gardens for the spectacle, and was exhibiting a show in the circus, while he mingled with the people in the dress of a charioteer or stood aloft on a car. Hence, even for criminals who deserve extreme and exemplary punishment, there arose a feeling of compassion; for it was not, as it seemed, for the public good, but to glut one man's cruelty, that they were being destroyed.[30]

As Tacitus observed, Nero's attempts to rebuild his popular support after the fire didn't work; revolutions emerged throughout the empire (including in Palestine), prompted in part by his heavy spending to rebuild Rome after the fire; he was soon deposed by the Roman Senate and committed suicide.

While the clues John provides seem to identify the beast as Nero, the meaning of "666" extends beyond the identity of any particular beast in history. Koester teases this out by contrasting the symbolic uses of the number *six* in the book of Revelation with the book's uses of the number *seven*:

Previously in Revelation, completeness and blessing have been associated with the number seven. The seventh seal brings reverent silence (8:1), and the seventh trumpet announces the kingdom of God (11:15). The number six, however, has more to do with imperfection and judgment, for the sixth seal and the sixth trumpet unleashed visions of wrath and devastation (6:12-17; 9:13-19). Following this pattern, the number 666 implies that the beast signifies unfulfillment and destruction.[31]

The riddle of the number 666, in the richness of its allusions, would have reminded our early church audience of the two threats to Christian faith from the Roman Empire: first, the obvious threat of torture, exile, or death for rejecting the rituals of Roman life: second, the more insidious threat of becoming an acolyte of the current manifestation of the beast by participating in the civic, business, and social customs of the Greco-Roman city.

✝

Early Jewish-Christian churches patterned themselves after synagogues but veered toward egalitarian and communitarian relationships within their fellowships depending on how tightly they embraced Jesus' teachings about sharing. These customs contrasted vividly with the customs of Roman

---

[30] *Annals* xv. 44, from Barrett, *The New Testament Background*, 15-6.
[31] Koester, *Revelation and the End of All Things* 132.

associations, on which they were modeled.

Roman rule over Asia Minor, the location of the seven churches to whom Revelation was addressed, was consolidated under Emperor Augustus after his victory in the Roman civil war in 31 BCE. Archaeological research has established that temples to Roman gods were quickly erected in the seven cities, an indication that their elites were urgently competing for Roman favor. As these elites were recognized by Rome through visits by the Emperor or his emissaries traveling along Rome's military roads, members of the elites, already "citizens" of their cities in the Greek way, became Roman citizens with those rights and perquisites, too.

A citizen's status and financial success depended on the willingness of another member citizen to extend his patronage to that man (and it was exclusively men for whom this system was designed). Business relationships or the common interests of artisans were advanced through associations, each of which would organize around the worship of a Greek or Roman god. City-wide civic associations of the elites, called *ekklesia* (a Greek word later appropriated by churches), were responsible for public works and for assuring that the city had food, water, and other necessities and amenities. Their hard work was rewarded by gifts and favors from the Emperor and his representatives, their patrons. Larger associations had meeting places, often temples dedicated to the god they worshiped. Smaller associations met in the homes of men whose houses were big enough for the meeting. Their dining and conversation were guided by the host, and the evening included worship of the emperor and the image of the Roman god who the men considered to be the spiritual patron of the association. The meeting usually concluded with heavy drinking.[32]

Christians might excuse themselves from these associations, but a lack of participation would mean exclusion from the business networks or apprenticeship systems the associations supported. Here we find the mark of the beast: "no one can buy or sell who does not have the mark, that is, the name of the beast or the number of its name" (Rev 13:17). By placing themselves outside the associations dedicated to pagan gods, Christians also faced social consequences: "Depending on the prevailing mood of the city and the time, this could result in social ostracism, exclusion from social events, having one's business boycotted, mob violence and lynching, or being reported to the local authorities."[33]

Supporting the patronage system and suffusing every part of life in Greco-Roman cities was the sacrifice of food to pagan gods. A priestly class continuously received foodstuffs they made sacred in fires; the food thereby *sacrificed* was consumed by the members of the sponsoring association or distributed throughout the city. Special occasions like ceremonies or sports

---

[32] Crossan and Reed, *In Search of Paul*, 303-6.
[33] Howard-Brook and Gwyther, *Unveiling Empire*, 118.

events called for sacrifices that were consumed by everyone present. Crossan and Reed describe a typical first-century feast at the Forum of Corinth, an extensive collection of temples, buildings, and open-air altars:

> Processions of priests and officials marched through the city and wound toward the forum's altars, where, with accompanying pomp, prayer, and libation, beast after beast was slaughtered. The meat was then distributed by key priests . . . first to honored guests and the city's leading citizens, who in turn took it to their neighborhoods or homes to pass it on to their clients. These in turn would preside over a banquet with their families, clients, and slaves. Many others would have barbecued right there in the forum and ate the meat as part of a public meal. The entire ceremony, of course, took place under the watchful eyes of the imperial family, whose statues stood in the forum and its surrounding temples.[34]

The Roman Empire provided peace, stability, and prosperity to its inhabitants, but *Pax Romana* brought a cost: it was created by violence and exploitation, enforced by torture and capital punishment, stitched together by sycophancy and favoritism, and maintained by a strict hierarchy of classes of people separated into male and female, slave and free, citizen and noncitizen, and patron and client.

Contrast the Roman Empire with the kingdom of God that Jesus described and which the churches of Asia Minor emulated. The kingdom of God was extended not by violence, but by word of mouth, and it was freely available to anyone who desired it. Like the Roman Empire, it had expanded rapidly through conquest, but the conquest was by love, not by military force. It organized itself through voluntary associations where members met to share a meal and worship God, but unlike Greco-Roman associations, the Christian associations were open to women as well as men, slave and citizen, Gentile and Jew, rich and poor, and within their assemblies, they were indifferent to status, gender, and race.[35]

Ideally, churches were supported by their membership using everyone's gifts. Their work helping the sick and the poor was out of love, not out of a desire for some earthly reward. Their shared meal, guided by a liturgy and not a wealthy host, was a ritual of mutual thanksgiving and community, not an exercise in power and privilege. The assembly shared their food at an inclusive table where they enjoyed fellowship and their resurrected Lord's forgiving presence; consumption of Rome's food, by contrast, immunized its consumers against exclusion by their patrons and extrusion from the protection of the Roman ruler's military might.

John the author of Revelation, as well as Paul the apostle, frequently compared and contrasted early churches with Roman practices. For example,

---

[34] Crossan and Reed, *In Search of Paul*, 301.

[35] Paul struggled mightily with the insinuation of a division of the wealthy and the poor during shared meals in the Corinth church and firmly repudiated it (1 Cor 11:17-34).

both described God, Jesus Christ, or their angels as clothed and worshiped like a Roman emperor or his emissaries. To some extent, John and Paul are using the stuff of everyday life in Asia Minor to help their readers and listeners understand God's lordship. However, both men were advocates of a kingdom that worked at cross-purposes to Rome's, and both acknowledged the great danger of Roman ways to believers. The kingdom they described was more hopeful, more an expression of *life* than the one offered by Rome, which offered only protection from *death*, and then, only by its threat. It explained why Jews mourning Rome's destruction of Jerusalem found hope in John's churches. It explained why Gentiles were so attracted to Paul's churches, even at the risk of slavery, exile, or death. A member of God's kingdom can't be separated from it, even by death, and in God's kingdom the beasts of Rome are conquered, not by legions but with forgiveness and love.

The angels' harvest

After the frightening visions of the beasts comes a vision of angels with messages announcing the beasts' defeat.

A first wave of angels flies down to mid-heaven, a sign that heaven and earth are in closer communication. One announces "the hour of his judgment has come"; a second announces the defeat of "Babylon the great," the kingdom of violence against which the kingdom of God must battle; and a third announces the doom of "those who worship the beast and its image" (14:7-9). The metaphor is military but the instrument of Babylon's defeat is the word of God: God has *decreed* that justice requires the defeat of the enemies of faith and their acolytes; therefore, the defeat must occur.

Before a second wave of angels descends, John speaks directly to the listeners in our first-century church: "Here is a call for the endurance of the saints, those who keep the commandments of God and hold fast to the faith of Jesus" (14:12). In form this recalls the earlier, equally direct address where John urged nonviolent resistance to the beast from the sea (13:9-10). John's call is confirmed by voices from heaven: "Blessed are the dead who from now on die in the Lord," and, "They will rest from their labors, for their deeds follow them" (14:13).

Introducing the second wave of angels is *one like the Son of Man*, who appears in the clouds wielding a giant sickle. The metaphor now is the harvest of wheat and grapes, staples of Palestinian agriculture. The first angel instructs *one like the Son of Man* to "use your sickle and reap" because "the harvest of the earth is fully ripe" (14:15). The harvest of wheat is a metaphor for salvation, God's protective gathering of the faithful; the passage recalls Isaiah's prophecy in his apocalypse: "On that day the Lord will *thresh* from the channel of the Euphrates to the Wadi of Egypt, and you will be gathered one by one, O people of Israel" (Isa 27:12, emphasis added). Similarly, Jesus used the harvest metaphor in one gospel account of his commissioning of missionaries to bring the good news to the villages of Galilee:

After this the Lord appointed seventy others and sent them on ahead of him in pairs to every town and place where he himself intended to go. He said to them, "The harvest is plentiful, but the laborers are few; therefore ask the Lord of the harvest to send out laborers into his harvest." (Luke 10:1-2)

The second angel in the second group also appears with a sickle, and in turn is instructed by a third angel, "the angel of fire," to "use your sharp sickle and gather the clusters of the vine of the earth, for its grapes are ripe" (Rev 14:18). Here the harvest metaphor focuses on the vineyard, in ancient Hebrew song and prophecy a place for repose under the arbor of God's love; it's described by Isaiah, again from his apocalypse:

On that day:
A pleasant vineyard, sing about it!
    I, the Lord, am its keeper;
    every moment I water it.
I guard it night and day
    so that no one can harm it;
    I have no wrath.
If it gives me thorns and briers,
    I will march to battle against it.
    I will burn it up.
Or else let it cling to me for protection,
    let it make peace with me,
    let it make peace with me. (Isa 27:2-5)

In this passage from Isaiah, God's attack on the vineyard is like the gardener's battle against the thorny weeds that would overwhelm it. God uses fire, a weapon in the ancient gardener's arsenal against weeds, which serendipitously explains the otherwise-mysterious "angel of fire."

The parallel agricultural metaphors of wheat and vineyard in the vision of the second wave of angels recall the parallel metaphors of agricultural tools used in the hopeful prophesy of Isaiah and Micah, the one inscribed on the statue outside the United Nations buildings in New York (see page 65):

They shall beat their swords into plowshares,
    and their spears into pruning hooks;
nation shall not lift up sword against nation,
    neither shall they learn war any more. (Isa 2:4)

Isaiah's farm implement metaphor is oriented toward peace, but when we return to the last angel in the vision of the harvesting angels in John's Revelation, the result of the harvest of the grapes seems to be a catastrophe:

So the angel swung his sickle over the earth and gathered the vintage of the earth, and he threw it into the great winepress of the wrath of God. And the wine press was trodden outside the city, and blood flowed from the wine press, as high as a horse's bridle, for a distance of about two hundred miles. (Rev 14:17-20)

Many modern readers of these passages follow the interpretation of end-times writers and conclude that this passage (indeed, the entire book of Revelation) predicts a bloodbath that ends history. Earlier messages of in-gathering and prosperity are apparently trumped by these metaphors of violence and death. To help us understand the apparent inconsistency, let me array the threefold messages of the two waves of angels and the call-and-response that separates them:

Message	A - First wave of angels	B - John and responding voices	C - Second wave of angels
	Rev 14:6-11	Rev 14:12-13	Rev 14:14-20
1	The hour of judgment has come.	Here is a call for the endurance of the saints, those who keep the commandments of God and hold fast to the faith of Jesus.	Use your sickle and reap [wheat].
2	Fallen is Babylon the great.	Blessed are the dead who from now on die in the Lord.	Use your sharp sickle and gather [grapes].
3	Those who worship the beast . . . will drink the wine of God's wrath.	They will rest from their labors.	Blood flowed from the wine press.

From this matrix, and by paying particularly close attention to the pivotal verse (John's direct address to his audience, "Here is a call for the endurance of the saints"), we learn that these visions ask the listeners of our first-century church to think anew about how the deaths of martyrs, Christians' hopes for justice, and the perseverance of Christians during times of trouble are linked. These visions do not necessarily describe the outcome of a future blood-soaked battle. If the metaphor of harvest is the nurturing one of Isaiah, then only two of the nine messages (A-3 and C-3) involve violence, and only one (C-3) appears to involve an active sort of violence, assuming "blood" is used literally and not symbolically (which is quite a stretch, considering the source). Moreover, the violence is secondary to the judgment that gathers the faithful who have chosen life; the remainder, despite abundant warnings, have chosen death and we should expect a ghastly metaphor for the consequence of their choice. The form of this vision of judgment is certainly apocalyptic, but it does not predict that violence will be directed by God against the enemies of the Christian (and Jewish) faith; instead, the outcome is the inevitable result of the administration of prophetic justice to people whose lives are oriented irredeemably toward injustice, violence, and death.

Having argued that, I must recognize another source for the metaphor in the vision of the second group of angels, the prophet Joel:

Put in the sickle,
    for the harvest is ripe.

Go in, tread,
    for the wine press is full.
The vats overflow,
    for their wickedness is great. (Joel 3:13)

In a parallel irony, a passage that immediately precedes this one in Joel *reverses* the prophecies of Micah and Isaiah about the agricultural implements associated with wheat and grapes:

Beat your plowshares into swords,
    and your pruning hooks into spears." (Joel 3:10)

The vision of the harvesting angels in Revelation certainly reinterprets the prophecies of Joel, Isaiah, and Micah, but we are presented thereby with a conundrum. Is this vision about pacific salvation or violent annihilation? Here, it helps to close the distance that separates us from early Christian beliefs. David Barr recognizes in the *wine press* metaphor some allusions that escape modern readers but would have been obvious to people listening to the reading of the book of Revelation in our first-century church. The harvest of wheat and grapes recalls the bread and wine shared in the Lord's Supper, and "outside the city," where the wine press is trodden, was an expression used by some early Christians to refer to the death of Jesus, who was crucified outside Jerusalem's walls.[36] Furthermore, from a contemporary numerological standpoint the length of the river of blood, in Greek 1600 *stadia*, represents the universality of Jesus' sacrifice on the cross. The square root of 1600 is forty or *ten* times *four; four* symbolizes *the earth* and *ten* symbolizes *totality*. Jesus' blood, manifest in the wine of the Lord's Supper, is available throughout the entire earth.[37]

The listeners in our first-century church, and we, face a choice. Does the *wine press* metaphor in Revelation recall the warmongering metaphor of Joel, or the *ingathering* metaphor of Isaiah? Is it redolent of violent judgment and destruction, or of nurturing salvation and a loving God's victory? Faced with pervasive and overwhelming evil, does a Christian select militant resistance or nonviolent endurance as a strategy? Even if violent resistance might potentially be effective, how consistent is that strategy with the ethical and moral teachings of Jesus? Can violence usher in the kingdom of God on earth? Shall we pick up the sword?

Like the passage about the sheep and the goats that John Kerry and John Hagee interpret so differently, the passage in Revelation about the chorus of angels has radically different meanings to end-times writers on the one hand and to those who put their faith to work consistent with the teachings of Jesus on the other.

Early in my book (on page 19), I repeated a story where Revelation's metaphor of the *wine press* figures in a visit by a group led by end-times

---

[36] Cf. Heb 13:11.
[37] Barr, *Tales of the End*, 130.

writer Tim LaHaye to the supposed site of the ultimate apocalyptic battle near Megiddo in Israel. A member of the group asks a journalist, "Can you imagine this entire valley filled with blood? That would be a 200-mile-long river of blood, four and a half feet deep. We've done the math. That's the blood of as many as two and a half billion people."[38]

The *wine press* metaphor also figured in my quote from the speech of Martin Luther King, Jr., on the steps of the Alabama State Capitol, twenty pages ago. Dr. King did not make cold-blooded calculations about battlefield deaths as he addressed people who themselves had suffered injury and indignity and had known colleagues, even children, who had been murdered because of the color of their skin. He was not demanding that God punish those who had shed innocent blood. He was crying out for patient endurance through nonviolent and loving resistance, quoting the "Battle Hymn of the Republic," a song whose words were written during the American Civil War using the *wine press* metaphor of the books of Joel, Isaiah, and Revelation:

> Mine eyes have seen the glory of the coming of the Lord;
> He is trampling out the vintage where the grapes of wrath are stored;
> He has loosed the fateful lightning of His terrible swift sword;
> His truth is marching on.[39]

The greatest risk in undertaking a study of Revelation is losing the thread of the faith that underlies its visions. That's why John's observation during the angels' harvest must stop us in our tracks: "Here is a call for the endurance of the saints, those who *keep the commandments of God* and hold fast to *the faith of Jesus*" (14:12, emphasis added). As we witness horrible visions with John, many of them motivated by a desire for justice for martyrs who died grisly, humiliating, and lonely deaths, we must remember the content of the faith that underpins this literature: what Jesus of Nazareth taught about *the commandments of God* during his ministry, and what Paul taught about *the faith of Jesus* during his evangelism.

Jesus taught that these are the *commandments of God*:

> "'You shall love the Lord your God with all your heart, and with all your soul, and with all your mind.' . . . 'You shall love your neighbor as yourself.'" (Matt 22:37-39)

Paul taught that this is *the faith of Jesus*:

> Neither death, nor life, nor angels, nor rulers, nor things present, nor things to come, nor powers, nor height, nor depth, nor anything else in all creation, will be able to separate us from the love of God in Christ Jesus our Lord. (Rom 8:38-39)

In Revelation, justice for martyrs is linked to the witness of the faithful

---

[38] "American Rapture," *Vanity Fair*, December 2005.
[39] See note 20.

who keep God's commandments to love and to forgive, and whose love of others is empowered by the faith of Jesus in a God who loves us. Love and faith in concert with God's will and grace will conquer in their apocalyptic battle with the empire of violence, which is doomed to crumble and spectacularly fail. Christians must not choose death or cause it, but they must persevere in the witness of their faith, which is love manifested by sharing and forgiveness. In a passage so oft-repeated that it risks being trite, Paul wrote to the church in Corinth: "And now faith, hope, and love abide, these three; and the greatest of these is love" (1 Cor 13:13).

Armageddon

After the angels' harvest, John sees the doors of heaven open and seven angels appear, each carrying a golden bowl filled with one of seven plagues. In accompaniment, a chorus of "conquerors" sings two songs, first the "Song of Moses" that celebrates the exodus of the Israelites from Egypt (Ex 15:1-18), and a second, which resembles it, the "Song of the Lamb":

> Great and amazing are your deeds,
>   Lord God the Almighty!
> Just and true are your ways,
>   King of the nations!
> Lord, who will not fear
>   and glorify your name?
> For you alone are holy.
>   All nations will come
>   and worship before you,
> for your judgments have been revealed. (Rev 15:3-4)

Recalling the plagues on Egypt that influenced Pharaoh's decision to permit the Israelites to leave Egypt, the first six of the seven plagues poured from the angels' bowls are these:

- On the earth: sores on the people who wear the mark of the beast and worship its image.
- On the sea: it turns to blood, and its creatures die.
- On the rivers: they turn to blood.
- On the sun: it intensifies, and scorches people.
- On the throne of the beast: his power ends, and his supporters howl.
- On the Euphrates River: the great river dries up, opening a pathway to invaders from the east.

Then, from the mouths of the dragon and the two beasts crawl warmongering, frog-like demons who gather armies from "the kings of the whole world" at a place that John says is called, in Hebrew, *Harmageddon* (16:16).

Harmageddon may be a corruption of *har Megiddo*, Hebrew for *Mount of Megiddo*. Megiddo is not a mountain but a plain among mountains in northern Palestine where the coastal road from Egypt joins the roads from Damascus and Tyre. The plain has been the site of important military battles throughout history. In modern times it was here that Ottoman armies were defeated first by Napoleon, in 1799, then by Allenby of England in 1917; in 1947, Israeli forces defeated Arab armies threatening Haifa in an important battle in modern Israel's war for independence.

Our early church listeners would know none of these battles, of course, but they might associate the place with ancient battles. In one, Joshua, inheritor of Moses' leadership, led armies that conquered thirty-one Canaanite cities including Megiddo (Josh 12:21). Canaanite power didn't end; Canaan still controlled strategic cities defended by significant armies on the plains among the Israelite tribes, who primarily occupied the hills. The insidious Canaanite threat, led by the general Sisera, was confronted by the ancient prophet Deborah, who was also a judge (Judg 4:5). Deborah authorized a general, Barak,[40] to call up an army from the Israelite tribes; he was reluctant to lead the fight alone, though, and asked Deborah to join him. She replied: "I will surely go with you; nevertheless, the road on which you are going will not lead to your glory, for the Lord will sell Sisera into the hand of a woman" (Judg 4:9). Her prophecy would be fulfilled in an unexpected way.

Canaanite armies led by their general, Sisera, confronted Deborah's and Barak's army at the Kishon River at the base of the mountains. Barak and Deborah held the heights and charged downhill. A cloudburst caused flash floods, disadvantaging Sisera's chariots. The Israelites slaughtered the entire Canaanite force, and Sisera ran for his life.

The woman who gets the glory for the Canaanites' defeat isn't Deborah, however. The enemy general fled on foot to the tent of a woman named Jael, the wife of an ally, Heber. Jael extended the hospitality that Sisera expects and that she is obligated by custom to provide. After she hides him under a blanket, she gives him some goat's milk, a strong soporific, and he falls asleep. Then, "Jael wife of Heber took a tent peg, and took a hammer in her hand, and went softly to him and drove the peg into his temple, until it went down into the ground" (Judg 4:21-22). Deborah and Barack celebrate the victory by praising God:

> "Lord, when you went out from Seir,
>   when you marched from the region of Edom,
>   the earth trembled,

---

[40] The victorious presidential candidacy of Barack Obama in 2008 sent many end-times believers to their Bibles in search of apocalyptic information about him. One factoid that circulated via the Internet was based on the meaning of his first name in Hebrew, which (like the name of Deborah's general) is *lightning.* End-timers seized on Luke 10:18, which quotes Jesus: "I watched Satan fall from heaven like a flash of lightning." (Actually, Obama's given name in Swahili, the language of his Kenyan father, means *blessed.*) Urban legends about Illinois lottery numbers and zip codes eerily similar to the number 666 corroborated the linguistic leap, and the equation of Barack Obama and the antichrist entered the electronic literature of our times. For an example, see the comments to this online post: www.usnews.com/articles/opinion/2008/10/28/seriously-actress-victoria-jackson-thinks-barack-obama-resembles-the-anti-christ.html

and the heavens poured.
the clouds indeed poured water.
The mountains quaked before the Lord, the One of Sinai,
before the Lord, the God of Israel." (Judg 5:4)

Except as the site of Deborah's and Joshua's ancient battles, there are no other references to a battlefield called *Harmageddon* in the books of the Old Testament. John could have used a prophecy of Joel that speaks of a battle in the "valley of Jehoshaphat," also an otherwise unknown place, to locate the ultimate battle between good and evil; *Jehoshaphat* is a Hebrew word translated *the lord judges,* and a passage that parallels the first refers to the "valley of decision," so Joel's prophecy would have enriched John's meaning (Joel 3:12, 14). Moreover, Joel's prophecy likens judgment on the day of the Lord to a *wine press,* the closing metaphor of the chorus of angels that precedes this battle passage in Revelation.

A reader is tempted to link John's visions about the ultimate battle between God and evil with the prophecies of Joel, but John has chosen a different location for the battle. Perhaps for John, the battle is not in the *valley of decision* because the decision has been made: victory, like Deborah's, is assured by God who strides across the earth accompanied by rumbling earthquakes and pouring waters and assisted by faithful collaborators who are cunning and brave (and women!).

The whore of Babylon

When the seventh angel pours the seventh bowl into the air, a voice from heaven thunders, "It is done!" (Rev 16:17). John sees an unprecedented earthquake that splits "the great city" (16:19), presumably Jerusalem, and destroys the other cities of the world. Huge hailstones crush people "as they cursed God" (16:21). The symbol of demonic power suddenly shifts away from the dragon and the beasts to another symbol used throughout the Old Testament for the enemies of God: Babylon, "'mother of whores and of earth's abominations'" (17:5).

Personifying Babylon in John's vision is a woman "clothed in purple and scarlet and adorned with gold and jewels and pearls," riding a "scarlet beast" that has seven heads and ten horns—the first beast, the beast from the sea (Rev 13:1). The woman holds a "golden cup full of abominations and the impurities of her fornication." She's "drunk with the blood of the saints and the blood of the witnesses to Jesus" (17:3-6).

Our early church audience would readily identify the caricature: the purple and scarlet robe, the gems and pearls, and the gold cup were blandishments of imperial aristocracy and power. An angel interprets the symbolism to John: the seven heads of the beast she rides "'are seven mountains . . . ; also, they are seven kings'" (17:9). The "seven mountains" refer to the seven hills of Rome, and the "seven kings" refer to the dynasty of Augustus, which still reigned at the time John wrote the book of Revelation. However, the number of mountains and kings—seven—symbolizes the hideous *completeness* of the vision. Our first-century listeners understand that the *whore of Babylon* is not just the Roman Empire, but all empires that claim totalitarian power by violence.

The angel tells John that the ten horns on the beast ridden by the *whore of Babylon* are ten kings who "have not yet received a kingdom, but they are to receive authority as kings for one hour, together with the beast. These are united in yielding their power and authority to the beast" who will make war with the Lamb (17:12-13). Because the woman "is the great city that rules over the kings of the earth, . . . the ten kings will devour her flesh and burn her up with fire" (17:16).

End-times writers are fascinated by how these passages might be applied to our own troubled times. They contain enticing details: the seven, or eight, or ten kings may represent the nations of the European Union, and the sequence of events involving the kings' abdication of power to the beast may predict mysterious summit meetings in Europe. These are clues that dispensationalist sifters of the Bible use to suggest that their end-times scenarios may be gaining traction in current events.

Another part of the vision of the *whore of Babylon* that fascinates some end-times writers is the location of the real-world Babylon in present-day Iraq.[41] It's a small city now; what remains of the great ancient city built of mud bricks is disintegrating. Saddam Hussein, the late dictator of Iraq, had a passing interest in restoring Babylon to its former glory and built a palace there for himself, not far from buildings and gates he ordered rebuilt in the ancient style. Events, of course, have since overtaken him.

To our early church listeners, *Babylon* communicated something entirely different but no less powerful. *Babylon* is used often in the Old Testament as a symbol of the threat of an evil, pagan empire whose power can't be resisted without God's help. In Genesis, Babylon is one of the first cities established following the Flood. However, the failure of the Tower of Babel, the summit of Babylon's cosmopolitanism, came to represent the hubris of pursuing salvation through civil engineering—which will ring true for Egypt and its pyramids, Rome and its temples, Nazi Germany and its stadiums, and Saddam and his palaces.

Babylon appears later in Genesis when it allies with other nations to subjugate the lands promised by God to Abraham. King Melchizedek of Salem (later Jerusalem) accepts Abraham's God and leaves the alliance; he's a *righteous king*, the translation of the two Hebrew words in his name, and the two men celebrate their new alliance with bread and wine. In the ancient story of Melchizedek, it is through separation from Babylon that a righteous kingdom is established.

---

[41] For example, Dyer, *The Rise of Babylon*, written before Hussein was defeated by invading American forces and executed by the new government.

In the eighth century BCE, Isaiah invoked God's wrath against Israel's neighbors, among them Babylon, whom the Lord addresses:

I will punish the world for its evil,
    and the wicked for their iniquity.
I will put an end to the pride of the arrogant,
    and lay low the insolence of tyrants. (Isa 13:11)

It was, of course, Babylon under King Nebuchadnezzar in the sixth century BCE that destroyed Jerusalem and the first temple and took Judah's leadership into exile, a watershed event in ancient Israel's history.

Babylon is not too different a symbol from the beast, or from the dragon, or for that matter, from Rome. These succeeding representations of the beast remind us of how the author of the book of Daniel used repetition in his apocalyptic visions. By using a succession of symbols for the powers of evil, biblical allusions multiply and enrich one another. Hearing these ancient and historical descriptions of oppression and empire, listeners in our first-century church understand that Rome is only the current manifestation of evil's domain.

As our early church listeners recognize Rome in its self-important pomp and drunken decadence as the target of John's lampoon, the whore of Babylon, they ruefully laugh; Rome wouldn't appreciate the comparison. Our first-century church has been given a memorable image of the power of empire to seduce, corrupt, and destroy—the causes of the assimilation, complacency, and persecution that threaten the seven churches to whom John writes.

Chapter 23
ALLELUIA!

With the defeat of Babylon, the choruses in heaven explode in celebration:

> Hallelujah!
> Salvation and glory and power to our God,
>   for his judgments are true and just. (Rev 19:1-2)

Modern Christians know this song—it's the "Alleluia." In Hebrew, the word means *praise the Lord*; as often as it's used in church or religious music today, it occurs only once in the New Testament, in this passage. Here is yet another example of the foundational importance of the book of Revelation in Christian worship.

After the Alleluia, a voice from the throne responds:

> Praise our God,
>   all you his servants,
> and all who fear him,
>   small and great. (19:5)

Modern Christians know a similar song—the "Doxology."

John is persuading his listeners that when Christians worship on earth, they join the unending worship of God by all the living creatures, elders, angels, and saints in heaven. Lampstands, an altar, burning incense, and a tabernacle had been borrowed from synagogue settings; so were many prayers, hymns, and responsive readings. Spontaneous calls from the congregation during worship, such as "Look! He is coming with the clouds!" and "Honor, glory, and blessing to the Lamb!" (5:12), became hymns.[42] As the book of Revelation is read (and sometimes sung), our early-church listeners recognize that the

---

[42] Dunn, *Unity and Diversity in the New Testament*, 145.

rituals of their church recreate the worship of God and the Lamb in heaven. In a larger sense, our listeners recognized that their worship service celebrates the same victory of God over evil that they witness in John's visions. In both worship and book, the New Jerusalem descends from heaven to earth and the kingdom of God comes near.[43]

By using the forms of worship of our first-century church in his visions of celebrations in heaven, John is persuading his listeners that when Christians worship on earth, they join the unending worship of God by the living creatures, elders, angels, saints, in heaven. Indeed, this is a teaching in the *Catechism of the Catholic Church*:

> In the earthly liturgy we share in a foretaste of that heavenly liturgy which is celebrated in the Holy City of Jerusalem toward which we journey as pilgrims, where Christ is sitting at the right hand of God, Minister of the sanctuary and of the true tabernacle. With all the warriors of the heavenly army we sing a hymn of glory to the Lord; venerating the memory of the saints, we hope for some part and fellowship with them; we eagerly await the Savior, our Lord Jesus Christ, until he, our life, shall appear and we too will appear with him in glory.[44]

Woven through the liturgical elements of Revelation are intensifying visions of the approaching conflict between God and God's enemies. By hearing and imagining John's visions, our early church listeners are also seeing and feeling (and with John's olfactory visions of incense, *smelling*) how their simple ceremonies of praise and fellowship are connected to the eternal, timeless celebration in heaven of God's victory over evil. In John's visions of conflict, our first-century congregation also witnesses how that victory is manifest in the struggle against injustice in the past, against empire in the present, and against evil's myriad manifestations in the future.

Revelation affirmed to early Christians that when they participated in liturgy, they participated in God's victory over evil as "conquerors." As Revelation closes and judgment concludes history, God's kingdom descends to earth, the nations are invited to the banquet table, and the Mass ends.

†

After the chorus of "Hallelujah!" an angel invites John to the "marriage supper of the Lamb" (19:9). Our first-century gathering expects John to describe the heavenly counterpart of their table fellowship, but instead of a celebrative banquet, John envisions a conflict where God defeats the dragon

---

[43] Two analyses of the influence of the book of Revelation on the Catholic Mass are Hahn, *The Lamb's Supper*, 118-21, and John Salza, "The Book of Revelation and the Holy Mass," online at: www.scripturecatholic.com/the_eucharist.html#eucharist—IIF.

[44] Vatican Archive, "Catechism of the Catholic Church," paragraph 1090. Online at www.vatican.va/archive/catechism/p2s1c1a1.htm

and the beasts. Members of our first-century church are provided with a vivid image of God's victory over evil that comes when they join together for the simple fellowship of their shared meal.

Leading an army of saints on white horses, a rider called "King of kings and Lord of lords," "Faithful and True," and "The Word of God" confronts the beast and his armies (19:11, 13, 16). From the mouth of the rider "comes a sharp sword with which to strike down the nations, and he will rule them with a rod of iron; he will tread the wine press of the fury of the wrath of God the Almighty" (19:15). The figure on the white horse is the judgmental aspect of *the Lord*, just as the Lamb represents the sacrificial aspect of *the Lord* and is not simply a symbol for Jesus Christ. That he has a sword in his mouth was introduced early in the book (at verse 1:16); it's a metaphor for the word of God, God's commandments and the good news. The iron rod of his rule recalls another earlier verse in the vision of the woman, the child, and the dragon (at 12:5): it is a reference to the rider's aspect as the expected Davidic king. The metaphor of the *wine press* is recalled from the vision of the angelic harvest (14:20); it represents the ingathering of the saints who have chosen life and the extrusion of those who have chosen death by collaborating with evil.

Mocking the invitations sent by a Roman patron to his clients for dinner at an association dedicated to a pagan god, an angel invites the birds of the world to feast on the corpses of the beast's armies at "the great supper of God" (19:17), itself an ironic twist of the "Lamb's Supper." The carrion-birds' feast recalls Ezekiel's prophecy about the unthinkably unclean demise of the corpses of Gog's armies, who are consumed by wild animals and birds of prey (Ezek 39:17-20). The two beasts are thrown into "the lake of fire that burns with sulfur" (19:20); the dragon is seized by an angel and thrown into a pit.

Here begins a curious sequence of events involving thrones, resurrections, and a thousand years (20:1-15). Thrones appear and are occupied by people empowered to judge, but no one is judged. Martyrs to the beasts' repression come to life and will reign "with Christ" for a thousand years, but others who have died, don't reign with Christ yet—they will come to life when the thousand years end. Then, the dragon, we're warned, will be let out of the pit "for a little while"; he'll join forces with Gog of Magog, the archenemy in Ezekiel, but will be defeated again and cast eternally into the lake of fire with the beasts. Finally, a general resurrection will occur, everyone will be judged, and those whose names aren't found in the "book of life" will be consigned to the lake of fire with the beasts and the dragon.

D. S. Russell finds the notion of a thousand-year reign unusual among other Jewish apocalypses of the time and supposes that it originates in a version of the second book of Enoch, a Jewish apocalypse written about the same time as the book of Revelation; in 2 Enoch, the span of human history is equated with the week of creation, and six thousand years of history are followed by a seventh, Sabbatical millennium, a thousand years of God's reign.[45] That there are two resurrections, that Satan must be defeated twice, and that there will be a penultimate, then an ultimate battle are novel ideas not found elsewhere in the Bible or in other Jewish or Christian apocalyptic literature.

The millennial passages in the book of Revelation reflect the crosscurrents of apocalyptic speculation in John's times. Perhaps they are a nod toward Christians who clung to Jewish beliefs in a messianic kingdom on earth that follows a day of the Lord. Perhaps the millennial passages were written to address the special issue of justice for martyrs, who these passages promise will be resurrected for the millennium while others are not, reflecting the kind of preferential treatment Paul gives the dead in his letters to the Thessalonians about the general resurrection at the end of time. Or perhaps it's a compromise apocalypse that appeases messianic believers in Jesus' return as an earthly theocratic ruler while preserving the finality of the fulfillment of time.

From the millennial passages of Revelation, dispensationalist writers draw their conviction that the end times culminate in a judicial decision of eternal damnation for those of us who haven't acknowledged to an evangelist that Jesus is our personal savior. But even casual readers of the book of Revelation will know that the losers in the ultimate conflict are not those who changed the channel at the "ask"; the losers are people who align themselves with the values of whatever manifestation of the beast presently confronts them, who are seduced by the beast with promises of power and wealth and purity while oppressing the poor, abandoning justice, and seeking war. Consistent with the prophets of the Old Testament and the gospels of the New, the book of Revelation assures *all* people that they are free to reject the messengers of death and to join the supper of the Lamb.

Biblical doom is not necessarily inevitable, personal, or bodily. It was invoked in prophetic times to warn Israel against injustice, and it was revealed in apocalyptic times to warn Christians against collaboration with evil. Throughout the Old and New Testaments, abandoning justice and righteousness is the prophetic choice of death; apocalyptic notions of the consequences of the choice of death are, not unexpectedly, *visions* of death, often ghastly. In Old Testament times, the choice of death had material consequences, in particular, the destruction of the first temple and Judah's exile to Babylon. In New Testament times, the result of the choice of death is spiritual: separation from the kingdom of God. That is the judgment of which John's visions warn.

✝

<hr/>

[45] Russell, *The Method and Message of Jewish Apocalyptic*, 293.

The Lord's victory transforms the world. John sees

"a new heaven and a new earth; for the first heaven and the first earth had passed away, and the sea was no more. And I saw the holy city, the new Jerusalem, coming down out of heaven from God, prepared as a bride adorned for her husband." (Rev 21:1-2)

A loud voice from heaven announces what the new heaven and the new earth signify:

"See, the home of God is among mortals.
He will dwell with them;
they will be his peoples,
and God himself will be with them;
he will wipe every tear from their eyes.
Death will be no more;
mourning and crying and pain will be no more,
for the first things have passed away." (Rev 21:3-4)

Heaven is no longer separated from the earth. People are not lifted into heaven, but God makes a home among them on earth. The nations no longer struggle on the earth's surface absent God's presence. Suffering and death are ended, and those who have suffered are comforted. This is the very essence of apocalyptic hope; it is what is celebrated at the wedding banquet, the shared supper of our first-century church, and the masses and holy communions of our churches today.

An angel takes John on a tour of the new Jerusalem. The city has twelve gates, one for each of the twelve tribes of Israel, each a giant pearl. On the wall's foundations are inscribed the names of the twelve apostles of the Lamb. The city's walls are jasper, the buildings of the city, gold. The angel has a measuring stick, recalling the opening of Ezekiel's prophetic vision of the perfect temple at the end of time (Ezek 40-48). Jerusalem is huge, its breadth the same as its length but equal also to its height, a cube 1500 miles on each side encompassing the world known in those times.

The New Jerusalem lacks a physical temple because worship is decentralized: "I saw no temple in the city, for its temple is the Lord God the Almighty and the Lamb" (21:22). The city requires no lighting: "the glory of God is its light, and its lamp is the Lamb" (Rev 21:23). Without night, the city's gates may always be open and the nations "will walk by its light, and the kings of the earth will bring their glory into it" (21:24). While preceding visions may give the impression that none but the righteous survive the final conflict, the New Jerusalem is available to everyone who chooses life, and at any time.

The angel shows John the "river of the water of life" flowing down the street from the throne of the Lord. Along the river grow rows of the "tree of life," their fruits ripening each month of the year, their leaves "for the healing of the nations" (22:1-2). The river fulfills the prophecy of Ezekiel about a river that will flow from the end-times temple (Ezek 47:1-2) and the prophecy of

Zechariah about a perennial stream that flows east and west (Zech 14:8). It also recalls a saying of Jesus only found in the gospel of John, who says Jesus exclaimed it in the temple at the close of the Festival of Booths: "Let anyone who is thirsty come to me, and let the one who believes in me drink. As the scripture has said, 'Out of the believer's heart shall flow rivers of the living water'" (John 7:38).[46]

✝

These days we take spectacle for granted. Eighty dollars will admit you to a show where a helicopter descends from the ceiling awash in light, singers wailing, music furious. You will emerge feeling bathed in emotion by what you've seen and heard.

The first century of the Christian Era, when Revelation was written, had spectacles too. They were spectacles of empire. An important man from Rome in a long white robe, his arm and head decorated with jewel-encrusted gold, would ride a thundering chariot accompanied by scarlet-clad warriors, their hob-nailed boots a staccato against pavement stones laid by slaves. With them marched musicians, horns blowing and drums pounding and cymbals crashing, all echoing off the walls of temples dedicated to hundreds of gods, a god for every purpose and some of them inclined to nasty tricks. The column would pass the elaborate mausoleums of dead aristocrats outside the city, then enter through a gate celebrating some great military victory. The column reached its destination at the city's temple complex, where priests roasted the meat of animals sacrificed to the gods, the smoke and aromas flowing down streets and up into the air. The huge quantity of meat was consumed by the powerful lord from Rome, then by his hosts the patrons of the city, then by their fawning clients in the associations. Eventually, as the fires burned low and the exalted company found their way home often drunk and debauched, what was left of the meat was distributed to the poor. Thus, *Pax Romana*, the peace brought by the swords of the Roman legions, was celebrated.

Christians were reluctant to eat the meat sacrificed to Roman gods. They belonged to another empire, the kingdom of God. Their supper was chiefly bread, the stuff of hospitality. They shared the bread with one another, rich and poor, male and female, sinners and saved. They washed the bread down with some wine, which symbolized to them the in-gathering of all God's creatures in the fulfillment of time. The dinner celebrated their Lord, a poor rural Jew who entered Jerusalem on a donkey and treated everyone, especially the poor and the despised, as God's precious children. Together, Christians then celebrated

---

[46] No Old Testament passage is precisely the one Jesus quotes. However, in form the quote inverts Zechariah's prophecy at 14:8. A reading of Zechariah 14 is part of the celebration of the Festival of Booths (see p. 132); if the two passages are related, an interesting equivalency is created: the believer's heart is the New Jerusalem.

the peace brought by the word of God and Jesus' sacrifice.

From time to time a Roman might confront a Christian. Why don't you participate in our sacrifices? Do you despise the peace and prosperity we celebrate? The Romans had killed Antipas of the church in Pergamum; it could happen to any Christian, or many Christians, at any time.

Where is our Lord? When will we have the safety and justice that God's kingdom will provide? *How long*?

Come to our church. Listen to the letter we have received from John. Imagine with us the visions that he has seen and heard. In our worship, sing the songs sung in heaven and experience God's victory over evil. Share our supper, which celebrates that victory. Help us build up one another and appreciate one another's gifts. Glimpse God's perfect place, his perfect time, where there is no darkness, no hunger, no sickness, no tears, no death. There is no evil, because it has been defeated by God's love for us.

Imagine that place and time when everyone, even people who have died, are together again sharing a supper fit for a wedding, a banquet where everyone in the world is welcome to come in peace. Witness the repudiation of every oppressivor, the empires of history, the empires of the future, and the empire now. Imagine a new Jerusalem descending from heaven, awash in light, our music soaring as heaven's voices join ours.

Become one of us.

Forgive one another, and share.

Praise the Lord!

Endure patiently.

The kingdom is coming.

Part Five

WHEN TIME ENDS

And the angel which I saw stand upon the sea and upon the earth lifted up his hand to heaven, and sware by him that liveth for ever and ever, who created heaven, and the things that therein are, and the earth, and the things that therein are, and the sea, and the things which are therein, that there should be time no longer.

—Revelation 10:5-6 KJV

Chapter 24
APOCALYPSE AND CATASTROPHE

Olivier Messiaen was a twentieth-century French composer whose interests ranged from Catholic mysticism to the songs of birds. He was drafted into the French army in 1939 when Germany invaded France, and the next summer he was captured and interned inside Germany. The Nazi victory over France was unexpectedly swift; German camps were unprepared for the number of prisoners they received, and they were crowded and poorly equipped. Winters during the war were unusually bitter. Messiaen and his fellow prisoners were isolated in primitive conditions while the mechanized butchery of twentieth-century warfare clanged and exploded around them.

Messiaen was nevertheless driven to compose. Learning that several accomplished musicians were interned with him and that a friendly German guard would get them instruments and a place to practice, he wrote a score based on the epigraph that opened this part of my book and they began rehearsals. Messiaen recollects:

> Conceived and composed during my captivity, the Quartet for the End of Time was premiered in Stalag VIIIA, on 15 January 1941. It took place in Gorlitz, in Silesia, in a dreadful cold. Stalag was buried in snow. We were 30,000 prisoners. The four musicians played on broken instruments: Etienne Pasquier's cello had only 3 [of 4] strings; the keys of my upright piano remained lowered when depressed. . . . It's on this piano, with my three fellow musicians, dressed in the oddest way . . . completely tattered, and wooden clogs large enough for the blood to circulate despite the snow underfoot . . . that I played my *Quartet for the End of Time*, before an audience of 5,000 people. . . . Never before have I been listened to with such attention and understanding.[1]

---

[1] Rischin, *For the End of Time*, 5.

The music was modernist, its melodies hidden, and its tonalities strange. Cellist Pasquier remembered:

> These people, who had never before heard such music, remained *silent.* These people, who were completely musically ignorant, sensed that this was something exceptional. They sat perfectly still, in awe. Not one person stirred. No doubt, these people reassumed their original personalities afterward, but there they were subject to a miracle: the miracle of the performance of this music.[2]

Separated from nation, village, and family, living hand-to-mouth as world war and holocaust swirled around them, the prisoners listened in silence to Messiaen's conjuring of the music of the end of time.

✝

The apocalyptic literature of the Bible was forged during three catastrophes that ancient Israel experienced in her history. One catastrophe was the enslavement and exile of Judah in the sixth century BCE, which gave us the prophetic conceptions of *the day of the Lord* and the archetype of the evil empire, *Babylon.* A second was the murderous repression of Judaism by Antiochus IV Epiphanes in the second century BCE that inspired the archetypes of *the beast* and *a son of man* in the book of Daniel. The third was the destruction of Jerusalem by the Roman Empire in the first century CE, which prompted Revelation's paradoxically hopeful visions of the defeat of the misshapen, violent, and debauched empires of death and the worldwide victory of God's word.

These catastrophes winnowed faith; they were the great wine presses of prophetic and apocalyptic metaphor that created competing vintages of beliefs that sustained Jews and Christians in the first century CE. One of these vintages, characterized by Jesus of Nazareth as "new wine" (Matt 9:17), reinterpreted prophecies about the day of the Lord and apocalypses about a cosmic battle between God and evil to proclaim the arrival, *now* and *on earth,* of the kingdom of God. God's present reign was revealed through Jesus' ministry of healing, sharing, and peacemaking among the poor and the despised who suffered most under the violence and injustice of the imperial system.

At the close of the book of Revelation when the defeat of evil is celebrated, John sees the New Jerusalem descending from heaven to earth: "And I saw the holy city, the new Jerusalem, *coming down* out of heaven from God" (Rev 21:2, emphasis added; cf. 21:10). To John, like Paul and the author of the gospel of Matthew, the perfect place in the perfect time is a work in progress, coming but not fully here, *already* but *not yet.*

The New Testament is clear about when time is fulfilled. Just as "the Lord,

---

[2] Ibid., 69, emphasis original.

God, is and was and is to come" (Rev 1:8), the apocalypse has happened, will happen, and is happening now. Today, as ever, apocalypse—*revelation*—occurs when people resist injustice, work for peace, heal the sick, visit prisoners, comfort the despised, and feed, clothe, and house the poor despite every indication that these efforts might not amount to much in a world dominated by injustice, violence, and grief. Our biblical heritage urges us to choose life despite the array of powerful forces that defend violence and poverty. Apocalyptic hope sustains people who are willing to patiently endure in the quiet struggle of mercy and forgiveness against the powers of hate and force, because the powers of evil are defeated.

This is counterintuitive, for we have been mired for centuries in theologies and doctrines that describe a reckoning that is postponed to the future and a salvation that transports a person to heaven to escape the trouble when it comes. Many early Christians similarly expressed their disappointments over Jesus' failure to return and fully implement the kingdom of God. Perhaps we've misunderstood. The author of our beliefs, Jesus of Nazareth, and his most eloquent interpreters in the New Testament speak of a choice for life made daily and of a kingdom of God that is here on earth. It has been this way for thousands of years, it is this way now, and it will be this way until time is fulfilled.

Recognizing the presence of God's kingdom and awaiting its fulfillment, Christians sustain their hope through simple but important daily practices. These practices are inarguably apocalyptic because they *reveal* God's present reign on earth, which is otherwise veiled. This part will identify the biblical basis of two: the Lord's Prayer, when a Christian asks that the kingdom of God come for everyone soon, and table fellowship, where hospitality and sharing reveal the kingdom's practical fundamentals. But first we must confront the apocalyptic belief that lies behind both: the hope for a general resurrection, where the final enemy, death, is defeated.

Chapter 25
RESURRECTION

While the idea of a transformed world, *utopia*, was familiar in Greco-Roman thought, the Jewish belief in the resurrection of the dead as the instrument of that transformation was alien. Romans took resurrection literally—dead bodies walking among us—and were aghast. Greek philosophy considered the soul immortal and the body a shell happily discarded at death. But *bodily* resurrection was difficult to accept. Even among the many first-century Jews who accepted bodily resurrection, the gospel of John reported that Jesus' resurrection of his dear friend, Lazarus, was astonishing and controversial (John 11:45-6).

One source of resurrection belief among first-century Jews was the catastrophic suppression of Judaism by Antiochus IV Epiphanes, who installed the "abomination that desolates" in the second temple and tortured and killed Jews who refused to recant their Judaism. Justice demanded that these martyrs, robbed untimely of their lives, live again (Dan 12:2). The promise of eventual justice through resurrection often drove a martyr's courage; a history of Epiphanes' repression and the Jewish resistance tells the response of one of seven brothers tortured to death for refusing to eat roasted swine: "And when he was at his last breath, he said [to his torturer], 'You accursed wretch, you dismiss us from this present life, but the King of the universe will raise us up to an everlasting renewal of life, because we have died for his laws'" (2 Macc 7:9).

That divine justice required making whole the broken lives of martyrs was one source of resurrection belief, but another source was the conviction that the perfection of the world at the end of time required a general resurrection of *all* the faithful who had died. Prophetic hope for the transformation of Israel, and then apocalyptic hope for the transformation of the world to a place of peace, justice, and prosperity, required a world inhabited by people transformed by God's spirit. Crossan and Reed write this about Paul's resurrection beliefs:

The general bodily resurrection was, first of all, about the justice of God amid the goodness of creation here below upon a transformed earth, and second, within that, it was about the martyrs who had died for justice and from injustice with their bodies tortured, brutalized, and murdered. Resurrection was not just about us and survival, but about God and this earth. It was not about the heavenly evacuation, but the earthly transfiguration of this bodily world. The soul's immortality . . . did not restore a world disfigured by human evil, injustice, and violence. For the Jewish and Pharisaic Paul, divine justice was necessarily about transfigured bodies upon a transfigured earth.[3]

Belief in resurrection was advanced, interestingly, by Pharisees, with whom Jesus often argued. Sadducees, the conservative party allied with the temple cult, did not accept resurrection and in one gospel story the Sadducees become a foil for a discourse on resurrection by Jesus. Hoping to confound the upstart prophet, some Sadducees ask Jesus about the post-resurrection marital status of a hypothetical widow. Her husband having died, consistent with the Law she is married by one of the late husband's brothers, and when he dies, by another, for a total of seven brother-husbands in succession. Which of the men will be her husband after the general resurrection of the dead? Jesus uses the question to reframe the concept of resurrection:

> Jesus said to them, "Those who belong to this age marry and are given in marriage; but those who are considered worthy of a place in that age and in the resurrection from the dead neither marry nor are given in marriage. Indeed they cannot die anymore, because they are like angels and are children of God, being children of the resurrection. . . . He is God not of the dead, but of the living; for *to him all of them are alive.*" (Luke 20:34-38, emphasis added)

"To him all *are alive.*" Note the inclusiveness of "alive," but also the use of the present tense. Again we are confronted by the elusiveness of God's time. While his contemporaries hoped for future messianic justice signaled by the general resurrection of the dead on a future *day of the Lord*, Jesus observed a transcendent and perfect time that encompasses the living and the dead, and is present. The reunion of the dead and the living involves bodies made whole, on earth. In Jesus' times, people believed that the perfect place, utopia, and the perfect time, eschaton, were kerpt from them by the barriers of worldly chaos and unfulfilled time. Jesus instead encouraged hope that God's ongoing transformation of the earth brings heavenly perfection to earth now, and that people could collaborate in that transformation now through praise, forgiveness, and sharing.

✝

The story of the resurrection of Lazarus, a friend of Jesus who lived with his sisters in Bethany, near Jerusalem, is pivotal in the gospel of John and opens

---

[3] Crossan and Reed, *In Search of Paul*, 344-5.

its final act. To establish the story's homely setting, allow me to introduce Lazarus's sisters, Mary and Martha, who appear in a story told in another gospel and set earlier in Jesus' ministry:

> Now as they went on their way, he entered a certain village, where a woman named Martha welcomed him into her home. She had a sister named Mary, who sat at the Lord's feet and listened to what he was saying. But Martha was distracted by her many tasks; so she came to him and asked, "Lord, do you not care that my sister has left me to do all the work by myself? Tell her then to help me." But the Lord answered her, "Martha, Martha, you are worried and distracted by many things; there is need of only one thing. Mary has chosen the better part, which will not be taken away from her." (Luke 10:38-42)

This passage is often interpreted as an allegory about people in the church who are interested in worship on the one hand and people who are doing the practical work necessary to keep a church going on the other. But we all know couples who live together and bicker about chores; besides its ecclesiastical point, this story reminds us that Jesus lived among ordinary people leading mundane lives.

On a day when the controversy over Jesus is swirling in Jerusalem and Jesus has gone into hiding across the Jordan River to let things cool off, the two sisters send word to him that their brother Lazarus is dying. Jesus arrives at their home in Bethany, but it is now four days after Lazarus's death and his body has been wrapped in burial clothes and entombed. Mary and Martha are providing hospitality to mourners; Martha, the practical one, welcomes Jesus and this conversation ensues:

> Jesus said to her, "Your brother will rise again." Martha said to him, "I know that he will rise again in the resurrection on the last day." Jesus said to her, "I am the resurrection and the life. Those who believe in me, even though they die, will live, and everyone who lives and believes in me will never die. Do you believe this?" (John 11:23-26)

Martha, who needs to get back to work in the kitchen, takes Jesus to her sister Mary, who not unexpectedly is incapacitated by grief. Observing Mary's bereavement, Jesus is angry, then sad, and then angry again, displaying a range of emotions common among people suffering loss:

> When Jesus saw her weeping, and the Jews who came with her also weeping, he was greatly disturbed in spirit and deeply moved. He said, "Where have you laid him?" They said to him, "Lord, come and see." Jesus began to weep. So the Jews said, "See how he loved him!" . . .
> Then Jesus, again greatly disturbed, came to the tomb. It was a cave, and a stone was lying against it. Jesus said, "Take away the stone." . . . He cried with a loud voice, "Lazarus, come out!" The dead man came out, his hands and feet bound with strips of cloth, and his face wrapped in a cloth. Jesus said to them, "Unbind him, and let him go." (John 11:33-44)

Resurrections were signs of the end-times, and Lazarus' resurrection was certainly viewed by the people who witnessed it ("Jews") as a sign that the end-times were near. Lazarus' resurrection occurs just before Passover, when Roman troops reinforced their garrison next to the temple to discourage trouble-makers among the hundreds of thousands of pilgrims who temporarily swelled the population. It creates a crisis for the Sandhedrin, the council of elders who oversaw Jewish affairs and were accountable to the Roman procurator for civil peace; the council worries that the Romans would view what Jesus was doing as an incitement to insurrection, and to forestall a typically brutal Roman response the chief priest Caiaphas begins the process that will cause the Roman authorities, who had the sole power for execution, to end his life.

Jesus and his followers temporarily leave the Jerusalem area as the plot thickens, but as Passover grows nearer they return. They stop to visit Mary, Martha, and the risen Lazarus in Bethany on the way back. During the visit Mary, the dreamy sister, anoints Jesus with perfume, recalling *messiah*, the *anointed one*. Jesus sits down to dinner with his three dear friends (John 12:1-8).

Let us imagine the supper that Jesus, Mary, Martha, Lazarus, and Jesus' disciples are having. As with the many other suppers enjoyed by Jesus in the gospels, there is conversation, celebration, laughter, and stories. Not just food is shared, but also the joy of being alive and together. And beyond the simple goodness of table fellowship, Jesus will *say* that the sharing is a good thing, a sign of God's reign.

This meal is shared by a friend who will be executed, a beloved brother and friend who not long ago died, and two women who love them both. It bridges the past, the present, and the future. Using the mundane manners of sharing food at a table, the friends pass plates of bread and saucers of olive oil to dip it in. They pour wine for one another, drink it, and pour more. The physical activity of sharing food is punctuated by conversations that recall their pasts together and confront the uncertainties of the immediate future. It will soon be Passover and all are devout Jews, so the recollection of God's grace during the exodus from Egypt suffuses the conversation.

As often happens in conversations among good friends in difficult times, the conversation has long silences. During the silences they think: we are suspended here before God and between two appalling deaths. One death, of Lazarus, a good man dead from disease but now resurrected, demonstrates presently the triumph of God's compassion and justice. The other death, of Jesus, then unjustly killed by crucifixion but who will be resurrected, will assure people that they are loved by God despite the power of evil and death.

Silence is a time when God comes close. When conversation pauses around the dinner table at Mary and Martha's home, a sacred place and time is created. The veil lifts. One resurrection has occurred and another will soon. Around a table of bread and wine, friends are reunited with God and one another and God's love for us becomes real; around the table, God's reign is revealed.

Chapter 26
TABLE FELLOWSHIP

Suppers, dinners, banquets, and feasts occur throughout the narrative accounts of Jesus' life. One—the Last Supper—is emblematic.

The Last Supper marks the conclusion of Jesus' teaching ministry, and it's recounted in each of the four gospels.[4] In those accounts, Jesus gathers his disciples to share a banquet. The occasion is Passover, a solemn Jewish festival commemorating God's liberation of the Israelites from slavery in Egypt. Unlike traditional celebrations of Passover, however, Jesus and his disciples don't celebrate it with their families; they take it with one another, in the "upper room" of the home of someone they don't know, a wilderness in the city.

The earliest account of the Last Supper is Paul's in his first letter to the church in Corinth, written about two decades after Jesus' death:

> For I received from the Lord what I also handed on to you, that the Lord Jesus on the night when he was betrayed took a loaf of bread, and when he had given thanks, he broke it and said, "This is my body that is for you. Do this in remembrance of me." In the same way he took the cup also, *after supper*, saying, "This cup is the new covenant in my blood. Do this, as often as you drink it, in remembrance of me." For as often as you eat this bread and drink the cup, you proclaim the Lord's death until he comes. (1 Cor 11:23-26, emphasis added)

The accounts of the Last Supper in the gospels of Matthew, Mark, and Luke are almost identical and agree that the sacrament took place during table

---

[4] Matthew 26:17-30; Mark 14:12-26; Luke 22:7-24; John 13:1-17:26. John's account of the Last Supper is very different from the others'; its sacrament is the washing of feet, not the sharing of wine and bread. Also, the supper in John is set on the evening before the Passover meal, while the other gospels set it on the evening of Passover. Still, the gospel of John refers to an existing sacramental practice when it earlier reports Jesus saying, "Those who eat my flesh and drink my blood abide in me, and I in them" (John 6:56).

fellowship:

> *While they were eating*, [Jesus] took a loaf of bread, and after blessing it
> he broke it, gave it to them and said, "Take; this is my body." Then he took a
> cup, and all of them drank from it. He said to them, "This is my blood of the
> covenant, which is poured out for many. Truly I tell you, I will never again
> drink of the fruit of the vine until that day when I drink it new in my Father's
> kingdom."
> When they had sung the hymn, they went out to the Mount of Olives.
> (Mark 14:22-26, emphasis added).

A non-biblical first-century Christian document called *Didache*, or
Teachings, includes a ritual for wine and bread that it calls a "thanksgiving" (in
Greek, *eucharist*). It was celebrated during table fellowship, but the instructions
for the ritual aren't based on Jesus' death. Instead, with wine God is thanked
for "the holy vine of David Thy servant," and the bread, broken, symbolizes the
hope that the "church scattered over the hills" will be gathered again.[5] An in-
gathering of the faithful, we remember, underlies the metaphor of the angels'
harvest in the book of Revelation (14:6-20), discussed in the previous part.

In these very early accounts, the sacrament doesn't stand alone; it is
embedded in a fellowship meal ("*while they were eating*"). The sacramental
statements about wine as blood and bread as flesh were likely later additions to
the story, but the event, a shared meal with bread and wine, and its occasion,
Passover, were likely historical. More importantly, these accounts of the Last
Supper recall prophetic and apocalyptic traditions that expand the significance
of this special meal.

First, the stories recall the apocalyptic history of Passover itself. Passover
commemorates events in ancient Egypt that freed the Israelite tribes from
slavery, protected them from Egyptian fury, and formed them into a nation as
they followed Moses through the Sinai desert toward Palestine. Those events
were apocalyptic because of what they *revealed*: the power of God and the
nation's dependence on God's grace. The disasters in Egypt that resulted in
their freedom—plague, locusts, rivers turning to blood, darkness at noon—
would later be prophesied for Israel as pointed reminders of the lessons of the
exodus and Israel's forty years in the wilderness of Sinai. They recur in visions
in the book of Revelation when the Lamb opens the seventh seal on the scroll of
God's decree, and with similar intent: to reveal God's power to defeat evil and
bring justice and peace to the earth.

Second, the Last Supper involves the sharing of bread. In the first century
CE, indeed in Palestine and Middle Eastern cultures then and today, bread was
the foundation of a meal and offering it to a guest was a sign of the extension
of the family's hospitality; sharing bread obliges even enemies to suspend

---

[5] "Didache," Roberts-Donaldson trans., Chapter 6. Online at: http://earlychristianwritings.
com/text/didache-roberts.html.

their enmity for the duration of the meal. Speaking of Jesus' practice of table fellowship, James D. G. Dunn observes:

> It is important to realize how significant this was for Jesus and his contemporaries. For the oriental, table-fellowship was a guarantee of peace, trust, brotherhood; it meant in a very real sense a sharing of one's life. Thus, table-fellowship with tax collector and sinner was Jesus' way of proclaiming God's salvation and assurance of forgiveness, even for those debarred from the cult. . . . *Jesus' table-fellowship was marked by openness, not by exclusiveness.* Jesus' fellowship meals were invitations to grace, not cultic rituals for an inner group which marked them off from their fellows.[6]

Finally, the Last Supper recalls two occasions during Jesus' Galilean ministry when he fed thousands of people by asking them to share small amounts of fish and bread. The first occurs (in Matthew's gospel) after Jesus had rowed out alone into the Sea of Galilee to mourn the death of his mentor, John the Baptist. John had been executed during a banquet, one very different from the one Jesus will soon lead.

Herod Antipas, the son of the late King Herod and the ruler of Galilee, is celebrating his birthday where he enjoys a dance by his stepdaughter so much that he decides to grant her whatever she wishes. She asks her mother, Herodias, for a suggestion. Herodias had married Herod despite a prohibition against marriage of people with their familial relationship (Herod was Herodias' half-uncle). John the Baptist had condemned the marriage as incestuous and was rotting in Herod's prison during the banquet as a result. Herodias suggests to her daughter that she ask for John's head on a platter, and she does. Despite the trouble John's assassination would cause Herod because of John's popularity with the Galilean masses, he complies.[7]

The execution of John the Baptist was not just the death of a friend, which like Lazarus' death would have angered and saddened Jesus; the death of a popular prophet like John was also a harbinger of how his own ministry would likely end. So, at this crisis in Jesus' life, he must mourn John but also reflect on his own mission and destiny. His violent death, too, is inevitable.

Jesus rows out onto the Sea of Galilee to find solitude, but crowds follow him expectantly on the lake's shore. Despite his emotional turmoil, love triumphs: "he had compassion for them and cured their sick" (Matt 14:14). Evening approaches and Jesus asks his disciples to feed the crowd. The disciples object that they have only five loaves of bread and two fish. He says:

> "Bring them here to me." Then he ordered the crowds to sit down on the grass. Taking the five loaves and the two fish, he looked up to heaven, and blessed and broke the loaves, and gave them to the disciples, and the disciples gave them to the crowds. And all ate and were filled; and they took up what

---

[6] Dunn, *Unity and Diversity in the New Testament*, 176-7, emphasis original.
[7] Matt 14:1-12

was left over of the broken pieces, twelve baskets full. And those who ate were about five thousand men, besides women and children. (Matt 14:18-21)

After sending his disciples back to the other side of the lake, Jesus sends the crowds home and retreats, finally, to a mountain overlooking the lake for prayer. Night descends; a storm comes up and threatens the boat carrying his disciples. They're amazed to see Jesus walking across the water to the boat; he says, "Take heart, it is I; do not be afraid" (14:27).

These two stories, the death of John the Baptist and the feeding of the five thousand, provide illuminating contrasts. In the first story, we learn that John met his grisly end at a royal feast where a king lasciviously enjoyed the dancing of his stepdaughter, succumbed to the vindictiveness of his wife whose relationship to him was incestuous, and ordered a ghastly execution that he fears will ignite rebellion. In the second, Jesus, mourning his mentor's violent death and realizing that the same fate awaits him, healed the sick and fed thousands with humble dinners brought by his disciples. Later, the disciples, frightened and alone in a boat in a storm, are encouraged by Jesus who calms the storm, and them.

Jesus' banquet celebrates the kingdom of God and is marked by compassion, healing, and a simple meal. The celebrants will encounter storms, but the storms will be calmed and the celebrants will gain courage. By contrast, Herod's banquet celebrating his worldly kingdom is marked by incest, lust, manipulation, violence, intimidation, fear, and death.

✝

Matthew's second account of the sharing of bread with thousands opens with Jesus on a mountain overlooking Lake Galilee, receiving visitors:

Great crowds came to him, bringing with them the lame, the maimed, the blind, the mute, and many others. They put them at his feet, and he cured them, so that the crowd was amazed when they saw the mute speaking, the maimed whole, the lame walking, and the blind seeing. And they praised the God of Israel. (Matt 15:30-31)

Evening draws near, and Jesus doesn't want the petitioners going home hungry. He asks his disciples how many loaves of bread they have with them:

"Seven, and a few small fish." Then ordering the crowd to sit down on the ground, he took the seven loaves and the fish; and after giving thanks he broke them and gave them to the disciples, and the disciples gave them to the crowds. And all of them ate and were filled; and they took up the broken pieces left over, seven baskets full. Those who had eaten were four thousand men, besides women and children. (Matt 15:34-38)

There's a gee-whiz factor in these stories that is difficult to overlook: because Jesus can do extraordinary things, he must have some special relationship to God. But we must remember the context of these events. Jesus' ministry was to the poor and the outcast. Almost everyone who came to him was subsisting on a single meal a day. Many who came to him for healing were homeless beggars because of their disabilities and status; they were desperately poor, in pain, and often slept without supper. In an era when poverty was considered a form of justice deserved by its victims, Jesus told the crowds that their poverty was a badge of membership in the kingdom of God. And on those evenings in the kingdom of God, the food was enough, not just for the disciples, not just for thousands, but also for leftovers. *Somehow.*

Many modern people find it impossible to accept these accounts as literally true, but at the same time, many other people insist that they are. Our rationalism may suggest that something physically impossible—feeding thousands of people with a basketful of bread and fish—could happen only if the *spiritual* bread of the good news was the food that was distributed.

Our modernistic blinders obscure why these stories were told and discount the acceptance of the miraculous among people in the first century. Karen Armstrong, a historian of religions, speaks of the dual character of events for people who lived before our modern age. History to the ancients consisted of the meaning of events (*mythos*) as well as their factual basis (*logos*). The mythological and miraculous aspect of a story was no less "true": it was the stuff that connected the facts of an event with its meaning. If anything, myth was more important to ancient people than the events in the story itself:

> In the premodern world, people had a different view of history. They were less interested than we are in what actually happened, but more concerned with the meaning of an event. . . . Thus, we do not know what really occurred when the ancient Israelites escaped from Egypt and passed though the Sea of Reeds. The story has been deliberately written as a myth, and linked with other stories about rites of passage, immersion in the deep, and gods splitting a sea in two to create a new reality. Jews experience this myth every year in the rituals of the Passover Seder, which brings this strange story into their own lives and helps them to make it their own.[8]

Our modernist blinders—which cause us to reject the story as impossible or insist on its literal truth—keep us from seeing the meaning of these stories to their first-century listeners. In the stories, Jesus was more than a compassionate man who reduced physical disabilities and fed the hungry (which is quite enough!); he also fulfilled Old Testament prophecies well known to the people he fed.

My biblical theology professor, Ulrich Mauser, recognized that these stories specifically recalled Old Testament prophecies of the Messiah as a shepherd-king who provides for the safety and material needs of his subjects. Those prophecies often invoked King David, who was a shepherd before he was a king. For example, Ezekiel prophesied (several centuries after the historical

---

[8] Armstrong, *The Battle for God*, xvi.

David): "I will set up over them one shepherd, my servant David, and he shall feed them; he shall feed them and be their shepherd" (Ezek 34:23). Matthew's account of Jesus' birth recalled these prophecies when visiting scholars who had followed a star to Judah tell King Herod that the star signified the birth there of the Messiah. Ready to eliminate this threat to his rule, he asks, "Where?" They respond, recalling a prophecy of Micah:

"In Bethlehem of Judea; for so it has been written by the prophet:
And you, Bethlehem, in the land of Judah,
  are by no means least among the rulers of Judah;
for from you shall come a ruler
  who is to *shepherd my people* Israel." (Matt 2:5-6, emphasis added; cf. Micah 5:2)

Herod, whose rule has been corrupt and brutal, is "frightened" (2:3) because Micah had prophesied *this* when the kingdom of God arrives:

He shall judge between many peoples,
  and shall arbitrate between strong nations far away;
they shall beat their swords into plowshares,
  and their spears into pruning hooks;
nation shall not lift up sword against nation,
  neither shall they learn war any more;
but they shall all sit under their own vines and under their own fig trees,
  and no one shall make them afraid. (Micah 4:3-4, emphasis added)

Herod, an autocrat, fears that his subjects will no longer fear him if the prophesied shepherd-king brings them *peace*. Mauser reads two biblical senses of *peace*: its strict meaning as the cessation of hostilities, and its fuller meaning of justice and well-being, the latter better reflecting the Hebrew sense of the word. With peace, fear among the oppressed abates and the tools of oppression become useless. Peace, Mauser writes, is the object of the kingdom of God; the shepherd-king is its instrument, and the provision of food in the wilderness is its emblem:

The feeding stories [about Jesus] are therefore primarily understood as royal acts in which the king cares for the elementary needs of his subjects, protecting them from the danger of starvation. But the miraculous element of the stories must not be rationalized away. It belongs to the epiphany of the king, who inaugurates the new world of peace, to set free the wonderful powers of heaven that are at his disposal, so that a desolate and arid land becomes the scene of a meal for multitudes who are preserved from hunger.[9]

†

---

[9] Mauser, *The Gospel of Peace*, 60.

Perhaps many among the thousands who gathered to hear Jesus' good news, to be healed, and to break bread together as night fell remembered a story about Isaac, Abraham's son. Rootless in Palestine, he and his tribe are banished from the lands of their enemies, the Philistines, during a famine and return to old settlements. They find that the wells they had dug have been filled by their enemies, but they dig them again, finding water to support a miraculous harvest. Hats in hand, the king of the Philistines and his adviser and military commander visit:

> Isaac said to them, "Why have you come to me, seeing that you hate me and have sent me away from you?" They said, "We see plainly that the Lord has been with you; so we say, let there be an oath between you and us, and let us make a covenant with you so that you will do us no harm, just as we have not touched you and have done to you nothing but good and have sent you away in peace. You are now the blessed of the Lord." So he made them a feast, and they ate and drank. In the morning they rose early and exchanged oaths; and Isaac set them on their way, and they departed from him in *peace*. (Gen 26:27-31, emphasis added)

Perhaps some of the thousands who shared supper with Jesus and his disciples recalled a story about Elijah, the prophet to whom Jesus was frequently compared. The story is set during a drought that Elijah had predicted if King Ahab reintroduced the worship of the Canaanite god Baal in Israel. Ahab isn't happy with Elijah, and God advises Elijah to leave town and hide. On the run, Elijah enjoys the hospitality of a starving widow and her son:

> When he came to the gate of the town, a widow was there gathering sticks; he called to her and said, "Bring me a little water in a vessel, so that I may drink." As she was going to bring it, he called to her and said, "Bring me a morsel of bread in your hand." But she said, "As the Lord your God lives, I have nothing baked, only a handful of meal in a jar, and a little oil in a jug; I am now gathering a couple of sticks, so that I may go home and prepare it for myself and my son, that we may eat it, and die." Elijah said to her, "Do not be afraid; go and do as you have said; but first make me a little cake of it and bring it to me, and afterwards make something for yourself and your son. For thus says the Lord the God of Israel: The jar of meal will not be emptied and the jug of oil will not fail until the day that the Lord sends rain on the earth." She went and did as Elijah said, so that she as well as he and her household ate for many days. The jar of meal was not emptied, neither did the jug of oil fail. (1 Kings 17:10-16)

As Elijah continues his stay, the widow's son weakens and dies. Elijah lays himself on the boy and prays, and God restores the boy to life. Elijah carries him downstairs and gives him to his mother: "See, your son is alive!" (17:23).

✝

We've started with bread and returned to resurrection. But that is the tapestry the New Testament weaves. The gospels aren't simply collections of stories that make a rational case for the divinity of Jesus, or demonstrate that he operated on some superior, symbolic level of existence as an actor in a cosmic drama. They may seem to, and they may sometimes say that they do, and many learned people may interpret them that way, but that is not how the gospel speaks to me in my times.

The gospels are collections of recollected sayings and stories that first-century Jews and Gentiles told each other about a famous prophet. They shared them at that point in Jewish history and in the apocalyptic spirit of their times. Jesus reminded them of the God who delivered the Israelites from slavery in Egypt, provided food in the wilderness, required them to be compassionate and just to the sick, poor, and oppressed, and would send a messiah.

But Jesus wasn't the messiah they expected. He refused worldly authority and taught that their acceptance of God's love and their forgiveness of one another brought the kingdom of God to earth. The kingdom was not an abstract vision separated from them by catastrophic events in the indeterminate future, which is what they heard from John the Baptist and a lot of other prophets, but a kingdom that is constantly *coming near* and *coming soon*. The kingdom had healed them, fed them, and reunited them with people they had lost. With this man's ministry, God's reign had arrived, and it was good news:

> Jesus answered them: "Go and tell John what you hear and see: the blind receive their sight, the lame walk, the lepers are cleansed, the deaf hear, the dead are raised, and the poor have good news brought to them." (Matt 11:4-5)

✝

Occasions to break bread are frequently the settings when Jesus debates, teaches, and tells parables, especially in the gospel of Luke. At a large banquet at the home of Levi, a tax collector, Jesus discusses his revolutionary teaching with critics who think he shouldn't dine with people many Jews despise. Using the apocalyptic metaphor of marriage feast (also used in the book of Revelation to announce "a new heaven and a new earth" [19:9; 21:1]), Jesus replies: "'You cannot make wedding guests fast while the bridegroom is with them, can you? The days will come when the bridegroom will be taken away from them, and then they will fast in those days'" (Luke 5:34-35).

At another dinner described in the gospel of Luke, this one in the home of the Pharisee Simon, "a woman in the city, who was a sinner" comes in, washes Jesus' feet, dries them with her hair, and anoints them with perfumed oil. These are, ironically, signs of the hospitality that the host had denied Jesus, who tells her, "Your sins are forgiven. . . . Your faith has saved you; go in peace." Simon's guests grumble: what kind of prophet lets a harlot wash his feet? How does he presume to forgive sins? Jesus replies with a parable: "'A certain creditor had two debtors; one owed five hundred denarii, and the other fifty. When they could not pay, he canceled the debts for both of them. Now which of them will love him more?'" (Luke 7:36-50)

At yet another dinner, Jesus is invited on the Sabbath, the day of rest, for a meal with "a leader of the Pharisees" (Luke 14:1). In front of his fellow guests, who were watching Jesus closely for violations of the Law, Jesus encounters a man with "dropsy," a swelling of tissues usually in the feet. Jesus asks, "Is it lawful to cure people on the Sabbath, or not?" (14:3). Faced with real needs, they're silent; he heals the man.

That dinner also serves as a metaphor for Jesus' scheme of forgiveness. He observes how the guests, in Greco-Roman fashion, "chose the places of honor" (14:7) in the banquet room and suggests that they might prefer to get the least-desired place, because from there the host might invite them to be first. Moreover, the host might want to invite "the poor, the crippled, the lame, and the blind" (14:13); they would be blessed by the host's invitation and become a blessing, in turn, to the host. These conundrums would have confused and perplexed the men at the Pharisee's dinner, and we can imagine Jesus' wry smile.

Jesus' disruption of the rigid hierarchy and rituals of Pharisee banquets symbolized the playful and revolutionary nature of his view of the kingdom of God, where thousands were welcome regardless of rules and customs that might separate them, where forgiveness and healing were celebrated, and where there was enough food for everyone.

But while suppers, feasts, and banquets provided Jesus with opportunities to debate, teach, and demonstrate the imminence of the kingdom, the messianic banquet was never far away from the lesson Jesus tried to convey to his fellow guests about the inclusiveness of the kingdom of God and the imminence of its peace. Isaiah's vision of a mountain-top feast celebrating peace among all the nations of the world perfectly expressed the prophetic hope for the outcome of history. A feast celebrating peace was what Jesus and his followers had in mind (but with simpler fare) when they celebrated their shared suppers, and it's worth recounting Isaiah's vision at length:

> On this mountain, the Lord of hosts will make for all peoples
> a feast of rich food, a feast of well-aged wines,
> of rich food filled with marrow, of well-aged wines strained clear.
> And he will destroy on this mountain
> the shroud that is cast over all peoples,
> the sheet that is spread over all nations;
> he will swallow up death forever.
> Then the Lord God will wipe away the tears from all faces,
> and the disgrace of his people he will take away from all the earth,
> for the Lord has spoken.
> It will be said on that day,
> Lo, this is our God; we have waited for him, so that he might save us.

> This is the Lord for whom we have waited;
> let us be glad and rejoice in his salvation. (Isa 25:6-9)

Isaiah's prophecy recalls, in turn, another ancient mountaintop banquet. During Israel's journey through the wilderness after the exodus from Egypt, God finishes his moral instructions to Moses, but before he begins instructions about worship and sacrifice, he invites Moses, his lieutenants, and the elders of the tribes of Israel to a banquet. In Jewish tradition, being in God's presence results in death except for the chief priest, who alone is permitted to enter the presence of God in the temple's Holy of Holies, and only on the Day of Atonement. Therefore, the leaders of Israel, in addition to Moses, must be granted safe-keeping for an encounter with the God who delivered them from Egypt.

> Then Moses and Aaron, Nadab, and Abihu, and seventy of the elders of Israel went up, and they saw the God of Israel. Under his feet there was something like a pavement of sapphire stone, like the very heaven for clearness. God did not lay his hand on the chief men of the people of Israel; also they beheld God, and they ate and drank. (Exod 24:9-11)

This table fellowship on the mountain was an unprecedented and unrepeated meeting among the leaders of Israel and their Lord. For Christians, a similar but simpler supper celebrates the intimacies and hospitalities God desires with us, and for us with one another. During our meals, which are safe places for fellowship and sharing, the shroud of death that separates us is destroyed, the veil lifts, fear abates, and God's reign of peace is revealed.

Chapter 27
ABBA!

"Your kingdom come" is the cardinal phrase in the "Lord's Prayer," a prayer Christians pray regularly together in church and elsewhere alone. With baptism, learning it was an important ritual of initiation into the earliest Christian assemblies. Baptism was a sign that a person had accepted the good news: "And baptism . . . now saves you—not as a removal of dirt from the body, but as [a pledge to God from] a good conscience, through the resurrection of Jesus Christ" (1 Peter 3:21).[10] Once baptized, a member learned the Lord's Prayer and prayed it three times daily: at sunrise, in the afternoon, and at night before going to bed.[11] The prayer succinctly describes the relationship Jesus wants his followers to have with one another, with the world, and with God.

The New Testament provides two versions of the Lord's Prayer in the gospels of Matthew and Luke. Joachim Jeremias, a twentieth-century German scholar, studied the two versions as part of a larger study of Jesus' conception of the kingdom of God and organized them into a matrix based on their similarities.[12]

Jeremias suggests that the prayer comes to us in different forms because the audiences for the two gospels were different.[13] Matthew was written for

---

[10] An English reading of the text is difficult; the reading I've chosen is the one preferred by the editor of 1 Peter in the NRSV Study Bible, David L. Balch, 2283. A free translation by Eugene Peterson reads: "The waters of baptism [save] you, not by washing away dirt from your skin but by presenting you through Jesus' resurrection before God with a clear conscience." *The Message// Remix*, 2218.

[11] Ibid., 137. An instruction to one early church to pray it three times daily is in *Didache*, ch. 8, online at: http://earlychristianwritings.com/text/didache-roberts.html.

[12] Jeremias, "The Lord's Prayer," in *Jesus and the Message of the New Testament*, 45-50. In my matrix, the NRSV is used.

[13] Crossan finds it difficult to believe, however, that such an important inheritance from Jesus' ministry would be transmitted so differently and in only two of the gospels. He suggests

a Jewish Christian community, who "have learned to pray in childhood but whose prayer stands in danger of becoming a routine"; Luke was written for a Gentile Christian community who "must learn to pray for the first time and whose courage to pray must be aroused."[14] In its brevity, directness, and relevance to the needs of very different communities, the Lord's Prayer has shaped the way Christians pray.

	Matthew 6:9-13	Luke 11:2-4
Address	Our Father in heaven,	Father,
"Thou" petitions	hallowed be your name. Your kingdom come. Your will be done, on earth as it is in heaven.	hallowed be your name. Your kingdom come.
"We" petitions	Give us this day our daily bread. And forgive us our debts, as we also have forgiven our debtors.	Give us each day our daily bread. And forgive us our sins, for we ourselves forgive everyone indebted to us.
Petition for preservation	And do not bring us to the time of trial, but rescue us from the evil one.	And do not bring us to the time of trial.

To uncover the Lord's Prayer in its earliest form, Jeremias focused on the differences between the two versions. One difference is the more formal address Matthew uses for God. A second is Matthew's addition of parallel material that restates Luke's original in different words, like Hebrew poetry or a responsive reading during worship. Both differences indicate that Matthew has expanded the original, perhaps for use in worship, but that Matthew's version also reflects an equally ancient form peculiar to his Jewish-Christian community. Jeremias concludes that Luke is the earlier prayer but that Matthew is more likely to have preserved the more ancient Aramaic original. This is the prayer that Jeremias proposes as one that likely underlies both:

> Dear Father,
> hallowed be your name.
> Your kingdom come,
> our bread for tomorrow, give us today.
> And forgive us our debts,
> as we also herewith forgive our debtors.
> And let us not succumb to the trial.[15]

---

the prayer originated in the post-resurrection churches and its purpose was to define their unique confessions (something Jesus was rarely interested in doing). Still, he thinks the prayer is consistent with other early sources about the nature of Jesus' faith and eschatology. Crossan, *The Historical Jesus*, 294.

[14] Jeremias, Lord's Prayer, *Jesus and the Message of the New Testament*, 44.

[15] Ibid., 49.

Dear Father

"Father," even Jeremias' gentle Germanism of "dear Father," doesn't do justice to Jesus' intimate relationship with God. The earliest manuscripts use the Greek *pater*, meaning *father*, but behind that use is the Aramaic word *abba*, the word a child in first-century Palestine would use to address the father in the family's home and the equivalent of "papa" or "daddy" among Americans. The term is affectionate, direct, and unpretentious.

An assertion of this degree of intimacy with the Lord was unusual among Jewish prayers of the time.[16] Dunn writes that "Jewish prayers certainly spoke of God as Father, but in a much more formal mode of address—God as Father of the nation—and without the directness and simplicity of Jesus' prayers."[17] Hence Jeremias' remark about the "courage" of early Christian petitioners who dared to address the Creator of the heavens and the earth with the childlike intimacy their own children used to addressed them.

That *Abba!*, "Dear Father," was how Jesus oriented himself to God in prayer is corroborated by its explicit use in one passage in Mark and, in translation by the Greek *pater*, in multiple passages throughout the gospels.[18] Two passages from Paul's letters also testify to the use by early Christians of *Abba!* to address God: "When we cry, '*Abba!* Father!' it is that very Spirit bearing witness with our spirit that we are children of God" (Rom 8:15-16); "Because you are children, God has sent the Spirit of his Son into our hearts, crying, '*Abba!* Father!'" (Gal 4:6). Also corroborating the child-to-parent orientation Jesus urged is this passage:

> The disciples came to Jesus and asked, "Who is the greatest in the kingdom of heaven?" He called a child, whom he put among them, and said, "Truly I tell you, unless you change and become like children, you will never enter the kingdom of heaven. Whoever becomes humble like this child is the greatest in the kingdom of heaven. Whoever welcomes one such child in my name welcomes me." (Matt 18:1-5)

Crossan believes this passage, which has parallels in Mark and Luke (and the noncanonical gospel of Thomas), speaks to the nature of the members of the kingdom of God—the meek, the poor, the sick—which Crossan flippantly calls a "kingdom of nobodies" to emphasize how radically Jesus' teaching diverged from the conventional wisdom. Moreover, Romans in Jesus' time considered children practically worthless and abandoned unwanted infants in garbage dumps with the prospect that they might be rescued by others for

---

[16] ibid., 51.

[17] Dunn, *Unity and Diversity in the New Testament*, 202.

[18] Mark 14:36: "He said, 'Abba, Father . . . .'"; parallels of this passage in Luke (22:41) and Matthew (26:39) omit "Abba." Other prayers by Jesus addressing "Father" include Matt 11:25/Luke 10:21 (Q), Luke 23:46, and John 11:41 et al. Therefore, Jesus' address of God as "Father" occurs in all source strata of the gospels, as Dunn points out.

development into slaves. Jews didn't practice infanticide, but still, Crossan writes, "to be a child was to be a nobody, with the possibility of becoming a somebody absolutely dependent on parental discretion and parental standing in the community."[19] The intent of the instruction to "become like children" is not simply to orient the person praying to the appropriate position of a child's respect for a parent, but also to create a feeling of absolute dependence on God as protector and nurturer.

The relationship of child and parent expressed by this passage, however, would later develop into elaborate theological (and paternalistic) notions about God as Father and Jesus Christ as His Son. Another passage from Matthew that often prompts theological speculation along these lines also occurs in Luke and is, therefore, from the early source Q:

> "I thank you, Father, Lord of heaven and earth, because you have hidden these things from the wise and the intelligent and have revealed them to infants; yes, Father, for such was your gracious will. All things have been handed over to me by my Father; and no one knows the Son except the Father, and no one knows the Father except the Son and anyone to whom the Son chooses to reveal him." (Matt 11:25-27; cf. Luke 10:21-22).

Jeremias suggests that in this passage, Jesus is appropriating a contemporary apocalyptic metaphor about the transmission of secret knowledge like one used twice in 3 Enoch, a Jewish apocalypse which was probably written about the same time as Matthew.[20] Marcus Borg provides a translation for the passage in the early Q source that sounds less theological and drives at the domestic intimacy of the relationship of Jesus and God:

> "I thank you, Father, for hiding these things from the wise and the clever and revealing them to the childlike. This is the way you want it. Everything has been put in my hand by my father. No one knows who the son is except the father, and who the father is except the son, and anyone to whom the son chooses to reveal him."[21]

The *Abba!* relationship, fundamental to Jesus' faith, catapults ahead through history to our time through the institution of the Lord's Prayer. The opening of the Lord's Prayer orients us in childlike dependence and directness with God. Yes, the God of judgment scorns those who choose death, who go through the motions of faith without extending justice and compassion to the poor and powerless, and who ally themselves with antichrists who reject love as the basis of their moral codes. But for those who choose life and love one another, God is a forgiving, nurturing, and joyous parent who teaches us, as a parent would his precious small child, the way.

---

[19] Crossan, *The Historical Jesus*, 269.

[20] Jeremias, *Jesus and the Message of the New Testament*, 71-3; the dating of 3 Enoch is from Russell, *The Method and Message of Jewish Apocalyptic*, 348.

[21] Borg, *The Lost Gospel Q*, 66.

Hallowed be your name. Your kingdom come.

After settling us into the nurturing relationship with God through the utterance of *Abba!*, the Lord's Prayer asks two things of God that are about God. The first is that his name be "hallowed." The second is that God's "kingdom come."

These two lines recall the *Kaddish*, the prayer said by Jews as the synagogue service ends. Jeremias translates an ancient form of the *Kaddish* from its original Aramaic:

> Exalted and hallowed be his great name
> in the world that he created according to his will.
> May he rule his kingdom
> in your lifetime and in your days
> and in the lifetime of the whole house of Israel,
> speedily and soon.
> And to this, say "Amen."[22]

The parallelism of the *Kaddish* helps us understand that the two "Thou-Petitions" are linked: our prayer that the kingdom come is another way of praying for the time when God's dominion will be praised.

For centuries, Israel's prophets had denounced libels on God by other faiths and demanded repentance by Israel so the nation could achieve its destiny as a light to the nations of the earth. Ezekiel, for one, warns that God's purpose for Judah's exile is to restore God's holy name:

> I will sanctify my great name, which has been profaned among the nations, and which you have profaned among them; and the nations shall know that I am the Lord, says the Lord God, when through you I display my holiness before their eyes. (Ezek 36:23)

As in Ezekiel, the time when God becomes king will be the time when God is universally recognized as holy. Therefore, the two "Thou-Petitions" have significance for the perfection of history. As in the *Kaddish*, Christians ask for the speedy arrival of a time, like Nineveh in Jonah's time, when God's greatness is praised and God's reign is recognized by Jews and Gentiles alike.

Jeremias says that "these petitions are a cry out of the depths of distress."[23] Christians and Jews in the first century were subjects of an imperial power that tolerated Judaism as long as it didn't seek to overthrow Roman power. Christians rejected the trappings of empire and its moral decay but risked slavery, exile, or death when confronted. God's kingdom couldn't come too soon, but over decades its tardiness had increasingly made the kingdom a cosmic, not a worldly, event. Its postponement had prompted the cry for justice, most vividly the cry from dead martyrs in the book of Revelation, "How long?" (6:10).

---

[22] Jeremias, *Jesus and the Message of the New Testament*, 52.
[23] Ibid., 53.

The opening chapters of Revelation encouraged Christians to endure imperial oppression and to avoid the patronage system while celebrating their love for God and one another. While the stunning imagery in the visions of the seven seals distracts us from them, the book's scenes of worship are its focus and have the "Thou-Petitions" as their theme. An ever-widening circle of worshippers praises the Lord's holiness as the cosmic battle rages to a hopeful conclusion and the New Jerusalem descends to earth. God's name is holy, and God's kingdom comes.

Jesus taught his disciples and, through generations of discipleship Christians today to join a collaborative relationship with God in prayer to hasten God's kingdom. In that prayer, we ask that the kingdom of our dear parent, *Abba!*, come near and soon. In the Mass or during Holy Communion, when we praise the Lord and participate in the Lord's Supper, Christians anticipate the mountaintop feast when all people celebrate the arrival of peace with the kingdom of God. But also in communion, Christians bring *Abba!* and kingdom to earth. The Mass is not about some future event in human history; it is a celebration of the kingdom conjured *now* as we prayerfully participate, singing songs of praise and sharing wine and bread.

Our bread for tomorrow, give us today. And forgive us our debts as we forgive our debtors.

Among the most radical claims that Jesus makes on his followers is that they forgive one another's debts. The Sabbath Law provided for the forgiveness of debts every seven years (and the Jubilee Law, restoration of ancestral lands every fifty), but as we saw in Part Two, the laws were only honored in their breach. Israel's prophets encouraged the nation and its leaders to be compassionate to the poor and the oppressed and they condemned the injustice that had caused their poverty. Jesus encouraged individual people to be compassionate toward others, forgiving even the debts of enemies, and he linked forgiveness to the coming of the kingdom of God. The faithful must give mercy if they hope to receive it.

Forgiveness of debts was no small matter in Galilee or Judea in Jesus' time. Crushing taxes led members of peasant families into debt, slavery, homelessness, and beggary. Jesus' advocacy for the forgiveness of debts attracted people to his ministry and is exemplified in this passage:

> "If you love those who love you, what credit is that to you? For even sinners love those who love them. If you do good to those who do good to you, what credit is that to you? For even sinners do the same. If you lend to those from whom you hope to receive, what credit is that to you? Even sinners lend to sinners, to receive as much again. But love your enemies, do good, and lend, expecting nothing in return. Your reward will be great, and you will be children of the Most High: for he is kind to the ungrateful and the wicked. Be merciful, just as your Father is merciful.
>
> "Do not judge, and you will not be judged; do not condemn, and you will not be condemned. Forgive, and you will be forgiven; give, and it will be given to you." (Luke 6:32-38)

Jesus' program for the relief of the impoverished wasn't limited to the forgiveness of debts or the sharing of bread. Forgiveness also extended to interpersonal wrongs, again in a passage from the early source Q:

> Then Peter came up and said to him, "Lord, if [my brother or sister] sins against me, how often should I forgive? As many as seven times?" Jesus said to him, "Not seven times, but, I tell you, seventy-seven times." (Matt 18:21-22; cf. Luke 17:3-4)

On the heels of this passage comes a parable about a merciful king and an unforgiving servant:

> "The kingdom of heaven may be compared to a king who wished to settle accounts with his slaves. When he began the reckoning, one who owed him ten thousand talents was brought to him; and, as he could not pay, his lord ordered him to be sold, together with his wife and children and all his possessions, and payment to be made. So the slave fell on his knees before him, saying, 'Have patience with me, and I will pay you everything.' And out of pity for him, the lord of that slave released him and forgave him the debt. But that same slave, as he went out, came upon one of his fellow slaves who owed him a hundred denarii; and seizing him by the throat, he said, 'Pay what you owe.' Then his fellow slave fell down and pleaded with him, 'Have patience with me, and I will pay you.' But he refused; then he went and threw him into prison until he would pay the debt. When his fellow slaves saw what had happened, they were greatly distressed, and they went and reported to their lord all that had taken place. Then his lord summoned him and said to him, 'You wicked slave! I forgave you all that debt because you pleaded with me. Should you not have had mercy on your fellow slave, as I had mercy on you?' And in anger his lord handed him over to be tortured until he would pay his entire debt. So my heavenly Father will also do to every one of you, if you do not forgive your brother or sister from your heart." (Matt 18:23-35)

The parable may appear to be allegorical because the king is called *Lord*, an appellation used for Jesus after his death and resurrection to recognize his divinity, but the story did not carry that meaning when it was told. It had a concrete, down-to-earth meaning to his listeners, lightened by an absurdity: a single talent, of which the first slave owed the king ten thousand, was worth fifteen years' labor; a denarius, by contrast, was worth a day's.[24] That the king would forgive several thousand lifetimes of wages was ridiculous, but the story's point is still made: if God is prepared to forgive the spiritual sins of a lifetime, then you must be ready to forgive the worldly debts of a brother or sister.

The threat at the end of the parable contrasts with Jesus' otherwise positive message. Threats aren't uncommon in Jesus' teachings; they're common enough to make credible the notions of dispensationalists about the eternal damnation of people who don't accept Jesus as their savior to escape the tribulations to come. However, the dispensationalist error is their belief that judgment will

---

[24] Dennis Duling, *NRSV Study Bible*, notes to 18:24, 28, 1891-2.

occur in a catastrophic future or at the end of a person's life. For Jesus (and for Paul and John of Patmos), judgment—the consequence of failing to heed the prophetic warning to choose life—comes in the *present*, and may be undone in an instant, God willing, when the person chooses life and forgives.

The centrality of forgiveness in Jesus' message extends to his healing ministry and appears in a story about a man who can't walk. Crossan identifies the assumption underlying the story, not alien to our times: people who are sick or disabled somehow earn the hopelessness and poverty they endure.[25] People in Jesus' time considered disability, leprosy, madness, and other afflictions to be manifestations of sin; one might receive the forgiveness of God through appropriate sacrifices at the temple, but this was another level of taxation that burdened the poor. The story of Jesus' healing of a paraplegic man is humorous because he is literally airlifted into Jesus' presence to get past the crowds who were listening to his teaching.

> Just then some men came, carrying a paralyzed man on a bed. They were trying to bring him in and lay him before Jesus; but finding no way to bring him in because of the crowd, they went up on the roof and let him down with his bed through the tiles into the middle of the crowd in front of Jesus. When he saw their faith, he said, "Friend, your sins are forgiven you." Then the scribes and the Pharisees began to question, "Who is this who is speaking blasphemies? Who can forgive sins but God alone?" When Jesus perceived their questionings, he answered them, "Why do you raise such questions in your hearts? Which is easier, to say, 'Your sins are forgiven you,' or to say, 'Stand up and walk'? But so that you may know that the Son of Man has authority on earth to forgive sins"—he said to the one who was paralyzed—"I say to you, stand up and take your bed and go to your home." Immediately he stood up before them, took what he had been lying on, and went to his home, glorifying God." (Luke 5:18-25)

We have to suspend our modern disbelief that paraplegia can be healed by words, for that is not the point of the story. Jesus was amused at the ingenuity the man's friends used to access Jesus' healing powers, and his first words were an assurance of forgiveness: the disabled man was no longer separated from God by neither a roof nor prevailing notions about his disability. Then, when Jesus heals the man, the theological dispute is ended; regardless of whether God alone can forgive people's sins, the healing is an objective sign of God's reign on earth. Accordingly, the man walks home "giving glory to God all the way."

Hallowed be your name. Your kingdom come. When Christians pray the Lord's Prayer, what God is asked to forgive is not the items on the list of our offenses against moral codes or interpersonal etiquette since the last time we confessed, because we can ask pardon for those things from the people we offended. What a faithful person asks God to forgive is the inability to live a

---

[25] Crossan, *The Historical Jesus*, 324.

life in complete and continuing obedience to God's will. Even when disability or some other problem prevents our full participation in human society and brings us the grief of loneliness and the hunger of poverty, God's forgiveness is available. We forgive others what they owe us; we ask in turn that God forgive our inability to live faithfully. Any grace God might grant in the mutuality of forgiveness between God and people brings the kingdom of God to earth.

✝

Just as *forgiveness* is a harbinger of the kingdom of God, so is *daily bread*. Bread signifies table fellowship and is fundamental to understanding Jesus' ministry. *Daily* bread recalls Israel's journey through the wilderness when God provided bread every morning to the starving migrants, and it speaks to the real needs of the poor for whom Jesus interrupted his prayers to serve by the thousands. *Daily bread* also has apocalyptic importance: not only is bread a part of the messianic banquet that reconciles all nations at the end of time, it is the focus of two biblical resurrections that revealed the nearness of God's kingdom in their times that we recalled earlier in this part: the resurrection of the blind woman's son by Elijah in the Old Testament, and the resurrection of Lazarus by Jesus in the New.

Joachim Jeremias sees a clear reference to the fulfillment of God's kingdom in *daily bread* in a report by a fourth-century church historian, Jerome (342-420 CE), about a gospel whose text has since been lost. While the lost gospel, "The Gospel According to the Hebrews," was written much later than the gospels in the New Testament and used Matthew as its source, it is unlike Matthew because it was written in Aramaic, the language Jesus spoke, so it may have preserved the earliest traditions. Jerome writes that the lost gospel's petition for daily bread used *mahar*, an Aramaic word meaning *tomorrow* and signifying the messianic banquet among first-century Jews. Jerome, quoted by Jeremias, writes: "In the so-called Gospel according to the Hebrews . . . I found *mahar*, which means 'for tomorrow,' so that the sense is, 'our bread for tomorrow—that is, our future bread—give us today.'"[26] In this interpretation, Christians ask for the fulfillment of the promised kingdom today, and Jeremias uses the lost gospel's text to reframe the second "Thou Petition" as, "Our bread for tomorrow, give us today."

But like most of Jesus' teaching, the petition for *daily bread* operates on several interrelated levels of meaning. While acknowledging *daily bread's* end-times associations, Donald Goergen emphasizes the petition's practical meaning to Jesus' disciples, who lived day to day and depended on the generosity of strangers for their food, clothing, and shelter. One may infer the importance of *actual* daily bread to disciples who followed these instructions:

---

[26] Jeremias, *Jesus and the Message of the New Testament*, 54.

He called the twelve and began to send them out two by two, and gave them authority over the unclean spirits. He ordered them to take nothing for their journey except a staff: no bread, no bag, no money in their belts; but to wear sandals and not to put on two tunics. (Mark 6:7-9)

It wasn't just his disciples, who chose their professions, who depended on *daily bread*. Although Jesus moved comfortably among tax collectors, estate managers, and others with wealth, his ministry in Galilee was mostly to peasants and beggars who lived in poverty and subsisted on one meal a day, if they were fortunate. Besides the practical importance of the petition to his disciples, Goergen recognizes Jesus' sensitivity to the poor in the petition of the Lord's Prayer for bread *today*:

> It was a petition that reflected the socio-economic reality of the petitioners, as well as dependency upon God. It was not a prayer taught the rich; it would too readily smack of irony or arrogance. Nothing would suggest that Jesus himself did not pray this way. He often could not be sure where his next meal would come from; he was certainly conscious that this was true of many who gathered to hear him preach.[27]

When Jesus' sermons extended into dinnertime, Jesus and his often skeptical disciples were in the position of feeding the crowds Jesus attracted with what little food they may have brought with them. Demonstrating the effectiveness of the petition to God for *daily bread*, there was always more than enough to eat.

Goergen also notes Jesus' use of "us" and "our" in the petition for *daily bread*. This is not a selfish prayer; if it were, it would have read, "*My* bread for tomorrow, give *me* today." For Goergen, the use of "us" reflects Jesus' concern for the poor with whom he identified. His purpose was practical as well as religious: while he spoke metaphorically of the hunger of the faithful for righteousness and the satisfaction of consuming the bread of life, he was always careful to assure that everyone had enough to eat before they went home.

Bridging the two levels of meaning of bread in the New Testament—the spiritual bread of the messianic banquet and the actual bread that feeds the poor—Goergen suggests that the two interpretations might be reconciled, quoting theologian Ernst Lohmeyer:

> "The bread, then, is earthly bread, the bread of the poor and needy, and at the same time, because of the eschatological hour in which it is prayed for and eaten, it is the future bread in this today, the bread of the elect and the blessed."[28]

Ulrich Mauser provides a third perspective on *daily bread* when he notes a "remarkable detail" in the story of the bread-like substance that the tribes of Israel gathered each morning in the wilderness after their exodus from Egypt.

---

[27] Goergen, *The Mission and Ministry of Jesus* 137-8.
[28] Ibid., 140.

Israel is starving in the Sinai wilderness when God tells Moses:

> "I'm going to rain bread from heaven for you, and each day the people shall go out and gather enough for that day. In that way I will test them, whether they will follow my instruction or not. On the sixth day, when they prepare what they bring in, it will be twice as much as they gather on other days." (Ex 16:4-5)

The *daily bread* of the exodus, humorously called *manna* (an Aramaic pun for "what is it?"), was a flaky substance that remained after the morning's dew evaporated. When the Israelites gathered it, they discovered that what they gathered was just enough to feed them for that day (or for two days when gathered on the sixth day of the week before the Sabbath, when food-gathering was prohibited). In fact, when some rebellious Israelites stored it without eating it that day, "it bred worms and became foul" (Ex 16:20).

Mauser writes that the daily ration of *manna* characterizes the wilderness tradition in the Old Testament; God is teaching Israel to live day by day to learn its utter dependence on God:

> [Israel] receives daily bread, and a daily portion only, from the hand of God. God's help does not miraculously change the wilderness into a paradise; the desert situation cannot be forgotten, not even for one day. . . . There is a promise of a better land ahead, a land flowing with milk and honey, but as long as the way through the wilderness lasts God's help has the form of daily rations of simple food.[29]

These three perspectives on daily bread from Jeremias, Goergen, and Mauser are expressed in the tenses of past, present, and future: the *manna* of memory and its lesson of abject dependence on God's grace in the wilderness; the present need of the hungry for a meal before bedtime; and the petition for "tomorrow's bread," the fulfillment of the kingdom of God. These three perspectives, and especially the fluidity of the time they represent, make possible the daily hopefulness we need to forgive others, work for justice, or make peace.

And let us not succumb to the trial.

The final petition in Jeremias' formulation of the prayer that Jesus taught his disciples is more familiar in the King James Version of it from Matthew:

> Lead us not into temptation,
> but deliver us from evil. (Matt 6:13 KJV)

Matthew added the second line to Luke's first, as he similarly expanded the other verses. For modern readers, the additional lines and their ancient English translations can raise barriers to understanding the prayer's original meaning. Is "temptation" an invitation to sin? Is temptation the primary manifestation of evil? Is temptation the fundamental threat to our faith? Why would God lead

---

[29] Mauser, *Christ in the Wilderness*, 22.

us into temptation? And importantly for this book, is the evil from which we ask deliverance (in Matthew's lengthened petition) the tribulation predicted by end-times writers?

Peirasmos is the Greek word translated in the KJV as "temptation," and Jeremias notes that it is used two ways in the New Testament:

- *Temptation*—being led into sin; and
- *Trial or testing*—faith or fidelity being put to the test.[30]

Only once, in a pastoral letter attributed to Paul, does *peirasmos* have the more restrictive definition meaning of "being led into sin":

> But those who want to be rich fall into *temptation* and are trapped by many senseless and harmful desires that plunge people into ruin and destruction. For the love of money is a root of all kinds of evil, and in their eagerness to be rich some have wandered away from the faith and pierced themselves with many pains. (1 Tim 6:9-10, emphasis added)

This exception makes the rule. The more common use of *peirasmos* is its second meaning, "time of trial." It significantly occurs in the gospels' narratives of Jesus' vigil with his disciples in the Garden of Gethsemane before his betrayal and arrest and is appropriately translated in the New Revised Standard Version of the passage:

> He came out and went, as was his custom, to the Mount of Olives; and the disciples followed him. When he reached the place, he said to them, "Pray that you may not come into *the time of trial*." Then he withdrew from them about a stone's throw, knelt down, and prayed, "Father, if you are willing, remove this cup from me; yet, not my will but yours be done." . . . When he got up from prayer, he came to the disciples and found them sleeping because of grief, and he said to them, "Why are you sleeping? Get up and pray that you may not come into *the time of trial*." (Luke 22:39-46, emphasis added)

Putting the use of *peirasmos* in a larger context, Jeremias quotes a saying ascribed to Jesus by a church Father, Tertullian (c. 160-c. 220 CE), that addresses the time of trial that Christians must expect:

> No one can obtain the kingdom of heaven
> who has not passed through the testing.[31]

This saying is consistent with other teachings of Jesus, who clearly identified the kingdom of God with people who were tested by poverty, oppression, sickness, disability, loss, hunger, or stigma. Christians called to a life of poverty, humility, and peacemaking or who reject injustice or violence are often at risk of persecution, and Christians called to service to the sick and the poor suffer their privations. A trial that tests one's faith is something a Christian has likely experienced and must continue to expect.

---

[30] Jeremias, *Jesus and the Message of the New Testament*, 58.
[31] Quoting Tertullian, "On Baptism," chapter XX. Ibid., 59.

Finally, the book of Revelation reflects the belief among first-century Christians that a time of trial would indicate the nearness of the kingdom of God: "'Because you have kept my word of patient endurance, I will keep you from the hour of trial that is coming on the whole world to test the inhabitants of the earth'" (Rev 3:10).

Let us not succumb to the trial. The final line of the Lord's Prayer asks God to preserve our faith if we must endure a time, like in the garden of Gethsemane, when our faith is tested at the risk of our lives. The churches addressed by Revelation are tested by assimilation, persecution, and complacency within the corrupt empire of Rome. For Jesus, like Israel, his test began in a barren garden, the wilderness.

✝

Matthew begins his account of Jesus' ministry in the desert outside Jerusalem: "In those days John the Baptist appeared in the wilderness of Judea, proclaiming, 'Repent, for the kingdom of heaven has come near'" (Matt 3:1-2). There, John baptized people to prepare them for the imminent arrival of the kingdom of God. Jesus' baptism is remarkable: John and others see the Holy Spirit "descending like a dove" and hear a voice say, "'This is my son, the Beloved, with whom I am well pleased'" (Matt 3:17).

After his baptism, Jesus joined John and adopted his austere lifestyle, living in the wilderness and wearing and eating what was available. The gospels dwell on how Jesus' calling to his ministry was unique from John's, but the theological issue distracts us from the most formative experiences in Jesus' life: the spiritual investment that occurred at his baptism in the wilderness outside Jerusalem, and his subsequent retreat to the desert, alone for forty days.

Gospel accounts of Jesus' internship with, then separation from John are contradictory; Mark's chronology indicates that John was arrested after Jesus returned from his stay in the wilderness:

> And the Spirit immediately drove him out into the wilderness. He was in the wilderness forty days, tempted by Satan; and he was with the wild beasts; and the angels waited on him.
> Now after John was arrested, Jesus came to Galilee proclaiming the good news of God, and saying, "The time is fulfilled, and the kingdom of God has come near; repent, and believe in the good news." (Mark 1:12-15)

John's arrest and brutal execution at the whim of Herod's dancing stepdaughter clearly indicated the trajectory Jesus' life would take, if he followed his calling. Despite his knowledge of his fate and strengthened by his forty-day testing in the wilderness, Jesus began at that point to proclaim the good news that God's kingdom had arrived.

Jesus' forty days in the wilderness recalls the forty days Moses spent with God on Mount Sinai (Ex 24:18); there, in a wilderness setting marked apocalyptically by earthquakes, lightning, and thunder, God revealed his name, YHWH, to Moses, an "event of unfathomable importance to Israel, because to know the name of a god was to these people, as to the other Near Eastern peoples of the time, a matter of supreme consequence."[32] An early covenant announced by Moses' protégé and successor, Joshua, recounts the history that resulted in the foundation of Israel and says, "And you lived in the wilderness for a long time" (Josh 24:7). By erecting booths of branches, open to the sky, celebrants of the Festival of Booths, the fall harvest festival and the occasion for Jesus' triumphal entry into Jerusalem on a donkey, recall the Jews' dependence on God in the wilderness, where God provided daily bread.

In the wilderness at Sinai, God offered Moses this covenant: God will make a place in Palestine for Israel to live, but Israel must never adopt the idolatrous religious practices of its other inhabitants. The covenant became the basis for the Law that set out detailed moral standards for Israelites as individuals and for their nation as a just society. Israel will repeatedly fail to keep its end of the deal. Even as Moses ascended the mountain to meet God, the Israelites created an image of God to worship, beginning a long series of idolatrous rebellions that Moses and a series of prophets confront with warnings that it is by God's grace alone that they survive. The tension between Law and idolatry, justice and oppression, good and evil, Christ and antichrist, began in the wilderness where Moses first formulated the prophetic choice: "'I call heaven and earth to witness against you today that I have set before you life and death, blessings and cursings. Choose life'" (Deut 30:19).

As controversy in Jerusalem escalates, Jesus re-enters the wilderness to make his prophetic choice.

---

[32] Mauser, *Christ in the Wilderness*, 24. With the addition of vowels, the Hebrew consonants YHWH can be translated to mean "I am who I am" (Exod 3:14). An NRSV annotator writes, "the name puns . . . and in the present context would seem to connote 'being there' for Moses and the Israelites." Edward L. Greenstein, "Exodus," *NRSV Study Bible*, 83.

Chapter 28
TIME ENDS

Jesus will confront the implications of his mission during his forty-day retreat in the wilderness following his baptism. Like John the Baptist, he will certainly be tortured, suffer, and die. Never does he avoid the wilderness after that; he continually seeks its solitude and silence for prayer. Then, in a repeated gospel motif, he emerges from his wilderness retreats to heal the sick, feed the hungry, and calm the frightened. In the wilderness, Jesus surrenders himself to the grace of God, and he emerges from the wilderness to forgive, make whole, and bring peace.[33]

The final wilderness Jesus will enter is existential. It begins after the Last Supper, when Jesus and the disciples go to the garden of Gethsemane. There, Jesus begins a prayerful vigil asking God, "My Father, if it is possible, let this cup pass from me; yet not what I want but what you want." A second time: "My Father, if it is possible, let this cup pass from me; yet not what I want but what you want" (Matt 26:39-42). Jesus enters the wilderness of the time of trial, endures it, and succumbs not to the trial but to the grace of God.

When the arresting officers appear, Jesus offers no resistance, although someone in his party swings a sword and cuts off an officer's ear. Jesus responds: "Put your sword back into its place; for all who take the sword will perish by the sword" (26:52). His disciples then abandon him; they will play no further role in his trial and execution.

Jesus is brought before the religious leadership of Jerusalem, led by Caiaphas the chief priest, who accuses him of falsely claiming that he's the Messiah. Perhaps as a sign of God's nearness, Jesus remains silent. Matthew reports: "The high priest stood up and said, 'Have you no answer? What is it that they testify against you?' But Jesus was silent" (Matt 26:62-63). Jesus is

---

[33] Mauser, *Christ in the Wilderness*, 107.

then taken before the civil authorities of Jerusalem, led by Pontius Pilate, and the religious authorities list Jesus' offenses. Pilate asked him, "'Do you not hear how many accusations they make against you?' But he gave him no answer" (Matt 27:12-14).

Jesus is taken to a nearby hill where he is publicly crucified: his arms are fastened to a beam that crosses an upright post, and he will asphyxiate when his shoulders, painfully exhausted, can no longer support his effort to breathe. Crucifixion was the method of execution preferred by the Romans for violent criminals, rebellious slaves, army deserters, and assassins, and it is the ultimate time of trial, an experience anyone would avoid at any cost. The scene is apocalyptic, recalling the prophets' descriptions of the day of the Lord: "From noon on, darkness came over the whole land until three in the afternoon" (Matt 27:45).

Jesus, dying, cries out the first excruciating line of Psalm 22: "'My God, my God, why have you forsaken me?'" (Matt 27:46). Only this once in the gospels does his prayer fail to address God as *Abba!*

Jesus falls silent. The earth quakes. Jesus has entered the wilderness of death.

†

Jesus' family, friends, and disciples will see him after he dies.

He greets his mother and his friend Mary with a brisk, "Greetings!" (Matt 28:9).

He joins some disciples as they walk along the road to Emmaus, about seven miles north of Jerusalem, but they don't recognize him. As they enter Emmaus,

> He walked ahead as if he were going on. But they urged him strongly, saying, "Stay with us because it is almost evening and the day is now nearly over." So he went in to stay with them. When he was at the table with them, he took bread, blessed and broke it, and gave it to them. Then their eyes were opened, and they recognized him. (Luke 24:28-31)

In another story, the disciples huddle inside a house, fearful of persecutors.

> Jesus came and stood among them and said, "Peace be with you." . . . The disciples rejoiced when they saw the Lord. Jesus said to them again, "Peace be with you. As the Father has sent me, so I send you." When he had said this, he breathed on them and said to them, "Receive the Holy Spirit. If you forgive the sins of any, they are forgiven them." (John 20:19-23)

Some of the disciples go fishing at dawn but have no luck. A stranger appears on the beach and offers some advice; their luck changes, and they bring the catch to shore. The stranger has started a fire to bake some bread and he cooks the fish they caught. Perhaps the sea is disturbed by the morning's freshets, like the sea at the creation was disturbed by God's breath. In the slanting rays of the rising sun, maybe the sea looks like a plain of jewels, like the visions of God's throne in Ezekiel and Revelation.

> Jesus said, "Come and have breakfast." Now none of the disciples dared to ask him, "Who are you?" because they knew it was the Master. Jesus came and took the bread and gave it to them, and did the same with the fish. (John 21:12-14)

✝

Let's compare two post-resurrection meals: the one Jesus enjoyed with his good friend Lazarus and his sisters, and the one his disciples have with the stranger, who is Jesus, on the beach.

In both meals, bread is shared in fellowship. At Lazarus' table, it's a meal among dear friends who are reunited after an appalling separation. With the disciples, it's edgy. They had run from the garden at Gethsemane when Jesus was arrested, had denied being his disciples, had abandoned the mission, had succumbed to the trial. Yet there he is, preparing a meal that they then share.

On the beach, we have the world as it is. Earlier, at the home of Lazarus, we have the world as it will be. We share, we forgive, and God's victory over death is revealed. *Then*, time ends.

APPENDIX 1: HISTORICAL TIME-LINE

Time frame	Larger World	Israel	Book
1800 BCE		Abraham founds his tribe in Palestine but soon enters Egypt.	
c 1280	Ramesses II is Pharaoh in Egypt	Moses leads the exodus of the enslaved Israelite tribes from Egypt into the Sinai wilderness.	
c 1250-1200		The Israelite tribes enter Palestine and militarily carve out homelands.	
c 1200-1020	Philistines settle in Palestine	Period of the Judges: Deborah	
c 1050-1000		Kingdoms of Samuel and Saul	
c 1000-922		Kingdoms of David and Solomon	
c 922		Death of Solomon; Israel splits into the northern kingdom, centered in Samaria, and Judah, centered in Jerusalem.	
869-850		King Ahab reigns over the northern kingdom; Elijah is a prophet.	
786-746		King Jeroboam II reigns over the northern kingdom.	Amos Hosea
742-687		Kings Jotham, Ahaz, and Hezekiah reign over Judah.	Isaiah (1) Micah
722-721	Assyrian Empire under King Sargon II conquers Samaria, the capital of the Northern Kingdom.	The northern kingdom is exiled to Assyria and absorbed,	
640-609		King Josiah (Judah)	Deuteronomy Samuel Kings Jeremiah Zephaniah
c 587	Neo-Babylonian Empire under King Nebuchadnezzar conquers Jerusalem.	Solomon's temple is destroyed; the elites of Judah are exiled to Babylon but are permitted to live separately and continue their traditions.	Isaiah (2) Ezekiel Jonah?
539	Cyrus, King of Persia conquers Babylon	Exiles are permitted to return to Palestine.	Isaiah (3)
515		The second temple in Jerusalem is dedicated.	Haggai Zechariah
465-425	Artaxerxes I is Emperor of Persia.	446: Nehemiah is authorized to fortify Jerusalem.	[final revisions:]

Time frame	Larger World	Israel	Book
		c 424: Ezra restores the Jewish cult and law and finalizes the five books of Moses.	Genesis Exodus Leviticus Numbers
336-332	Alexander the Great of Macedonia conquers Babylon, Persia, and Palestine.		Joel
200-198	200: the Seleucid Empire gains control of Palestine.		
175-164	Antiochus IV "Epiphanes" is king of the Seleucids.	167: Epiphanes profanes the temple; Mattathias begins the Maccabean revolt. 164: the temple cult is restored by Judas Maccabeus and the temple is rededicated.	Daniel
134-104		John Hyrcanus of the Maccabean dynasty is chief priest.	1 Maccabees
64		The Roman general Pompey militarily subdues Palestine, occupies Jerusalem and installs Antipas, a Jew, as king.	
37-4 BCE	31: Augustus is victor in the Roman civil wars and is proclaimed the first Emperor of the Roman Empire.	Herod the Great, son of Antipas, is king of Judea and Galilee, but still under Roman hegemony. He rebuilds the temple.	
c 3 CE		Jesus of Nazareth is born.	
6		Rome begins directly administering Judea.	
14	Augustus dies and is declared a "God" by the Roman Senate.		
c 32	Tiberius in Emperor (14-37 CE)	John the Baptist is executed by Herod Antipas, tetrarch of Galilee and son of Herod the Great.	
c 33		Jesus of Nazareth is executed at the recommendation of the chief priest Caiaphas and the direction of Pontius Pilate, Roman procurator for Judea	
33-42	Caligula is Emperor (37-41)	The Apostolic ministry is led by Peter, Stephen, and James in Jerusalem.	
c 47-65	Claudius is Emperor (41-54)	Paul, a convert from the Pharisees, organizes churches throughout the Roman Empire.	1 Thessalonians
64	Nero is Emperor (54-68)	Rome burns; Emperor Nero blames and persecutes Christians in Rome; Paul and Peter are martyred in Rome c 65.	

Time frame	Larger World	Israel	Book
66-70	Vespasian is Emperor (69-79)	Great Jewish Revolt; Jerusalem is besieged then sacked by the Romans, who destroy the second temple in 70 CE.	Gospel of Mark Gospel of Luke Acts of the Apostles 2 Thessalonians
81-96	Domitian is Emperor		1 & 2 Peter Gospel of Matthew Gospel of John Revelation 1 & 2 John
132-134 CE		Bar-Kochba's Revolt, the last revolt of the Jews; Jews are expelled from Jerusalem, which becomes a Roman city.	

APPENDIX 2: REVELATION'S SCENES OF WORSHIP

Scenes of Worship	Scenes of Evil's Destruction	References
Greeting: Alpha and Omega		1:1-8
The Ancient One and the Son of Man		1:9-20
Messages to the Seven Churches		Chapters 2 & 3
--The Scroll--		
❶ "Holy, Holy, Holy"		Chapter 4
❷ The Lamb	The Lamb begins to unseal the scroll.	Chapter 5
	Seals 1-4: the four horsemen. Seal 5: martyrs sing, "How long?" Seal 6: environmental catastrophe.	Chapter 6
	An angel seals 144,000 servants of God.	7:1-8
❸ "Salvation...!"		7:9-17
	The seventh seal: heaven quiets for a half hour. Seven Angels with trumpets appear. An Angel hurls a censer to earth.	8:1-5
	Trumpets 1-4: heavenly catastrophes.	8:5-12
	A loan eagle cries "Woe!" three times.	8:13
	Trumpet 5: torturing locusts. Trumpet 6: fire-breathing cavalry. John is asked to measure the temple.	9:1-11:14
❹ "The kingdom of the world has become the kingdom of our Lord."	The seventh trumpet:	11:15-19
	The woman, a dragon, and her son. The beasts from the sea and the earth.	Chapters 12 & 13
❺ "New song."		14:1-13
	The angels' harvest.	14:14-20
❻ "Song of the Lamb"		15:1-8
	Bowls 1-6: plagues and disasters	16:1-16
	The seventh bowl: worldwide catastrophe.	16:17-21
	The whore of Babylon and Babylon's defeat.	Chapters 17 & 18
❼ "Hallelujah!"		19:1-10
	The battle of Armageddon.	19:11-21
	The Millennium.	Chapter 20
The New Creation		21:1-8
The New Jerusalem		21:9-22:7
Benediction: Alpha and Omega		22:8-21

WORKS CITED

Actemeier, Paul J. and James Luther Mays, eds. *Interpreting the Prophets*. Philadelphia: Fortress, 1987.

Armstrong, Karen. *The Battle for God*. New York: Random House, 2000.

Barr, David. *Tales of the End: A Narrative Commentary on the Book of Revelation*. Santa Rosa: Polebridge, 1998.

Barrett, C. K., ed. *The New Testament Background*. San Francisco: HarperSanFrancisco, 1989.

Beker, J. Christiaan. *Paul the Apostle: The Triumph of God in Life and Thought*. Philadelphia: Fortress, 1980.

Borg, Marcus J. *Jesus: A New Vision*. San Francisco: HarperSanFrancisco, 1991.

Borg, Marcus J., ed. *The Lost Gospel Q*. Berkeley: Ulysses, 1996.

Boyer, Paul. *When Time Shall Be No More: Prophecy Belief in Modern American Culture*. Cambridge MA: Harvard University Press, 1992.

Bright, John. *A History of Israel*, Third Edition. Philadelphia: Westminster, 1981.

Brown, Raymond E. *An Introduction to the New Testament*. New York: Doubleday, 1997.

Brueggemann, Walter. *An Introduction to the Old Testament: The Canon and Christian Imagination*. Louisville: Westminster John Knox, 2003.

Chilton, Bruce. *Rabbi Jesus: An Intimate Biography*. New York: Doubleday, 2000.

Collins, John. *The Apocalyptic Imagination: An Introduction to Jewish Apocalyptic Literature*, Second Edition. Grand Rapids: Eerdmans, 1998.

Crossan, John Dominic. *The Historical Jesus: The Life of a Mediterranean Jewish Peasant*. San Francisco: HarperSanFrancisco, 1992.

Crossan, John Dominic, and Reed, Jonathan L. *In Search of Paul*. San Francisco: HarperSanFrancisco, 2004.

Dunn, James D. G. *Unity and Diversity in the New Testament*, Third Edition. London: SCM, 2006.

Dyer, Charles H. *The Rise of Babylon: Is Iraq at the Center of the Final Drama?* Chicago: Moody, 2003.

Foerster, Werner. *From the Exile to Christ*. Philadelphia: Fortress, 1964.

Funk, Robert W. *Honest to Jesus: Jesus for a New Millennium*. Rydalmere, Australia: Hodder and Stoughton, 1996.

Goergen, Donald J., O.P. *The Mission and Ministry of Jesus*. Wilmington, DE: Michael Glazier, 1986.

Hagee, John. *The Revelation of Truth: A Mosaic of God's Plan for Man*. Nashville: Thomas Nelson, 2000.

Hagee, John. *From Daniel to Doomsday: The Countdown Has Begun*. Nashville: Thomas Nelson, 1999.

Hagee, John. *Jerusalem Countdown: A Prelude to War*. Lake Mary, FL: Frontline, 2006.

Hahn, Scott. *The Lamb's Supper: The Mass as Heaven on Earth*. New York: Doubleday, 1999.

Howard-Brook, Wes, and Anthony Gwyther. *Unveiling Empire: Reading Revelation Then and Now*. Maryknoll, NY: Orbis Books, 2005.

The Interpreter's Bible. New York: Abingdon, 1952.

Jeremias, Joachim. *Jesus and the Message of the New Testament.* Minneapolis: Fortress, 2002.

Jewett, Robert. *Jesus Against the Rapture.* Philadelphia: Westminster, 1979.

Jones, David Hugh, ed. *The Hymnbook.* Richmond: Presbyterian Church, 1955.

Koester, Craig R. *Revelation and the End of All Things.* Grand Rapids: Eerdmans, 2001.

LaHaye, Tim and Jerry B. Jenkins. *Left Behind: A novel of the earth's last days.* Carol Stream, Ill: Tyndale, 1995.

LaHaye, Tim. *Revelation Unveiled.* Grand Rapids: Zondervan, 1999.

Lindsey, Hal. *The Everlasting Hatred: the Roots of Jihad.* Murrietta: Oracle, 2002.

Lindsey, Hal. *The Late Great Planet Earth.* New York: Bantam, 1981.

Lindsey, Hal. *The Apocalypse Code.* Palos Verdes, CA: Western Front, 1997.

Mack, Burton L. *Who Wrote the New Testament? The Making of the Christian Myth.* HarperSanFrancisco, 1996.

Marsden, George M. *Understanding Fundamentalism and Evangelicalism.* Grand Rapids: Eerdmans, 1991.

Mauser, Ulrich. *Christ in the Wilderness.* London: SCM, 1963.

Mauser, Ulrich. *The Gospel of Peace.* Louisville: Westminster John Knox, 1992.

McGinn, Bernard. *Antichrist: Two Thousand Years of the Human Fascination with Evil.* San Francisco: HarperSanFrancisco, 1994.

[NRSV Study Bible] *The HarperCollins Study Bible: New Revised Standard Version.* New York: HarperCollins, 1993.

Petersen, David L. *The Prophetic Literature: An Introduction.* Louisville: Westminster John Knox, 2002.

Peterson, Eugene H. *The Message//Remix: The Bible In Contemporary Language.* Colorado Springs: Navpress, 2003.

Podhoretz, Norman. *The Prophets: Who They Were, What They Are.* New York: Free Press, 2002.

Reicke, Bo. *The New Testament Era: The World of the Bible from 500 B.C. to A.D. 100.* Philadelphia: Fortress, 1968.

Rischin, Rebecca. *For the End of Time: The Story of the Messiaen Quartet.* Ithaca: Cornell University Press, 2003.

Russell, D. S. *The Method and Message of Jewish Apocalyptic.* Philadelphia: Westminster, 1964.

Seow, C. L. *Daniel.* Louisville: Westminster John Knox, 2003.

Wojcik, Daniel. *The End of the World As We Know It: Faith, Fatalism, and Apocalypse in America.* New York: New York University Press, 1997.